ANDRES KÜNG

A DREAM OF FREEDOM

Four decades of
national survival versus Russian imperialism
in
Estonia, Latvia and Lithuania
1940–1980

BOREAS PUBLISHING HOUSE
CARDIFF   NEW YORK   STOCKHOLM   SYDNEY
TORONTO
1981

Copyright © 1980 Andres Küng

Published in 1981 by
BOREAS PUBLISHING HOUSE
63, Ninian Road
CARDIFF CF2 5EL
Great Britain

ISBN 0 906967 05 8

Text set in 12/13pt VIP Palatino, printed and bound
in Great Britain at The Pitman Press, Bath

ANDRES KÜNG was born on September 13, 1945, in Ockelbo, Sweden. His Estonian parents left their country as political refugees during the German occupation in September 1944.

He attended the Estonian Elementary School in Stockholm, a Swedish secondary school and graduated from the Stockholm School of Economics in 1967. Later studied languages in various universities in Sweden and abroad.

He was editor-in-chief of Swedish Broadcasting Corporation's cultural programme *OBS* in 1969–1972 and news-editor of the Swedish TV programme *Children's Journal* since its start in 1972. He is also a co-editor of a number of other television programmes and is a columnist for Swedish and Estonian newspapers in Sweden. He has travelled in some hundred countries and speaks a dozen languages.

Since his debut in December 1969 he has published 24 books in Swedish, many of which have been translated into English, Estonian, Finnish, German, Icelandic, Japanese, Latvian and Norwegian.

In August 1977 he was appointed Honorary Member of the underground resistance movements of Estonia, Latvia and Lithuania. He has been awarded a number of important cultural prizes and recently received a life-scholarship for outstanding journalistic and literary achievements from the Swedish Association of Writers.

He lives in Malmö, Southern Sweden, and is married to Lena, an assistant TV-producer. They have two children, Daniel, born in 1974 and daughter Emilie, born in 1978.

BOOKS BY THE SAME AUTHOR
(all originally published in Swedish):

LATIN AMERICA – REFORM OR STAGNATION?, 1969

LAPP POWER!, 1970

THE OPPRESSED OF THE EARTH, 1970, co-author with Olof G. Tandberg

ESTONIA – A STUDY OF IMPERIALISM, 1971, also in German and Icelandic

BANGLA DESH – AN ASIAN DILEMMA, 1971

WHAT HAPPENS IN BALTICUM?, 1973, also in Estonian, Finnish and Latvian

AN UNBALANCED CONTINENT, 1973, co-author with David Widmark

SWEDEN, MY NATIVE LAND!, 1974

THE CASE OF CHILE, 1974

A PROMISED AND LOST LAND – Report from Palestine, 1974

BRUCE!, 1976, also in English, Finnish and Norwegian

THIS IS SWEDEN, 1976, drawings by Lennard Frantzen

THE BOLIVIAN EMIGRANTS, 1977

THE THIRD ISRAEL, 1977, also in Finnish

WHAT HAPPENS IN FINLAND?, 1977, also in Estonian and Finnish

THE CASE OF ENGSTROM – SARELD, 1978, also in Finnish and Japanese

ASTRID, ANGEL OF MARSEILLE, 1978

A DREAM OF FREEDOM, 1978, also in English and Finnish

THE CASE OF AGAPOV, 1978, also in Finnish

THE TV-COLLEAGUES, 1978

A LONG WAY TO FREEDOM, 1978, also in Finnish and Norwegian

CHRISTIAN MARTYRS OF EAST AND WEST, 1979, also in Finnish and Norwegian

A PROTEST FROM BALTICUM, 1979

SAVED, 1980

Contents

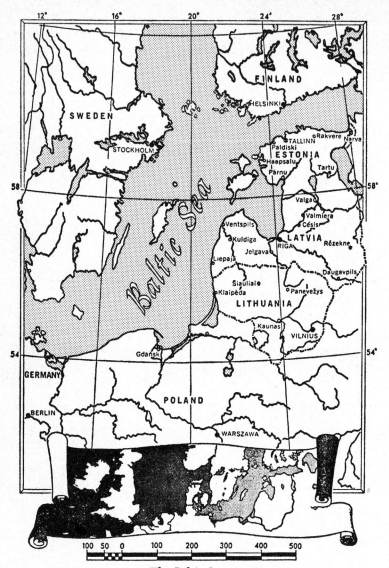

The Baltic States.

Foreword
by Peter Reddaway

Andres Küng has written a book which will serve an unusually wide range of readers: students and academics, journalists, government officials, businessmen, and visitors of all types to the Baltic area.

His description of life in the Soviet republics of Estonia, Latvia and Lithuania is both remarkably comprehensive and highly readable. He has digested a large volume of official and unofficial sources, and, blending in his personal experiences from travel in the area, he produces a narrative in which the judgments are judicious and balanced. He has overcome the notoriously difficult problem for writers on Soviet affairs, that of assessing the true substance beneath the layers of propaganda and prejudice which coat many of the sources, especially the official ones and some of those produced by emigrés. This is no mean feat, as emotive themes such as Russification, colonial domination and economic exploitation are naturally central to the book's concerns.

Mr. Küng has marshalled a vast quantity of hard facts, but he presents them with skill, so that the pace does not slacken and our interest is stimulated, not lost. At well chosen moments he slips in popular jokes which both amuse and illuminate.

The reader will come away from Küng's book with a detailed understanding of the extensive differences and similarities between the three Baltic peoples he describes. Each has its own special problems, its own strengths and weaknesses, its own successes and failures. But Küng is convinced, as I am, that despite the worrying level of non-native immigration, each is resisting assimilation and retaining its identity. The success is greatest among the Lithuanians, then the Estonians, then the Latvians, in that order. But even for the Latvians some of the more alarmist prognoses seem unfounded. Sudden moves towards greater assimilation and Russification would, it seems, be strongly resisted here too, just as they were in Georgia in 1978 when the authorities yielded to a mass demonstration of protest against a slight down-grading of the status of the Georgian language. More positively, the development of dissent and samizdat publications hold out hope for a more vigorous and explicit development of national cultures than is possible through the heavily censored official media.

Mr. Küng is naturally guarded about the prospects for the national independence which both he and most Soviet Balts would clearly ideally like. At present independence is an unrealistic goal, and it will clearly remain so until the Soviet empire eventually goes – as it must – the way of its tsarist predecessor.

Finally, Küng gives us not only detailed pictures of the history, economics, religions, politics, cultures and dissent groups of the Baltic republics; he also provides an annotated bibliography for further more specialized reading. This crowns his achievement in writing a book of unusual worth to both specialist and layman.

Peter Reddaway
London School of Economics and
Political Science.
November, 1979.

CHAPTER 1

The trial against the Estonian Democratic Movement

The building in Tallinn, the capital of Soviet Estonia, is surrounded and the courtroom is guarded by the KGB and walkie-talkie militia. Only members of the secret police, KGB, and selected activists from the local party organization are admitted to the room together with some relatives of the prosecuted.

Unwanted persons are not allowed to the courtroom. Some are not even admitted to the courthouse or are led out if they manage to get in. During the morning twilight, some are forcibly removed from the courtroom door. No announcement of the trial is placed on the board of announcements of the Supreme Court.

Any taking of notes is forbidden and the courtroom is closely scrutinized by the KGB. The following report is based on material put together collectively in Estonia and smuggled out.

The Defendants
The trial is conducted primarily in Russian. The trial documents are in the same language. The defendants and the witnesses are also permitted to address the court in Estonian. The defendants are:

Kalju Mätik, born 1932 in Tallinn. Estonian. Single. Graduated from the Tallinn Polytechnical Institute (=TPI), works as an electrical engineer and as lecturer at TPI.

Sergei Soldatov, born 1933 in Estonia's historic border town with Russia, Narva. Father a Russian, mother an Estonian. Married, father of a son of 16. Graduate of the Leningrad Polytechnical Institute. Mechanical engineer, lecturer at TPI and interpreter.

Mati Kiirend, born 1939 in Tallinn. Estonian. Married, two children, ages 10 and 1. Graduate of TPI, thermal engineer, lately engaged as an artist for motion picture ads.

Artom Yuskevich, born 1931 in Volynia. Ukrainian. Married, father of a daughter, age 17. Technical college education. Member of the Communist Party. Works as an interpreter.

Arvo Varato, born 1932 in Tallinn. Estonian. Married, has three children, ages 12, 5 and 2. Graduate of Tartu State University. Physician.

Brief of Accusations

The prosecutor reads the indictment which has been signed by Lt. Col. L. Nikitin, head of the KGB Section of Investigations. According to the brief of accusations, the defendants organized in 1970–72 anti-Soviet activities with the purpose of undermining and weakening Soviet power and the governmental and social order of the Soviet Union. Having entered into criminal association with each other they participated in the discussion, drafting, duplication, dissemination, and concealment with the purpose of distribution of the anti-Soviet program of the Estonian Democratic Movement. They wrote anti-Soviet and slanderous articles and turned these over to other defendants for inclusion in the (underground) periodicals *Eesti Rahvuslik Hääl* (Estonian National Voice), *Eesti Demokraat* (Estonian Democrat), *Demokrat* and *Luch svoboda* (Ray of Freedom), the latter two in Russian.

In an attempt to involve the United Nations in Soviet internal affairs, the defendants discussed, drafted, duplicated, distributed and stored memoranda to the UN General Assembly and Secretary-General Kurt Waldheim. These memoranda contain malicious slander regarding the foreign, internal and nationalities policy of the Soviet Union. Those documents were widely echoed in the bourgeois and emigré press, and were broadcast by anti-Soviet radio stations like Voice of America and Radio Liberty.

Following is the anti-Soviet literature confiscated from the defendants: N. Berdyayev *Sources and Meaning of Russian Communism*; Milovan Djilas, *The New Class*; Andres Küng, *Estonia as an Example*; Aleksandr Solzhenitsyn, *Gulag Archipelago*; Andrei Amalrik *Will the USSR Survive Until 1984?*; Yuly Daniel, *Moscow Speaking*; Mazepa-Bakavaisky, *Russian Colonialism and the Problem of Nationalities*; *The Judgment of History – The Judgment of God*; *2000 Words* (the Czech manifesto of 1968); *The Liberation War of Estonia 1918–20*; *The Year of Suffering of the Estonian People*; various periodicals and newspapers from the time of Estonian independence between the two World Wars and the time of German occupation during World War II. Also some typewriters and a camera were from the defendants.

This was the brief of accusations. Before we go on to describe the trial itself, let us also have a short look at the central documents of the case: the memoranda to the UN General Assembly and to the Secretary-General.

The Program of the Estonian Democratic Movement
Despite the rapid communications of today, voices from the Baltic States often reach us with considerable delay, if at all. Dissident messages to the West must seek illegal and devious ways, sometimes via several countries, to avoid Soviet censorship. The two memoranda to the UN from Estonia took almost two years to reach us.

3

The memoranda carry the seals of two underground organizations, the Estonian Democratic Movement and the Estonian National Front. They are written in English and dated Tallinn, October 24, 1972. I will quote them without changing their language. The memorandum to the UN General Assembly stresses the right of national self-determination and recalls Estonian national independence before World War II. It ends thus:

> The Estonian Democratic Movement and the Estonian National Front demand the UN to take effective steps in order to abolish the immoral, inhuman and illegal Soviet colonial rule in Estonia and to compel the Soviet Union not to hinder the restoration of the legal rights and national sovereignty to the Estonian nation.
>
> Estonians will never accept the colonial status of their fatherland. At present, when even the smallest nations of the world have been recognized the right to national independence, the Estonian nation looks forward to urgent and real help from the United Nations Organization.[1]

The memorandum demands the restoration of the independent Estonian state with the frontiers fixed by the 1920 Tartu Peace Treaty between the Republic of Estonia and Soviet Russia. It also demands the admission of Estonia, as a former member of the League of Nations, to United Nations membership. The memorandum also states:

> To these ends the Estonian Democratic Movement and the Estonian National Front consider necessary:
> a. to liquidate the existing colonial administration, which does not correspond to the art. 21 par. 3 of the Universal Declaration of Human Rights, depends

[1] See Appendix for full text.

4

entirely on the Soviet central government and is an instrument of the latter's imperialistic and chauvinistic aims;

b. to liquidate the Soviet military bases on Estonian soil and to withdraw from Estonia all Soviet military personnel (who, under the agreement between Estonia and the Soviet Union were stationed for 10 years only, the agreement expired in 1949);

c. up to the formation of national organs of government through free democratic elections to place Estonia temporarily under UN administration and to introduce into Estonia the UN peace-keeping forces;

d. pending the UN administration, the opportunity for return to Estonia of all persons of Estonian nationality, who have been forcibly deported from Estonia (including those detained for political reasons) or who have left Estonia at their own will, and also to all other persons who have been citizens of the Estonian Republic, and to their descendants;

e. to restore normal political life and to create conditions for really free democratic elections (under the supervision of the UN observers) in order to form a representative body of the Estonian people – the Constituent Assembly.

Such then was the "malicious slander regarding the foreign, internal, and nationalities policy of the Soviet Union", that brought Kalju Mätik, Sergei Soldatov, Mati Kiirend, Artom Yuskevich, and Arvo Varato to the attention of the KGB. While the Soviet leader Leonid Brezhnev met other world statesmen to sign the final act of the European Security Conference in Helsinki, then 50 miles to the south, on the other side of the Finnish Gulf, Soviet secret police were persecuting the Estonian Democratic Movement and the Estonian National Front. The trial against these groups was preceded by mass interrogations, house searches, and job dismissals in different districts of Estonia. Among the dismissed were: Ülo Vooglaid, director of the sociological laboratory of Tartu State University; Heljo Tauk, a well-known musicologist who had been a teacher at the State Conservatory in Tallinn; Tunne Kelam, a member of the editorial staff of the Soviet Estonian Encyclopaedia; Oleg Trjutrjumov, administrator of the Estonian Radio Symphony Orchestra, and Paul Motsküla, a journalist, translator and publicist.

The investigations lasted for several months. The KGB was reinforced from other parts of the Soviet Union. Finally, all was ready for the trial in Tallinn, October 21–31, 1975. This only two and a half months after the solemn signing of the Helsinki declaration, where the Soviet leaders pledged to facilitate the freer flow of information across the frontiers.

Interrogations

Mati Kiirend is the first to be interrogated in court. He renounces his testimony given during the investigation. He signed the report, dictated to him under pressure, and now protests against the methods used by the investigators. Kiirend refuses to testify in court on matters of substance.

Kalju Mätik also refuses to give evidence on matters of substance, since he does not consider the materials slanderous or anti-Soviet. He cites commonly accepted concepts of freedom of speech and press.

Judge Afanasev (interrupting Mätik): "It is for the court to decide whether the materials are anti-Soviet or not. You just have to respond from whom you got them and to whom you gave them!"

Mätik points out the incompetence of the KGB investigators. They have considered anti-Soviet even an article from the periodical *Eesti Kommunist*, in which the abuse of power during the time of the Stalin personality cult was illustrated. He demands a public, unbiased, and competent discussion of the articles with an indication of anti-Soviet, slanderous passages or untruthful facts. He remarks that the articles and documents for which he is prosecuted are unknown to the public.

Judge Afanasev: "The Court will decide about that. If you are not going to testify, I shall ask the Prosecutor to read from the file."

Prosecutor Kessler reads about the circulation of democratic materials. Later during the trial, witnesses are called. Several of them testify that the defendants have given them material to read or to duplicate. Others, such as Ott Arder, are less cooperative.

Judge Afanasev:	Did Soldatov offer you anything to read?
Witness Arder:	I gave him more to read.
Prosecutor Kessler:	Did Soldatov say that faith could be exploited for democratic purposes, for making society better?
Witness:	What faith?
Prosecutor:	The faith in God, of course.
Witness:	I do not remember. The isolation on the part of the believers in a spiritual and meditative way of life and their insignificant interest in social and governmental problems are well known.
Prosecutor	Did you see Soldatov writing on the typewriter?
Witness:	I cannot remember.
Prosecutor:	You testified that Soldatov gave you an article to read

	called "Freedom, Man, the Individual". When was that, in 1972?
Witness:	I do not remember.
Defendant Soldatov:	Did you find anything that might be termed anti-Soviet in the article? Is a particular state or party mentioned therein?
Witness:	No, it is not an anti-Soviet article.

The Defense

After a week, it is time for the Prosecutor to sum up and for the defendants to defend themselves. Prosecutor Kessler stresses the role played by international imperialism in the present case. He maintains that the US Central Intelligence Agency in 1968 entrusted a certain Garanin with the task of fabricating and publishing a document. It was to convey the impression of being composed by democratic dissidents in the Soviet Union. After this a democratic movement actually came into being, according to the Prosecutor. He demands heavy prison sentences for Mätik, Soldatov, Kiirend and Yuskevich and a shorter, suspended sentence for Varato.

Arvo Varato has admitted his guilt and assisted the KGB during the investigation. His defense counsel asks the court to regard this and Varato's family background as extenuating circumstances. Arvo Varato was born into the family of a small merchant, whose shop and house were confiscated after the Soviet take-over of Estonia, Latvia, and Lithuania in the summer of 1940. In this condition of dissatisfaction with Soviet rule, Varato grew up "under the influence of bourgeois ideology, from childhood on he perceived everything in a distorted and exaggerated form." Since Varato has confessed his guilt and sincerely repented his crime, and promises to refrain from criminal activities in the future, the defense counsel asks the court to be lenient with him, especially in view of the fact that he has assisted in the investigation.

The other four deny their guilt and reject the official defense lawyers. They are permitted to conduct their own defense. They reject all accusations, both in their pleas for the defense and their last words before the passing of sentences.

Artom Yuskevich speaks of the freedoms enumerated in the Constitution of the Soviet Union and shows that his activities did not violate this Constitution: "Whereas everybody can interpret the Bible as he sees fit, nobody is entitled to interpret the Constitution to suit himself. But this is what is being done to accuse us."

Yuskevich further states that he had not been a democrat before, but became one on December 13, 1974, when he was arrested and packed into a van, with arms tied and twisted. He also complains about the conditions in the KGB prison, where the preliminary interrogations took place. He had asked for a bedsheet in vain for three months. The lights were bad, the food inedible. The room in which they are held during the trial is as dirty as a public lavatory . . . He is stopped by the judge at this point.

In his final statement, Yuskevich stresses that as a materialist and dialectician, a Communist and Soviet citizen, he holds the opinion that an open discussion of problems and criticism are necessary prerequisites for the development of society. Working in various firms he had criticized shortcomings. His criticisms had helped to solve problems and eliminate errors. But now, when he criticized injustice and shortcomings of the state and society, this was branded as anti-Soviet activity, hostile to the state.

9

"My ancestors fought in 1917, with weapons in their hands, for Soviet power. Now I am being convicted as a criminal for having availed myself of the rights achieved. During the Civil War, censorship was temporarily introduced and this temporary measure has existed to this very day. The biography of many an outstanding person ends with a short notice: died in 1937–38 or 1948. Many events of these times are now condemned, and are regarded as mistakes. This is true also of the political show trials. After five, perhaps ten years, a real court will feel ashamed of this trial also!"

Kalju Mätik also denies that the duplicated materials are anti-Soviet or slanderous. The data in them have been collected from Soviet newspapers and other public sources, such as the Soviet Constitution, other official documents, a speech by the then Soviet president Podgorny and so on. Mätik also stresses that the activity of the democrats was not designed to overthrow the Soviet regime, nor did it violate the Soviet Constitution: "The constitution guarantees the right of the constituent republics to secede from the Soviet Union. We demanded a referendum. This is not the same as to overthrow the regime, especially since it is claimed that 99·8% of the population support the Communist Party."

Mätik further speaks about himself and those of his friends who had become victims of Soviet repression. Mätik mentions three classmates who were arrested in the late 1940's, one of them because he had read a biography of Stalin, published in independent Estonia. He himself grew up with his mother, who was an artist: "Artists in capitalist countries are, as is well-know, poor people." A. Jõeäär, a former leftist Social Democrat, later to become People's Commissar and Minister of Justice was a great friend of our family, continues Mätik. Jõeäär was imprisoned in the 1940's.

Judge Afanasev (interrupting Mätik): He was not!
Mätik: I may be mistaken.

The fate of many persons imprisoned or deported in early Soviet years is still not known with certainty. Tens of thousands of Estonians were deported in cattle vans from Estonia to Siberia on June 13, 1941, and then again during the forced collectivization of agriculture in 1948–1949. Similar mass deportations took place from Latvia and Lithuania.

In his final statement, Mätik says that during the investigation he was told that the activities of the democrats were of a Utopian kind. If this were so, says Mätik, then you would only have to ridicule us, but not condemn us. When our activity is now hindered, it is because we are not alone. The movement has a broader basis and our demands may obviously become reality one day!

Mati Kiirend can hardly believe it possible to indict people for activities that are in line with the Constitution. He stresses, like his friends, that the Estonian Democratic Movement bases itself on the Soviet Constitution and the UN Charter on Human Rights. They want to help eliminate injustice and shortcomings in the interests of the development of society.

Kiirend also gives some facts about himself. His father was executed by the Germans, who occupied Estonia in 1941–44. Their apartment was burnt down during the Soviet bombing raid on Tallinn, in March, 1944. Since then he has lived in a narrow, damp, and dark flat in an old house.

Having lost her husband and living in anti-sanitary housing conditions, Kiirend's mother fell ill with consumption and other diseases and was sometimes bedstricken. Some years ago Mati Kiirend himself fell ill with tuberculosis. After his marriage, his wife and his child had to share the same small flat, although it was a real challenge even to find place for a pram in the room. Finally, Kiirend and his wife started knocking the doors of private houses in Tallinn, like beggars, hoping to find a room of their own to rent. They found none, until Yuskevich put a room at their disposal.

Mati Kiirend also tells of administrative harassment of relatives and friends. Already before his indictment, his wife had been transferred to a less paid job, although she had never been involved in the democratic movement, apart from translating one phrase from German. Finally, Kiirend begs the court to be lenient towards Yuskevich, who suffers from ill health.

Sergei Soldatov fails to see anything criminal in his doings: "Violence is contrary to everything I stand for concerning the development of society and man – I was guided by moral and ethical principles". Soldatov states that he has chosen the word as his weapon, according to the principles of humanism. He does not consider his activity hostile to the state or governmental order. He recognizes the rights of activity and representation for the Communists and even considers this necessary in all countries. However, he is for the same rights for all parties. "As a believer, I forgive everybody and I bear no resentment against anybody. I have confidence in the humaneness of the court and I beg that the punishment of my prosecuted friends be alleviated."

The Verdict
The verdict is given on October 31, 1975. All the defendants are found guilty and are sentenced according to paragraph 68:1 of the Criminal Code of the Estonian SSR. The counterpart of this paragraph in the Russian Criminal Code is the well-known paragraph 70 that deals with "anti-Soviet activity". Mätik is also sentenced according to paragraph 207:1 of the

Soviet Estonian Criminal Code for "illegal storing of weapons" – a rifle, model 1944, was found in his shed.

Kalju Mätik and Sergei Soldatov are sentenced to 6 years in a strict regime labor camp. Mati Kiirend and Artom Yuskevich to 5 years in a labor camp with a strict régime. Arvo Varato is given a 3-year suspended sentence, with a 5-year probationary period. Varato is warned that if he during this period participates in any anti-Soviet activity the three years will be added to any other sentence.

Kalju Mätik is deprived of the rank of a lieutenant and Kiirend of the rank of a lieutenant of the Soviet Army reserves. Typewriters are confiscated from all defendants, the rifle and its ammunition, and photographic equipment from Mätik, and several newspapers and periodicals from Varato.

The term of punishment is counted from the date of arrest. This means that Kiirend and Yuskevich can look forward to camp life until December, 1979. Mätik will not be released before December, 1980 and Sergei Soldatov, who was the last to be arrested, will remain a prisoner until January, 1981.

The Struggle Goes on
"The Tallinn 4", as they have become known after their trial, seem to remain spiritually unbroken in the labor camp. Soldatov, Mätik, Yuskevich, and Kiirend all signed an "Appeal to World Public Opinion, to People of Good Will, to All Who Cherish the Principles of Democracy, Liberty and Human Rights". This appeal was signed by nineteen political prisoners of Potma prison camp in February, 1976. Soldatov and Mätik were the first signatories.

We the undersigned have been declared exceptionally dangerous criminals because we have read books ban-

13

ned in the USSR, because of our views and convictions which we shared with our friends, and because we permitted ourselves to give our reality a different meaning from what has been absolutely decreed.

In other words, we were sentenced for what is the rule in true democracies, the right of expressing personal opinions.

We were accused of "defamatory invention" and of having read defamatory books, although neither the investigators nor the court, in their fear of self-exposure, attempted to scrutinize or to analyse scientifically the incriminatory evidence and the literature concerned.

The investigators, the public prosecutor, the court – they all act in collusion to serve one and the same purpose. They all play their well-learned roles. They are permitted to act in such a manner solely to maintain a deceptive outward guise of jurisdiction.

We are detained in prisons, in concentration camps with a severe régime, in mental hospitals, completely isolated from the outside world.

We are forced to work, with extremely poor food and virtually without pay, for 48 hours or more a week. We are forced to attend political retraining lessons daily. We are being punished for the smallest offenses, we are taunted and tortured with hunger and with cold.

We beg you to come forth to defend us and to demand that the leaders of the CPSU and of the Government of our country observe the final act of the Helsinki Conference, that they adhere to the Declaration of Human Rights and to the International Convention of Political Rights. We beg you to demand our release as a practical proof of the implementation of the above documents, both in form and in spirit, and to demand the cessation of political persecution, hatred, and deportations.

February, 1976
(Signed) Soviet Political prisoners

CHAPTER 2

Why I wrote this book

This is not a history book. Its main theme is the present situation in the Baltic States. I will therefore not narrate the history of the Baltic States. It has been well described elsewhere. In those books you can read about the glory of medieval Lithuania, which was, at the time, one of the great powers of Europe. You can read how the Estonians and Latvians lost their ancient independence in the 13th century and were over the centuries reduced to being serfs on their own land at the hands of foreign masters. But their condition, both economic and social, gradually improved when liberalism swept over Europe in the 19th century. Having stubbornly kept their ethnic identities, Estonians, Latvians, and Lithuanians went through a period of national re-awakening. The stage was set for a liberation struggle in the Baltic area, then merely outlying provinces of Tsarist Russia.

Independence was finally achieved when the Russian and German empires collapsed simultaneously during World War I. The small national liberation armies of Estonia, Latvia, and Lithuania managed to push back the invading Soviet Russian forces from the East, and the invading German troops from the South. Soviet Russia signed peace treaties with each of the three Baltic States in 1920 and promised to respect their sovereignty "forever".

This "forever" lasted for some twenty years. Then

once again the Baltic peoples were crushed between the German hammer and the Russian anvil. The red and brown dictators, Josef Stalin and Adolf Hitler, signed their non-aggression treaty in 1939. In a secret additional protocol to his infamous Molotov-Ribbentrop pact, they agreed to the partition of Eastern Europe. The Baltic States were allotted to the Soviet Union. This was the beginning of the end for the independent Baltic States. First they were forced to sign mutual assistance treaties with the Soviet Union and to lease military bases to the Red Army. And in June 1940, the Soviet Union presented ultimatums to the Baltic States and the Red Army marched into Estonia, Latvia, and Lithuania in force. At the same time, Paris fell to the Nazis, so the world hardly noticed what happened to the Baltic nations.

The Western allies did not recognize the Soviet annexation of the Baltic States. Until this day the diplomatic representations of the independent Baltic States are formally recognized by the United States, Great Britain, Canada, and some other Western powers. No Western state, except for Finland, Sweden, and New Zealand has legally recognized the incorporation of the Baltic States into the Soviet Union.

The worst of Stalinist repression struck the Baltic nations during the early years of Soviet occupation. The Balts had to be taught to obey their new masters. The means are now well-known – mass deportations, imprisonments, and arbitrary terror. The rest was to be silence.

The repression finally achieved results. The anti-Soviet guerilla struggle faded out after a decade. It was the most long-lived and heroic guerilla struggle in post-war Europe but almost totally unknown in the West. The Western borders of the Baltic states were hermetically sealed and the Baltic guerillas received almost no outside support.

A "Conspiracy of Silence"

For the Soviet leaders, the best international news from their Baltic Republics was no news. Therefore, no foreign correspondents were allowed to visit these newly annexed territories, with their unreliable native populations.

Most Baltic families had friends or relatives who had fled to the West during the Second World War. But no contacts whatsoever were allowed between exiles and their homeland as long as Stalin lived. My mother and her sister had fled from Estonia in 1944. They did not hear a word about the fate of my grandmother for more than a decade. This was a typical case. No one was allowed to leave the Baltic Republics and no exiles were permitted to visit their old homeland.

After Stalin's death in 1953, things began to change. The surviving deportees in the Siberian camps began to return home. A few older people, who were "economically useless", received permission to unite with their families in the West. Private letters started to move again, although under the watchful eye of the Soviet censorship.

Until this day, however, no Western television team has been permitted to visit the Baltic Republics of the Soviet Union. In 1972, I was asked by Danish and Dutch television companies to do a report on the Baltic states today. But the Danish state television was not allowed to send any crew to film on the spot. Nor was Finnish television, although it scrupulously avoids any information that may be regarded as anti-Soviet. And we had only wanted them to film the finest in today's Estonia, the fantastic Song Festivals. Even this was not permitted. It has thus been impossible to get any news films without the express approval of the Soviet censorship. And the censorship naturally tries to stop any critical information about Soviet conditions. They have been remarkably successful in the Baltic case. Foreign correspondents stationed in Moscow occasionally visit Estonia, Latvia, or Lithuania and comment upon the passive resistance against the Soviet régime. But they have to obey strict travel regulations and do not master the local languages, which limits their effectiveness.

Occasional newspaper articles do not have the same impact as newsfilms. People saw and were shaken by the television coverage of the Vietnam war. Such newsreels as the one from Saigon, where a South Vietnamese police officer shot a prisoner through the head in the middle of the street had a tremendous impact. Horrifying sights, such as Buddhist monks burning themselves to death in protest of governmental policies, helped to create a widespread revulsion against the Vietnam war. But how many people have seen newsreels – or even a single picture – about the self-burnings by Lithuanian catholics which have taken place in anguished protest against the Soviet rule? None, because Western news photographers and cameramen have no access to Lithuania.

Such protests against the Soviet régime pass almost unnoticed in the West. Western media should more actively seek out critical information about closed societies such as the Soviet Baltic Republics, since such information is seldom served on a silver platter.

Through the resourcefulness of unknown persons living in Latvia, the West was provided with an original newsfilm. In late 1975 and early 1976, television viewers in the United States, Canada, Great Britain, West Germany, and France saw an unusual sight. The film was short – not more than three minutes long – but it gave westerners their first real glimpse of life in a Soviet labor camp. Viewers saw

18

columns of prisoners, the camp's watchtowers and gates, trucks with barred cages in which prisoners are transported to and from work sites, armed guards, and watchdogs. The film was secretly shot in Latvia, near Riga, and smuggled out to the West.

Until recently very few Balts have been able to travel to the West, where they can tell about life in their homelands. The Soviet authorities try to restrict foreign travel by both economic and political means. Any Soviet citizen who wishes to get an external passport to visit the West must pay an application fee of 30 roubles. This amounts to one-fifth of the average monthly wage in 1980. If the application is turned down, the money is not reimbursed. If it is accepted, the applicant must pay another 181 roubles to get his external passport. This means more than a months wages for an average worker. These economic restrictions affect all Soviet citizens, but they are especially annoying and restrictive for the Balts, who often have relatives in the West, and are thus able to get invitations.

Many Balts are not allowed to travel abroad, even if they could afford it. Those who have been in Siberian camps, or have otherwise been denounced as "enemies of the state", are still regarded as security risks and forced to stay home. But quite often persons with a clear past, and even Party members, are refused an external passport. Their applications are turned down without explanation. Even those reliable elements who manage to get permission to go abroad normally have to leave their family at home as a kind of hostage.

The exile Balts are also a rather poor source of information about current developments in their former homelands. Firstly, there is a natural tendency to react emotionally to the situation, to exaggerate or to have blind spots. Secondly, not many have dared or wanted to visit their occupied homeland. They do not want to activate their often traumatic memories from the days of flight, deportations, and Stalinist terror. Many are also afraid to be kept by the Soviet authorities in Estonia, Latvia or Lithuania against their own wish. It should be pointed out that the Soviet authorities officially regard former Baltic citizens living abroad and their children as Soviet citizens, even people like me who were born in the West after the Second World War. Third, exiles who have visited the Baltic States often refrain from publishing their impressions to protect their relatives back home. Many of them are not even willing to talk openly. I can speak freely since I have "chosen" to have no contacts whatsoever with friends or distant relatives in Estonia.

I visited Estonia twice in 1970, the first time to make a radio program for the Swedish Broadcasting Corporation where I was then chief editor of a daily debating program. I was fascinated by the country, the people and the political situation. I could move around freely in the capital Tallinn and speak to anybody I wanted to. I speak fluent Estonian, and also some Russian. I could therefore speak in confidence with people, without any official interpreter/censor. I remember an aged official who was moved to tears when he heard that I speak my Estonian mother tongue without accent, although I was born and grew up in Sweden.

A woman grabbed me by the arm and said: "Go home and write about everything you have seen, heard, or felt. Tell the world that we have survived and will never become Russians or Communists!"

This emotional plea, that was repeated to me by other people, made me write my first book on Soviet Estonia. Since that book was published in Sweden in 1971, I have not been allowed to return to Estonia nor to any other part of the Soviet Union. This blacklisting, however, cannot force me to silence. This book on the three Baltic States today is my reply.

Why Should the Baltic States Interest Us?
Why should Europeans, Americans, Canadians, Australians as well as other peoples be interested in the Baltic States? They are after all very little known in the West, especially now that they are no longer shown as independent states on the world map. And, furthermore, they are often seen as mini-nations.

Yes, the Baltic nations are indeed small. But their total population of 7·5 million is substantially larger than the population of European nations like Denmark, Norway or Switzerland. It is more than twice that of Ireland, Israel or New Zealand. The population of 16 Latin American nations is smaller than that of the Baltic States. And 33 new nations in post-colonial Africa, among them such focal points of recent international concern like Angola or Rhodesia-Zimbabwe, have less people than the Baltic States. The Baltic population is half that of Australia and a third that of Canada, two countries that have received a substantial number of immigrants from the Baltic area since the turn of the century and now have very active Estonian, Latvian and Lithuanian communities in their midst.

As I have travelled round the world I have often noticed how the Baltic States have become so little known that they seem almost exotic. The Estonians, Latvians, and Lithuanians have become the forgotten nations of Europe. And yet they are situated so close to the heart of that continent and are so much part of its history.

Today the Baltic Republics play an interesting role within the Soviet Union, which occupied and incorporated the three independent nations in 1940. The Baltic role in today's Soviet Union can be summarized by saying that the Baltic Republics play a negligible part in Soviet politics, a very special role in economics, and a rather important and influential socio-cultural role.

In the social and cultural field the Balts act as "westernizers", as promoters and transmitters of Western ideas and traditions, and of current international trends. For the hundreds of thousands of Russians and those of other Soviet nationalities who have settled either permanently or temporarily in Estonia, Latvia, and Lithuania, or who visit them as tourists or on state business, the Baltic Republics are a substitute for the West. After all, geographically they form the westernmost part of the Soviet Union and they constitute the area most recently incorporated into the Soviet Union, while they retain their western orientation and heritage.

The knowledge and information acquired in the Baltic Republics by visitors or temporary residents from other parts of the Soviet Union filters back east, carried throughout the vast reaches of the Soviet Empire.

On the other hand, the visits of Baltic theatrical troupes, rock and jazz bands, scientists and scholars, students, athletes, government officials, as well as the exhibitions of Baltic art, also contribute towards the dissemination of western attitudes and modern characteristics into other parts of the Soviet Union.

Estonia and Latvia are the most urbanized and industrialized republics of the Soviet Union and also have the highest living standard. Lithuania is vigorously catching up with her two sister republics in modernization and there are indications that she will in the near future surpass them in many areas of development. The Baltic Republics have been pioneers in the use of automation, computer technology, and in industrial and agricultural reforms and innovations. They have experimental plants where new production methods and technology are tried out for the Soviet economy. The social, industrial, economic, and agricultural development in Baltic Republics may therefore indicate future trends for the Soviet economy and society as a whole.

The Baltic Republics today trade with more than eighty foreign countries. This foreign trade is now controlled by all-Union agencies in Moscow or Leningrad. But in the future the autonomy of Baltic enterprises might be increased, so that they can trade directly with the outside world. Then they will become important trading links to the huge Soviet market.

Besides these socio-cultural and economic features, the situation and development of ethnic relationships within the Baltic Republics bears watching. Moscow has professed as one of her main political and social goals the creation of a unified Soviet nation. This amalgamation process is constantly furthered by official Soviet policies.

This merger of nationalities is a slow process, since half the population of the Soviet Union is composed of nationalities other than Russians, and the non-Russian share of population in the Soviet Union is steadily increasing. Soviet behavior towards Estonians, Latvians and Lithuanians, as well as the degree of ethnic cohesiveness and resistance shown by the Balts gives us some indication of how this great struggle in the field of Soviet nationalities policy will resolve itself.

If the Soviet Union should permit freer international exchanges in tourism and other kinds of visits, and the trends of the past decade have been in this direction, the Baltic Republics may become important centers for western tourism, as well as very attractive places for western scholars and students.

The Baltic capitals with their history written all over them are now open for western tourists. Vilnius, the renaissance and baroque city of Lithuanian Grand Dukes has now a population of 450,000 and its modern quarters contain some of the best laid out new construction in the Soviet Union. Riga, a bustling metropolis of 800,000, is the centre of Latvian culture with many of its buildings reaching back into the medieval times. Tallinn, the capital of Estonia on the shores of the Gulf of Finland, has an unusually well preserved inner town full of medieval gothic architecture surrounded by the ancient city walls and bastions topped with the hill fort of Toompea (Dome Hill), which is a sight by itself. The 440,000 citizens of Tallinn are now renovating the old town and constructing modern buildings in preparation to host the yachting races of the 1980 Olympics.

Two or three other cities in each Republic are open for western tourists, but only for very short day trips with no provisions nor permits for overnight accommodations. Before the war many foreigners, especially Scandinavians, used to vacation in the Baltic seaside resorts. But such beautiful beach resorts as Palanga in Lithuania, Jurmala in Latvia, and Pärnu and Narva-Joesuu in Estonia are not prepared to host western vacationers. Some are even off-limits. Each summer these are filled with Russians who come in great numbers to the "Baltic Riviera".

The Baltic countryside, with such gems as the recently founded national parks – Ignalinas Lithuanian National Park, the Gauja River Latvian National Park, and the Lahemaa Estonian National Park – is also off-limits to foreign tourists. But this restrictive Soviet policy, dictated from Moscow, might ease up in coming years.

Different Perspectives

When describing the present situation in the Baltic states, or for that matter in any other country, one is soon faced with a difficult question. From what perspective should the immediate past and the current situation be seen and projected? What standards should it be measured against? And what aspects of society should be stressed?

The picture one paints of contemporary Estonia, Latvia, and Lithuania from the vantage point of the open, democratic welfare societies in the West will be very different from the picture you get when your point of departure is the very difficult situation in the Baltic states themselves which existed during the first two decades of Soviet rule.

For most Europeans and North Americans, the comparison with the Western world seems probably most natural, since our society is the best frame of reference. Exile Balts, who for psychological reasons tend to have a negative understanding of life in the contemporary Soviet Baltic Republics, also prefer the Western comparison. It may be, however, that they thereby have set up an idealized standard, a higher level of aspiration than their compatriots at home.

"The Baltic nations have of course the same right to liberate themselves from their present domination by Soviet Communist colonialism as we in Africa, Asia, and Latin America liberated ourselves from Western colonialism", President Senghor of Senegal told me in 1976. For him the parallels between Eastern and Western colonialism were easy to see, as was the moral right of the Estonians, Latvians and Lithuanians to national self-determination and political independence.

For the people in Estonia, Latvia and Lithuania, immersed in the daily realities as they are, the most important thing seems to be that the semi-starvation, mass terror, and hopelessness of the Stalin era have passed into history. The social and economic development in the 1960's after all brought significant improvements within the narrow limits of the Soviet system. Many people feel that they can now breathe again and hope for the future. This observation is not intended as an excuse for the dark sides still ominously present on the Soviet Baltic scene, but only as a reminder that oppressed people might be less unhappy than they should be.

By Soviet norms the Baltic Republics are doing rather well. Their living standards are higher than those of other Soviet Republics. They have better than average incomes, more spacious housing, a greater choice of consumer goods. This difference is readily apparent to the Russians, who are immigrating to Latvia and Estonia in large numbers.

According to Soviet bookkeeping the Baltic per capita national income is on par with Scandinavia. This is, however, a Soviet statistician's mirage and the Balts know that they have vastly less purchasing power than the Scandinavians. They feel economically exploited and ethnically threatened. And above all they want to make their own decisions in economy, in social policies and in the cultural life. This, however, is denied to them.

Observers from the developing countries of the Third World, on the other hand, would probably be impressed by the fast transformation of the pre-war, mainly agricultural Baltic States into modern industrial societies with highly developed technology. They might, however, also recognize the colonial character of the Baltic dependence on Moscow.

In this book I will try to take into account all these different perspectives.

26

CHAPTER 3

Between East and West

Estonia, Latvia and Lithuania are the youngest of the Soviet Republics, and the only ones to have been independent nations between the two World Wars, 1918–1940. They are also the most westerly, both geographically and culturally. Russians sometimes speak of the Baltic Republics as "the Soviet abroad" (*Sovetskaya zagranitsa*).

Western influence is noticeable in many ways. One example is the way the people dress and look. Such Western apparel as the miniskirt and jeans showed up early in the Baltic Republics. The old women of the grandmother dressed in black, so typical of the Russian street scene, are less conspicuous in the Baltic Republics. The Baltic ready-made clothing industry is in the fore of Soviet fashion. The Estonian fashion journal *Siluett* (Silhouette), published in both Estonian and Russian, has a wide circulation in Moscow and Leningrad.

The Western orientation of the Baltic Republics has geographical, linguistic, and historical origins. The Baltic region is not geographically or geologically part of Russia, but rather a Western European outpost and a part of Scandinavia, forming a wedge in Northern Europe between the Slavic and Germanic areas.

The area around the Baltic Sea is a homogeneous physical, and, to some extent, ethnogeographical region. The Swedish geographer Sten de Geer called this region Balto-Scandia. The Baltic lands are divided from Scandinavia only by the narrow Baltic Sea and its gulfs. If you look at a geological map you will find that the seabed of the Baltic Sea is a bridge, joining geologically similar areas in Scandinavia and in the Baltic states. Courland, the western province of Latvia, lies less than a hundred miles across the Sea from Gotland, the largest of the Swedish islands in the Baltic Sea. In the north, Estonia is divided from Finland by the Gulf of Finland, which in some places is no more than fifty miles across. The northern half of the Baltic region has an archipelago, just like the Scandinavian peninsula and southern Finland. Lithuania and Latvia have thousands of lakes, just like Sweden and Finland.

A marked ethnogeographical boundary runs through the areas of swamp and forest east of Latvia and Lithuania, and continues northward through the large lake called Peipsi (Peipus) and the Narva River on the border between Estonia and Russia. The lower Nemunas (Neman), the great river of Lithuania, is the boundary of the Baltic area to the southwest. It is therefore incorrect to call the Baltic region "the border states of Russia", as some have done, or a German "Ostland" as the Nazis did during the Second World War.

Neither should the Baltic countries be regarded as a Russian area historically. Russia is in fact only the latest colonial power to rule the Baltic countries. The Russian domination began as late as the 18th century. The nucleus of the Russian Empire, the Great Principality of Moscow, itself only ceased in 1480 to be a vassal of the Khanate of the Golden Horde. By that time Lithuania had been in existence as an independent kingdom or principality for 250 years, and remained so for almost another 100 years – until union with Poland in 1569.

Tsar Peter the Great captured the northern Baltic provinces (Estonia and Livonia) from Sweden in the Great Northern War (1700–1721), but this did not bring about any considerable immigration of Russians. The rest of the Latvian area and Lithuania were annexed by Russia during the first and third partitions of Poland in 1772 and 1795. Local power in the Baltic provinces, until the independence of the Baltic States after the First World War, was not in the hands of Russians, but of the Baltic Germans in Estonia and Latvia, and the Polonized gentry in Lithuania. The special position of the Baltic provinces within the Tsarist Empire was marked, for instance, by their retaining their own legal systems (except in Lithuania, where Russian law was introduced in 1840). By the time the Baltic peoples regained their independence in 1918, they had been under Russian rule for less than two centuries.

Non-Russian Cultures
The languages, alphabet and religion of the Baltic peoples are different from those of the Russians. The Balts use the Latin alphabet, unlike the Russians, who use Cyrillic letters. The explanation for this is a religio-cultural one. Those peoples who were Christianized from the Byzantine Empire and became Orthodox received the Cyrillic alphabet, based on Greek script; those who were Christianized from Rome, became Catholic and adopted the Latin alphabet. Thus the different alphabets also indicate from where different European peoples have gotten their basic cultural impulses.

Latvian and Lithuanian constitute the Baltic language group within the Indo-European language family. The Baltic languages were earlier far more widespread. To this group belonged Old Prussian, which disappeared in the 17th century through delib-

29

erate Germanization. The Baltic languages are of great linguistic interest. Lithuanian is considered to be the living language closest to the original Indo-European. The Baltic language group is considered a separate entity and different from the Germanic, the Slavic, and the Romance languages.

Estonian is linguistically not a Baltic language, not even an Indo-European one. Estonian belongs to the Finno-Ugric family of languages, together with Finnish, Lapp, Hungarian and several languages spoken in the Soviet Union. Among the latter are Mordvinian, which is spoken by more than one million Mordvinians living in their Autonomous Republic and neighboring areas southeast of Moscow, and Komi and Mari, spoken by two distinct peoples in the northeastern part of the European Soviet Union.

So we must distinguish between the linguistic label "Baltic languages" (a sub-group of the Indo-European language family), and the languages spoken in the Baltic countries. The difference is not only of academic interest. One must keep in mind that Estonians do not understand Latvians and Lithuanians speaking their native tongues, and vice versa. Latvian and Lithuanian, although closely related, cannot be mutually understood, except on a very elementary level.

These differences of language, as well as of folklore and religion, make it obvious that the collective names "Balts" and "the Baltic countries" do not cover the kind of homogenous group that most non-Balts assume. The main bond between the Balts is their geographical proximity, and the historical fate they have often shared, especially in the twentieth century.

Estonians and Finns
The Estonian and Finnish languages are very close. This is the basis for the cultural affinity between the two nations. The Estonians have through the cen-

turies found it very useful to have a larger sister nation and neighbor just across the Gulf of Finland. They have often been inspired by Finnish culture.

The national anthem of independent Estonia, *Mu isamaa, mu õnn ja rõõm*, is sung to the same tune as the Finnish national anthem. During the Stalin era it was therefore forbidden in Estonia to play the Finnish national anthem. Delicate situations arise even today when Finnish national teams visit Estonia and the public stands up for the "wrong" national anthem and joins in more enthusiastically than when the Soviet Estonian anthem is played.

The geographical and linguistic proximity to Finland is still useful to the Estonians. On most of the roofs of apartment houses in the Estonian capital there are television aerials turned towards Helsinki. The Finnish television broadcasts are not jammed. There is hardly any need for it since Finnish television abstains from what could be considered by the Russians as "anti-Soviet propaganda". But the Finnish programs are still somewhat of a safety valve. They act as a relay for Western cultural impulses and news to Estonia. Most Estonians understand Finnish well enough after some practice to understand radio and television programs. One detail that illuminated the popularity of these programs for me was the great demand for the Saturday issues of the Finnish Communist newspaper *Kansan Uutiset*. The weekday issues can always be had in Tallinn, but the Saturday issue was sold out for two Saturdays in a row during my visit. I was told that all copies of the Saturday *Kansan Uutiset* are normally sold out on the very same day they reach the news-stands. The explanation given for this surprising popularity was that *Kansan Uutiset* on Saturday publishes the Finnish television program for the following week.

The Estonians have a similar relationship to other Finno-Ugric peoples within the Soviet Union as the

Finns do to the Estonians themselves. The incorporation of Estonia into the Soviet Union was, for example, an asset for the Finnish culture in Karelia. The Karelians, who use the Finnish language for written communication, came into contact with a larger, linguistically related nation within the Soviet Union. The cultural exchange between Estonia and Karelia consists of visiting theatre companies, translations of literature, scientific co-operation, and tourism.

Estonia is also a source of cultural inspiration for the other Finno-Ugric peoples in the Soviet Union. Almost half of the doctoral and candidates' dissertations in the Volga-Finnic Mari language have been presented at Tartu State University in Estonia.

Estonian ethnographers, linguists and students carry out research among the Mari, the Komi, the Mordvins, and other linguistically related people in northern and central Russia. One group of Estonians, for example, was surprised to find out that people in the Vepse villages (a small nationality closely related to Estonians) were listening to the Estonian radio broadcasts from Tallinn.

Links with the West
Paradoxically, the Second World War strengthened the Western orientation of the Balts, in spite of their countries being incorporated into the Soviet empire. To begin with, the Soviet occupation only alienated the native population from everything Russian. And most Baltic families obtained some personal connection with the West through relatives or friends who had fled abroad during the Second World War.

When the Soviets had taken over, almost all contact with the West was prohibited. Even sending letters to the West was considered compromising. Letters that all the same were posted to Western addresses were scrutinized by governmental censors.

Only at the beginning of the sixties were tourists from the West again allowed to visit the Baltic Republics, and then certain larger cities only. Other large cities, almost all small towns, and all of the Baltic countryside has remained a forbidden area to Western tourists, to this day. At the same time the censorship of letters was relaxed. Older non-productive people began to get permission to emigrate and join their children in the West. A direct sea link, operating during the summer season between Helsinki and Tallinn, was established in 1965. Cultural and sports exchanges with the West were initiated.

Estonia is the Republic within the Soviet Union that has the closest contacts with the West. In the first place, Estonia is situated closer to a Western country, namely Finland, than any other Soviet Republic. Historical contacts across the Baltic Sea with Scandinavia were mainly directed to the northern parts of the Baltic countries, mostly to Estonia, but also to Latvia, and because of this the Estonians and Latvians feel a certain affinity with Swedish culture. Also, Sweden is one of the main centres of cultural life among exiled Estonians. Most exile Latvian and Lithuanian intellectual leaders and cultural personalities reside in the United States or Canada, where large and very active Lithuanian, Latvian and Estonian communities are to be found.

Source of Cultural Inspiration
The 1960's brought a cultural renaissance in the Baltic countries in the arts, literature, music, theatre, and the study of national heritage. The Baltic countries, especially Estonia, have for a long time played a leading role in Soviet jazz music and modern art. The first Soviet jazz festival ever was held in Tallinn, Estonia, when jazz to the Soviet authorities was still

33

an expression of "bourgeois decadence". The first Soviet performances of Bertolt Brecht's hardly orthodox plays took place in Estonia. The Lithuanian and Estonian playwrights were the first to experiment with the theater of the absurd. Estonian composers pioneered the use of the twelve-tone technique. At art exhibitions in the Baltic Republics you can find paintings and sculptures that would have given Khrushchev apoplexy. (In 1962, when viewing an art exhibition in the manége building in Moscow, he noticed some abstract paintings and hurled vulgar abuse at the artists, saying that abstract art could quite well be produced by donkeys, if only their tails were dipped in a jar of paint.) In the 1970's Lithuanian architecture and town planning became known as the most modern and advanced in the Soviet Union.

There is, however, a difference in tolerance between Estonia and Lithuania on the one side, and Latvia on the other. The Latvian cultural climate is harsher than the Estonian or Lithuanian. This might be because Russian and Russian-born Latvian Communists, faithful to Moscow, have a stronger position within the Communist Party in Latvia than in Estonia or Lithuania.

This difference in the latitude given to creative artists and writers in the Baltic Republics is of interest to anyone trying to predict the future of the non-Russian peoples in the Soviet Union. Does the development have to be strictly within the guidelines handed down from Moscow, which would also mean Russification? Or is it possible to safeguard and to carry forward, more than hitherto, the non-Russian people's cultural heritage also?

Will Nationalism Die?
What non-Russians call Russification is often the result of the strong centralization of all expressions of

34

Soviet life to Moscow. In the days of the Tsar the Baltic provinces were to a considerable extent autonomous, although belonging to the Tsarist Empire. Today the central authorities in Moscow have more numerous and also more effective means of influencing the development in the Baltic Republics and other outlying areas. This is the great difference between the Tsarist and Soviet attempts to Russify the non-Russian areas and cultures of the empire.

According to Soviet propaganda, the nationality problem has already been solved and all Soviet peoples live in harmony with each other in the best of all possible worlds. A number of scholars in the West, on the other hand, are convinced that nationalism in the non-Russian areas will continue to exist as a threat to the Soviet state. The national differences make the Soviet Union a giant with feet of clay.

The well-known Soviet dissident Andrei Amalrik maintains in his book *Will the Soviet Union Survive Until 1984?* that the disintegration of the Soviet empire will begin in the 1980's as a consequence of a protracted war with China. "Simultaneously, the nationalist tendencies of the non-Russian peoples of the Soviet Union will intensify sharply, first in the Baltic area, the Caucasus and the Ukraine, then in Central Asia and along the Volga," adds Amalrik and says that the non-Russian nationalities will aim for separateness.[1]

Perhaps Amalrik and other doomsday prophets exaggerate. The events of recent years do, however, indicate that the Baltic question will remain an irritating problem for the Soviet authorities. And the spirit of resistance of the Estonians, Latvians and Lithuanians is far from broken.

[1] Andrei Amalrik, *Will the Soviet Union Survive until 1984?*, New York, Harper & Row, 1971, p. 63.

Nationalism or Socialism?

The guiding principle of cultural life for the many nations of the Soviet Union is usually summarized in the slogan, "National in form, socialist in content". Spiteful tongues maintain that this merely grants the right to praise the Soviet Union, Communism and Russian culture in all possible languages.

Baltic intellectuals often try to emphasize the national part of the formula.[2] Several writers have tried historical themes. Others have praised their mother tongue as the main expression of national culture and identity.

One example of the attitude to the native language is expressed by the young Estonian poet Hando Runnel, here in a free English translation by Rein Taagepera of University of California:

> What can console my people
> If one of its gems were lost?
> What could console me in particular
> If my native tongue became extinct?
>
> Our wise friend has a ready answer,
> It's good that it's going this way;
> It's all so perfectly progressive
> And directed by the great cause.
>
> It serves all nations and countries
> That small fry and sharks may live
> But if some do die then only so as
> To stamp out war and self-delusion.
>
> But if some do die then only
> In order to fulfil a noble dream
> Which says the many are one
> Or at least they will become one.

[2] See, e.g., Andres Jüriado's study "Nationalism vs. Socialism; The Case of Soviet Estonian Drama", a paper presented at the AABS Conference on Baltic Studies in Toronto, 1972.

Yet what could console a people
If its tongue became extinct?
As for us there would be no solace
If my native tongue were lost.

The Case of Arvi Siig

An interesting example of how writers can, in spite of the Soviet censorship, transmit a nationalist message to attentive readers, was given by another young Estonian poet, Arvi Siig. He published a poem in the cultural weekly *Sirp ja Vasar* which at a cursory glance seems to be quite an innocent poem about Masha, the matron of a day nursery. She is described as a good woman, though she really ought to retire as she does not understand the children and is mostly concerned with keeping them in order, rather than trying to help them or teaching them anything.

It could have been a coincidence that Masha is a Russian name, while all the children have Estonian names. More interesting is that the initials of the children's names, taken in the order they appear on the scene, together form the Estonian word for "people" or "nation". In order to deceive the censor a classical ruse thus changes an innocent poem to an expression of what even an Estonian Party member feels down deep of the Soviet nationality policy.

Another interesting example of how a gifted and daring writer can, in a formally unobjectionable poem, transmit a controversial message, is Siig's poem, "Che". Written in honor of the Latin American revolutionary, who on several occasions openly criticized the Latin American Communist Parties and also the Soviet Union, this poem was published in January, 1970 by the Estonian literary journal

Looming (Creation). The first two verses are given here in a free English translation by Rein Taagepera:

> Che, Che Guevara!
> The world is black – black.
> The glory of revolution
> is only
> a line out of its miscellania.
> Jan Hus must have perished in the same way,
> although in a different way.
> The black and white list will
> contain your name, Che Guevara.
>
> There was a promise of dawn.
> Winds and clouds were restless.
> In the jungle
> and at the top of the stone jungle
> the new day flashed.
> Over your body they march again,
> as they marched
> into a certain small country –
> the troops of the world gendarme.

This poem passed the scrutiny of the censors because it was possible to read it as critical of the United States. But anybody used to reading between the lines immediately discovers the double meanings. The march of foreign troops into a small country describes as equally well the invasion of Czechoslovakia as of the Dominican Republic, which is mentioned towards the end of the poem. In order that the reader is left in no doubt of this possibility of interpretation, Che Guevara is compared to Jan Hus, the Czech reformer. And wasn't Tsarist Russia called the "gendarme of Europe" after Russian troops helped put down the liberal revolutions of 1848?

By honoring Che Guevara and placing the imperialist methods of the United States and the Soviets side by side, the poem becomes not only a national protest against an earlier invasion, but also reminds us of the New Left critique of the Soviet Union.

The Latvian national midsummer celebration Jani (or Ligosvetki) was forbidden for many years. The authorities thought it unworthy for a Soviet people to devote themselves to "heathen traditions". Only in 1968 was the time of the summer solstice again allowed to be celebrated. Otherwise the Soviet authorities have normally tried to take over national traditions and adapt them to socialist conditions. They want to fill old bottles with new wine, but many people still prefer the old well-known brands. The Baltic Song Festivals are the main example of a native cultural event having been given a new Soviet gloss on the surface.

Almost 30,000 singers and some thousand musicians took part in the 1969 Centennial Song Festival in Tallinn. Nearly a quarter of a million people attended (Estonia only has 1.4 million inhabitants). Not even Fidel Castro in Cuba is able to collect almost one-fifth of the nation in one and the same place. Furthermore, over one-third of the population in Estonia is now non-Estonian and takes little part in Estonian cultural events or cultural consumption.

Eight out of ten Estonians, but hardly more than one out of ten Russians in the Republic, have, for example, read one of the classic works of the Estonian literature by Oskar Luts.[3] Similar figures are valid for the novel *Tôde ja ĉigus* (Truth and Right) by the greatest Estonian prose writer, A. H. Tammsaare.

The Russians in the Baltic Republics are well catered for culturally. 60% of the films shown at the cinemas in Latvia are in Russian, 35% are in Russian with Latvian subtitles and only 5% are in Latvian. More than half of the Latvian radio programs are

[3] These figures are taken from a survey published in the theoretical journal *Eesti Kommunist*, No. 7, 1969.

Russian broadcasts relayed from Moscow, while barely a quarter of the transmission time is taken up by programs in the Latvian language.

The Alphabet
A problem that concerns Estonians, Latvians and Lithuanians in the Baltic Republics is the apprehension about the position of the Latin alphabet they use.

A number of Soviet peoples have been forced to change to the Cyrillic alphabet used by the Russians. Among the latter are nations as large as the Uzbeks (over nine million people in 1970), the Tatars (nearly six million), and the Azerbaijanis (over four million). In the twenties and thirties these people used the Latin alphabet (and before that the Arabic), but in 1938–40, Stalin decreed that they should change to the Cyrillic alphabet.

Some of the Estonians I talked to in 1970 were afraid that the Latin alphabet might be done away with in their Republic also (and if so, most probably in Latvia and Lithuania, too). Such an event would make it more difficult for the Balts to keep in touch with the Western world. It would also cut off some of the connections with the Baltic peoples' past. A change from the Latin alphabet would considerably increase the coercive aspect of the present Russification of the Baltic Republics.

Such a step was actually attempted already in Tsarist times. In Lithuania and in the Latvian province of Latgale it was forbidden to use the Latin alphabet for forty years (1864–1904). The authorities did not succeed in crushing Lithuanian nationalism and resistance to Russification with this decree. People refused to change to the Slavic characters. Newspapers, magazines, and books were printed abroad and smuggled in. The Baltic exile publish-

40

ing and cultural activities make a good foundation for an enterprise of this kind if the need for it should rise again, but the Soviet regime has far more effective means of control and repression than did the Tsarist régime at that time.

"Internationalist Education" – a Catchword for Russification

At present the Soviet propaganda against the "remains of bourgeois nationalism" and for "internationalist education" is stronger than ever. It shows that the nationalities problem is not solved. This campaign is especially strong in the Baltic Republics because of the national resistance to Russification and to the domination of all facets of Baltic life by Moscow.

At the 23rd Party Congress in 1966, the conflicting national problems were mentioned only in passing. At the 24th Party Congress in 1971, nationalism was one of the main items on the agenda. A new large campaign with the watchword "internationalist education" was embarked upon on the eve of the 50-year anniversary of the Soviet Union.

Estonia, Latvia and Lithuania were likened to some cozy corners in the spacious and modern house which is the whole of the Soviet Union. The message was that the interests of the local Republics must always give way to the common interests of "the Great Socialist Fatherland". The Soviet Union must be every Soviet citizen's only Fatherland, irrespective of his or her nationality.

In March 1972, the Central Committees of the Estonian and Latvian Communist Parties discussed in plenary sessions how the new campaign for "internationalist education" was going to be carried out. The First Secretary of the Latvian Party, Augusts Voss, said:

Propagandists, agitators, political information officers, all workers on the ideological front must in a brilliant and convincing manner stress the great Russian people's important role in building up Socialism and Communism in our country. We are proud to be members of a society that has arisen for the first time in the history of the world, of the Soviet people; we are proud to have one and the same Socialist Fatherland, to be members of the great internationalist army building a new society. We must place the interest of the whole state first; no nationalist, local patriotic and isolationist manifestations can be allowed.[4]

This speech by Voss was a faithful repetition of the central slogans and a typical example of how fond Communist leaders are of military terminology.

Two days earlier, a Soviet Estonian newspaper published a speech by the local First Secretary, Johannes Käbin. He too demanded "patriotic pride in our Great Socialist Fatherland" and an uncompromising fight against "manifestations of nationalism" and "chauvinism".[5] Neither Voss nor Käbin specified what was meant by "not permitted manifestations of nationalism". Were these speeches only a dutiful repetition of slogans sent to them from Moscow?

The Baltic leaders have repeatedly demanded "increased ideological alertness". During the 1976 Party Congress Augusts Voss again warned against a "creeping contra-revolution" in Latvia.

Käbin's speech was published under the heading, *Primus inter pares*, first among equals. The Baltic peoples are often forced to honor the Russians as an "elder brother". To paraphrase George Orwell, all the peoples of the Soviet Union are equal but the Russians are more equal than the others.

[4] *Sovetskaya Latviya*, March 14, 1972.
[5] *Sovetskaya Estoniya*, March 12, 1972.

CHAPTER 4

Education and indoctrination

The number of university and college students in the
Baltic Republics has multiplied since the Second
World War. In 1975 there were in Estonia about
23,000 students at six institutions for higher learning,
in Latvia 41,000 students at ten institutions, and in
Lithuania nearly 60,000 students at twelve institutions for higher learning. Since the end of the 1930's,
student numbers have grown by four times in Latvia,
five in Estonia, and ten times in Lithuania. According
to official statistics, Estonia, Latvia, and Lithuania
have about 170 students per 10,000 inhabitants, twice
as many as Great Britain, France, or Italy and three
times as many as West Germany.

Five Reservations
One has to be careful when comparing present education statistics with figures for the period of national
independence between the two World Wars or for
Western countries.

Firstly, the development in Soviet Baltic education
is only a continuation of the trends from the Tsarist
times and the era of Baltic independence. The Estonians and Latvians were already in the 19th century
the best educated people in the Tsarist Empire.
According to the 1897 census figures, the highest
percentage of people who could read resided in the
Baltic provinces of Estonia (92%), followed by Livo-

nia (91%) and Curonia (85%), while the rest of the Russian Empire lagged far behind. And only one-fifth of the Estonians and Latvians were unable to write, compared to four-fifths in the whole of Russia.

When the Baltic states were incorporated into the Soviet Union in 1940, only 2% of the Estonian population was illiterate, 7% of the population of Latvia and 14% of Lithuania, in comparison with 13% of the population in Soviet Union. Most of the illiterates in Estonia and Latvia were Russians in the areas bordering on the Soviet Union.

Before independence native Balts had, by and large, been cut off from higher education, but the development during the two decades of independence was all the faster. Latvia had more university students in relation to her population than any other country in the world, and Estonia followed closely. In the middle of the 1930's Estonia had one university student per 332 inhabitants, compared with one per 522 in Norway, one per 657 in Denmark and one per 885 in Great Britain.[1] There are today twice as many students in Estonia as in Great Britain, according to Soviet figures, but according to the above figures there were more than two and a half times as many students in Estonia as in Great Britain before World War II. The gap between Great Britain and Estonia has according to these statistics decreased since the war.

Secondly, the large increase in the number of students during the Soviet period is partly due to the general increase of population. Thirdly, admission of students from other parts of the Soviet Union inflates the enrollment of Baltic universities. The total number of students in the Baltic republics is thus bigger than the number of native students. This on the other

[1] Hampden Jackson, *Estonia*, Allen and Unwin, London, 1938, p. 236.

hand is partly offset by Baltic students studying elsewhere in the Soviet Union. Fourthly, many students take only short correspondence courses and would in other countries not be counted as full-time students. One third of the students at Tartu State University in southern Estonia study in this way, and about the same proportion at other Baltic institutes for higher learning. Fifthly, the education explosion is a general phenomena in the post-war world; it is far from limited to the Baltic republics or to Communist regimes.

With all these reservations in mind, education remains one of the areas where the Communist governments of the Baltic republics have been most successful. Most of the Estonians I talked to during my visits to Estonia considered that the best achievement of the Soviet period was that most people can now get the education or training that they wish to have. Groups that lack this advantage are, amongst others, religious youths, former political prisoners, and "class enemies", often including their children and relatives. Baltic students often face transfers to Russian institutions of learning or places of work, usually for the first three years after taking a degree.

Soviet and Scandinavian Schools
Since I grew up in Sweden, I will attempt to draw some lines of comparison between the Scandinavian and the Soviet educational systems. The Soviet, and thus also the Baltic, schools differ from Scandinavian schools in many basic concepts.

1. The Scandinavian school is said to be trying to educate the pupil for independent and critical thinking; this is not encouraged in Soviet schools.

45

2. The Soviet school is a true mirror of the society around it, stressing the respect for authority and officials. The children in Baltic schools wear school uniforms and have to stand in attention when they answer the teacher's questions.

3. Emphasis is placed on competition as a means of getting as good results as possible from all pupils. Yearly competitions are held to select the best pupils in languages and natural sciences. These pupils are then looked after by the universities while still at school. The school notice boards are used to praise specially good pupils and to denigrate "bad" ones, for example those who regularly attend church.

4. The system of a heavy homework load is still practised in Soviet schools. The teachers I spoke to said that homework could not be abolished without seriously lowering the standards of knowledge.

5. Factual knowledge is the supreme value. The Soviet school is still to a high degree a process of learning facts. Theoretical subjects are more highly valued than practical ones, by teachers, pupils, and parents alike. One exception is the promotion of art and music studies, where Baltic schools have gone further than other schools in the Soviet Union.

6. An obvious difference between Baltic and Western schools is the role of the Russian language. The Baltic native languages are voluntary in Russian language schools in the Baltic Republics and are normally taught to Russian children two hours a week from the first year. The Russian language is also theoretically a voluntary subject in native schools. But in reality every Baltic schoolchild has to study it. The teaching of Russian begins with four to five hours a week in the

first year. Experiments are being carried out on teaching Russian already in the nurseries.

7. The teaching of Marxism-Leninism begins in the compulsory school and is intensified at university, then usually with an obligatory six to seven hours a week. A medical student, for example, cannot get his medical degree without passing an examination in Marxism–Leninism as well as taking a short course in the history of the Communist Party. The "sacred writings" of Marx and Lenin are also studied in the Communist youth movement, Komsomol. Those who do not join are regarded as politically unreliable and jeopardize their future careers.

8. Pupils in Soviet high schools are already taught military skills. They learn to handle automatic guns and practice markmanship with small arms. Many male students at universities or other institutions of higher learning also go through officers' training at the same time.

9. Boarding schools are encouraged. They make it, among other things, more difficult for parents to "poison" their children with bourgeois and religious values.

10. There are special schools which emphasize the teaching of natural sciences, languages, sport, and music. The special teaching in a language school starts in the second term of the first year. The number of hours that a foreign language is taught is three times as large as in ordinary schools, and classes are small, at the most twelve children in a group. They also study the literature, culture, geography and history of the country in question.

   In schools which specialize in mathematics, physics, or chemistry, streaming occurs in the ninth year.

Teaching is carried out in co-operation with university lecturers. The pupils in these "elite schools" can after graduation continue with individual studies at institutions of higher learning.

Such special schools mostly recruit children from towns and the intelligentsia. The Soviet school authorities, and those in the Baltic Republics, seem to think that the advantages from the point of view of both society and pupils outweigh the disadvantages of socially biased recruitment. The elite schools provide society with highly qualified and most valuable specialists.

The teaching in schools is organized according to the background and ability of the children by other means than special schools for bright children. A leading idea is that children of different abilities should not follow the same courses. There is no comprehensive schooling as in the Western welfare states.

Within the general school system there are a number of specialized classes for deeper penetration of various subjects from the ninth year. From the seventh year pupils can also choose voluntary extra courses in one or more subjects. In Estonia there were courses in about a hundred such extra subjects at the beginning of the 1970's.

Eleven-Year School
The main difference between Baltic and other Soviet schools is that the eleven-year high school has been retained in the Baltic Republics. In the rest of the Soviet Union the school years were cut back to ten in 1965. The extra year at school is thought to be important for maintaining the teaching of their native languages and other national subjects.

Baltic educators and cultural personalities pointed out to Moscow that the time of schooling in the non-Russian Republics must be longer as the educational content is greater. Non-Russian children learn, over and above their own mother tongue, the Russian language and literature. Baltic educators warned that if the eleventh year of schooling were discontinued, Baltic children's knowledge of Russian would be diminished, though what they feared at heart was perhaps that the reduction of a year would affect national subjects most.

Falsification of History
Soviet education meets its most important problems in qualitative rather than quantitative questions, that is to say, problems that cannot be measured in figures alone. Balts dislike the fact that education is used for Communist and pro-Russian indoctrination. Somebody said to me that the Soviet school is "the Church of the new Communist Creed". In all societies, however, education has the task of fostering certain ideological values. The problem is not whether such indoctrination is good or bad, but rather whether "right" or "wrong" values are being promoted, and how and why.

One typical example of how indoctrination works in the Soviet school system is the re-writing and re-education of Baltic history. The period of Swedish supremacy in Estonia and northern Latvia from 1561 to 1721 used to be popularly called "the good old Swedish times". This period is today described as a time of "military and feudal oppression", when serfdom and colonial exploitation became worse than ever. The incorporation of the Baltic provinces into Tsarist Russia in the early 18th century, on the other hand, is said to have been of enormous beneficial importance for the Baltic peoples. A typical quotation: "Influences from the democratic culture in Russia were of decisive importance for Estonia's national culture and raising of the people's cultural level".[2] If a higher "democratic culture" was thus ascribed to Russia already in the darkness of the Tsarist era – what heights have been reached since the Great October Revolution?

The independence of the Baltic States is described as a time of "bourgeois class dictatorship" and "dependence on western imperialism". The Molotov–Ribbentrop Pact, which was the beginning of the end for Baltic independence, is never mentioned. The Soviet occupation in 1940 is called a "spontaneous proletarian and socialist revolution". The mass deportations during the Stalin era are hardly ever mentioned. The independence between the two World Wars is usually said to have been of a "formal" nature while "real sovereignty" begins only in 1940, when the Baltic peoples are said to have cast off the heavy yoke of imperialism. This is a typical case of Soviet "newspeak", where words and concepts are given a different meaning from the western one.

The re-evaluation of history is not restricted to the Baltic countries, but concerns the history of all non-Russian peoples.[3] The history of the Russian people is also rewritten in order to show that the Bolsheviks have never erred and have always been a driving force. Historiography is not fixed – it can be changed according to the political climate. The earlier truly Marxist and internationalist historical writing was prohibited by Stalin already in the 1930's. It has since mostly been based on pro-Russian tenets.

The teaching of national history (and geography) in the Baltic Republics was prohibited after 1940. It was

---

[2] *Eesti NSV Ajalugu*, ed. G. H. Naan. Tallinn, 1959, 2nd ed., pp. 131–132.

[3] See Lowell Tillet, *The Great Friendship, Soviet Historians on the non-Russian Nationalities*, University of North Carolina Press, North Carolina, 1969.

reinstated in Estonia and Latvia at the end of the fifties (in Lithuania already in 1944). The number of lessons devoted to national subjects is fewer than during independence, because now more material about the Soviet Union must be included in the timetable.

Not only do the children learn quantitatively less about their own countries, but what they do learn is sometimes false, and often misleading. Even Party activists in Estonia admitted – when I asked them in private – that schoolbooks sometimes contain out-right falsifications. One example is the description of the events in 1939–40.

Some people who admitted to such falsifications discounted the impact of such official double-talk. "Everybody is still able to distinguish between lies and truth," I was told by a history teacher. This may be so; but, for example, the exact wording of the Molotov– Ribbentrop Pact is still a secret in the Soviet Union, and therefore the Balts have only a general idea of its contents.

Some teachers refuse to teach their pupils according to the lies and propaganda in the schoolbooks. Jonas Lauce, the assistant headmaster of a school in the Lithuanian town of Birzai, even wrote and used a heretical text about the occupation and the anti-Soviet guerillas. He was sentenced to two years in prison.

If teachers do not themselves dare to give a truthful picture, they can try to skip the propagandistic parts. "I can always tell my pupils that the history course is too extensive," another teacher told me. "So we simply have no time to deal with everything in class. You can read about the 1939–40 events for yourselves and ask your parents to help you check that you've understood it all." This truth may be able to survive even under Soviet conditions. But for how many generations?

Russification in Schools

Indoctrination at school is not limited to history books. A few years ago the following passage could be read in an Estonian grammar for the eighth year:

> The Soviet people are building Communism and their common language is Russian. Russian science is the most advanced in the world. Soviet science, based on Russian science, is leading in the world. How can the peaks of science be reached without knowing Russian? You should study the Russian language thoroughly.[4]

This eulogy of things Russian was found in an Estonian schoolbook for Estonian children.

Many Russian schools have been established in the Baltic Republics, mainly for Russian immigrant children. More than half of the schools in the Estonian capital teach in the Russian language only. Russian schools are less common in the rural areas, but in Estonia as a whole more than one-third of all pupils attend Russian schools. The Russian schools and the number of pupils in them correspond with the Russian population figures.

Since the middle of the sixties there are bilingual schools in the Baltic Republics. In some classes the children are taught in Russian and in others in their native language. Baltic nationalists dislike this type of school. They see it as an attempt to Russify their children.

Such bilingual schools are commonest in Latvia, where there are several hundred of them. These schools come under attack in the Letter of Seventeen Latvian Communists (see pp. 169):

[4] J. Valgma, *Eesti Keele Grammatika*, Tallinn 1955, pp. 119–120. I do not know if this book is still in use today in a later edition, but at least the message of the quotation is still current.

So-called united schools, kindergartens, and children's homes have been established in the cities and in the countryside. In practice this means that the kindergartens, homes, and schools with Russian as the language of instruction have remained the same as before, but that in all establishments and schools where the language of instruction is Latvian, Russian groups and classes have been created. Subsequently here, too, all business (such as pedagogical councils, teacher-student meetings, and Pioneer gatherings) is conducted in Russian. Excepting some country districts in Kurzeme, Zemgale and Vidzeme, there are few Latvian schools left.

National Schools?
According to the 1918 revolutionary decree all Soviet peoples had the right to education in their own native language. Four decades later a new law was adopted, and according to this law national schools are no longer obligatory. According to the letter of the law parents have the right to choose the school and the language in which their children get their education. Two thirds of the children in the Soviet Union attend Russian schools, though only just over half the population is Russian.

All non-Russian Republics have Russian schools, but there are no ethnic schools for non-Russians who live outside their native Republics. This affects, for instance, 160,000 Lithuanians, 90,000 Latvians and 80,000 Estonians. In the 1920's, there were some 190 Latvian schools in Soviet Russia and a number of cultural associations for Latvians. All these schools and other institutions were closed in connection with the Stalinist terror in the thirties. Since then Estonians, Latvians, Lithuanians and other non-Russians in Russia proper have been forced to attend Russian schools. Some Baltic parents, within and outside the Baltic Republics, voluntarily choose Russian schools for their children, hoping that this will help them to attain leading posts in society.

Small nationalities and people such as Karelians are no longer taught in their native language. Some thirty peoples, among them most Finno–Ugric and Turkish peoples, are taught in their native language only for the first three years of school. Between the two World Wars these people had schooling in their native languages as far as the elementary school level.

Some Estonians I talked to were worried about the teaching of the native language and other national subjects in the future. The majority of the children beginning school in Estonia in ten years time are expected to be non-Estonian. Will all schools in the Republic then become Russian? This does not seem likely, but some people fear it. Or will the authorities decide for each school if teaching in Estonian will be permitted, and if so to what extent? Will Estonian in that case be compulsory or only optional?

Universities
Higher education and research are most important for the future of any small nation. The Lithuanians are proud that the University of Vilnius, founded in 1579, is the oldest in the Soviet Union. And the University of Tartu in Estonia, founded in 1632, was an important center of learning already in Tsarist times. Its importance today is indicated by the size of its university library, which contains three million books. Within the Soviet Union this is surpassed only by the university libraries of Moscow, Leningrad and Kazan. The Tartu State University is an all-Union centre for research and training in sports medicine, Scandinavian studies, Finno–Ugric subjects, and some branches of physics. During the Soviet period

the greatest achievements have been made in the natural sciences. Research in the humanities, arts, and social sciences has been hampered by ideological censorship.

The large increase in student numbers during the Soviet era has already been mentioned, but university study is not open to everyone. The Russian language is obligatory in university entrance examinations. Also considered are the student's civic activities, mainly within the Communist youth movement. Thus it can be said that there is a certain ideological selection and also a tendency to favor those with a good knowledge of Russian.

The extent of Russification in higher education should not be exaggerated. When I visited Tartu in the summer of 1970, the lists of new students were just being put up. Nine out of ten of the names on these lists were Estonian. The Rector of the University told me that four-fifths of the courses were held in Estonian. There are parallel Russian language courses in medicine, mathematics, physics, Russian language and literature. The Russian-speaking students are taught in separate groups, not together with the Estonian students.

At the Riga Polytechnic Institute they teach thirteen of the day-time courses in Russian only, eight in Latvian only, and sixteen in both languages. At the Technical Institute of Daugavpils all courses are in Russian, while the other Latvian institutions for higher education in technology or natural sciences are bilingual. There are no courses taught in Russian only at the Latvian State University in Riga. Among the subjects taught in Latvian only are philosophy, French, geography, biology, biochemistry and archaeology.

In Latvia today, four out of five doctoral theses and other academic dissertations at lower levels are written in Russian. Russian is the world language nearest at hand to make research more widely know – Scandinavian doctoral theses also are often written in a world language, usually English. In 1976, however, a new ruling went into effect in Estonia. All doctoral dissertations are now required to be presented in Russian, or to be supplied with a full-length Russian translation.

In all three Baltic Republics the native peoples are over-represented in higher education, while local Russians are clearly under-represented. Russian immigrants often have a poor basic education and are thus not prepared for academic study. Also, higher education is mainly in the native languages, which the Russians seldom master.

Student Protests

The world-wide phenomenon of "student revolt" never became as widespread in the Baltic Republics as in the West, mainly because Soviet student organizations are controlled by the Party. Student leaders who criticize the authorities can be quickly disposed of, without the students being able to do anything about it. Demonstrators face severe sanctions and would risk their later careers.

Political protests by students would not receive any attention from mass media as they do in the West, because all Soviet mass media are totally controlled by the government.

Spontaneous student demonstrations of a political nature occurred in Lithuania in connection with the Hungarian uprising of 1956. This street demonstration by Lithuanian students in Kaunas, which took place in November, 1956, is described with surprising frankness in a novel by Vytautas Rimkevičius called *Studentai* (The Students), published in 1957. It is also known that quite a few Estonian high school students were expelled and some of them arrested and sentenced to labor camps because of their nationalist activities in the wake of the Hungarian uprising. Among them was the controversial young poet Jonny B. Isotamm who spent some six years in a forced labor camp in Mordovia.

In 1969 some students in Tallinn tried to join an official demonstration with the slogan "Tallge TAPA KOMMUNISTI". This means "Subscribe to the Tapa Kommunist", the Communist paper in the small town of Tapa – a hardly remarkable or revolutionary demand. But it is also a play on words, as "Tapa" is both a place-name and the imperative form of the verb "to kill" in Estonian. If you disregard the first word and only read the last two, written in capitals, the slogan means "KILL THE COMMUNIST".[5] And this is certainly a somewhat more controversial appeal. The demonstrators were not allowed to continue their studies.

Similar partly mocking, partly serious demonstrations take place almost every autumn during the students carnival in Tartu. In 1969 some students adapted the old slogan "Yankee go home!" to local conditions. The satirical placard read "Jänkid Peipsi taha!", (Yankees to the other side of Peipsi!). Since Peipsi is the Estonian name for the large lake separating Estonia from Russia, Estonian onlookers immediately recognized the students' slogan as an indirect way of saying "Russians go home". This demand is often voiced in private conversations. The students who carried this placard were expelled from the university.

In the summer of 1970 I watched a basketball tournament in Tallinn in which a team representing the

[5] *Estonian Events*, No. 27, August 1971.

United States, the national teams of Estonia and Latvia, as well as the Soviet junior national team, took part. The Soviet team was booed as soon as they appeared on the court. A young man near me almost got himself into trouble. His neighbor, a Russian militiaman, got furious when the young Estonian greeted the Soviet flag with a catcall. He tried to pull the boy out of the stands, but I managed to stop this at the last minute by holding up my camera and saying a few words in English. The militiaman became confused, and to be on the safe side he left the boy alone.

Afterwards I asked the boy what would have happened if he had been brought in. He threw up his hands and said: "They would probably have made a note in the files that I am unreliable and should not be permitted to travel abroad. But I wouldn't be allowed to do that anyway, because my father has been in a concentration camp in Siberia for almost ten years."

After the games I talked to players from the different teams. The Americans were overwhelmed by the support from the public, especially during the match against the Soviet team. The leader of the team remarked: "It's always the same when we play in the Soviet border states. You should have been there when we played in Kiev, the capital of the Ukraine. The roof was nearly lifted off when we made the winning basket against the Russian team."

I also met with similar pro-American reactions among students, even if they did not look at American society as an ideal. I therefore asked the Rector of Tartu State University, Arnold Koop, why students and other young people so rarely are critical of the United States. Why, for example, were there no demonstrations to be seen in Estonia against American actions in Vietnam?

The Rector's answer was: "We don't need any demonstrations here. We have experienced war ourselves, and therefore we are all obviously in opposition to the American war in Vietnam. War is actually forbidden in Soviet law. Our love of peace is shown by the fact that even toy weapons used to be not allowed in our country."

I then asked why toy weapons had been allowed again. Had the Soviet Union become less peace-loving? "They were allowed again to familiarize the child with the harsh realities of life," was the answer. If demonstrations against the war in Vietnam were not needed, I insisted, as everybody so obviously was against it, why was it then necessary to have demonstrations and placards and "voluntary" over-time work to the honor of Lenin? According to the Rector this was quite another matter. Lenin was almost holy "not only in our country (in his usage meaning the Soviet Union, not Estonia), but to friends of progress the whole world over."

In June, 1972, two hundred Lithuanian students were arrested in Vilnius because of their anti-Soviet acts during an international handball tournament. They had cheered the foreign teams and booed the Russian-composed Soviet teams. They also refused to stand up when the Soviet national anthem was played. After the games the students took to the streets, carrying anti-Soviet placards and hoisting the flag of independent Lithuania.

A similar incident took place in Tallinn in 1972. Students at the Tallinn Polytechnic Institute were watching the World Hockey Championship game between the Czechoslovak and Soviet teams on tele-vision. When the Czechoslovaks beat the Russians there was a wild outburst of joy from the Estonian students. When some fellow Russian students repri-manded them for their unpatriotic behavior the tick-lish situation turned into a student riot. Estonians started throwing furniture out of the dormitory win-

59

dows and setting it on fire. They also went marching through the streets. It took militia units and fire brigades to quell the students. A great number were arrested and subsequently expelled from the Institute.

These happenings are generally not reported in the Soviet press. Exceptions to this rule can be sometimes found in local papers. I am providing here, in direct translation from the Estonian, several quotes from the newspaper of the Tartu State University, culled from late 1968 and early 1969 issues. These refer to the Estonian student carnival in October, 1968, which got out of hand. One must also keep in mind that the political situation was tense in the wake of the Soviet invasion of Czechoslovakia, which took place some months earlier.

> There is no need to hide the fact that ideological battle is nowadays very sharp in the whole world, as well as at home. In a very complex situation, in an atmosphere of provocative rumors and incitements, in the atmosphere of general hooliganism prevailing in the city of Tartu where windows are broken and posters are being defaced, we can still claim that the Student Festival as a whole was ideologically successful and disciplined.

> The mood of the (student) audience was peculiar. They did not respond to the pleas of the performers to give them a fair hearing. The theme of the performances – peoples' friendship and the danger of war – was clearly stated and the loudspeaker system was operating fairly well. From close by one could hear: "This is not what we need! Enough! Can't we go to the students club." . . .' Expressions of impatience continued even then when there were pleas from the rostrum for a minute of quiet in order to pay respect to the soldiers fallen in battle.

> We were constantly trying to drown out with our singing the stupidities of younger students . . . it is

60

terrible when students go to their great festival singing *Kalle-Kusta* and the people standing and watching the demonstration from the roadside try to join with a boisterous rendition of *Ōllepruulija*. (For clarification: *Kalle-Kusta* and *Ōllepruulija* are popular Estonian student songs from the independence period. *Kalle-Kusta*, by the way, is sung to the tune of the American song *Battle Hymn of the Republic*.)

K. Ird made some critical comments about the performance of the student ensemble *Rajacas*. He pointed out that some parts of the performance gave grounds for nationalistic interpretation . . .

. . . some divide peoples into chauvinistic and nationalistic ones. They act against the Soviet order. Precisely these people came out during the Student Festival carrying openly some nationalistic banners. ("Chauvinistic" of course refers to the charges, voiced by Estonian students, that Soviet rule over the Baltic States is Russian chauvinism.)

I have quoted the Tartu State University newspaper at some length because it uniquely reflects the restless and defiant mood which prevails among the Baltic – in this case Estonian – students under the Soviet occupation.

CHAPTER 5

Literature and art as the Party tells you

Literature and other forms of artistic expression have re-emerged in the Baltic Republics since the death of Stalin in 1953. Many valuable literary works have been published during the period of cultural thaw that followed. The simple "production literature" has not dominated the scene to the same extent as before. Some of this newly won freedom was lost after the fall of Nikita Khrushchev in 1964, and during the tightening of Party controls in the 1970's.

No book can be published, no play performed or art exhibition opened, without having first been censored. The people and the creators do not have the last word about the content and form of culture. They are subordinated to the political will of the Party, and must serve "socialism". All publishing firms are state-owned and under the control of the Communist Party.

The fact that a number of Baltic creative artists and writers have in recent years managed to produce and publish artistically valuable works tells us more of their abilities than of the attitude of the authorities toward artistic freedom. No doubt more and better works would have been published or created without censorship and Party control. Therefore this positive development in art and literature has taken place in spite of, rather than because of, the official cultural policy.

The situation in the arts was much worse during the years immediately after the war, especially during

1949–1954. Writers accused of "bourgeois national-ism", "decadence" or "estheticism", were forbidden to publish, were ejected from the Writers' Union, imprisoned, deported or silenced in other ways. Only one-seventh of the pre-World War II authors appeared on the publishers' list during the Stalin era. Even writers who went to Russia with the Red Army during the Nazi occupation, and then returned, were accused of "bourgeois nationalism". The very worst year in Estonia was 1952, when only three literary works in the Estonian language were published. (In the same year eighteen new Estonian literary works were published abroad by the Estonian exile com-munity in the West). In Lithuania only five new novels were published between 1945 and 1952. Most publications that appeared were Communist tracts, written to official order to honor Communism, the Party and the Soviet Union.

Today the situation is more exciting and interest in things cultural has increased greatly. The demand for culture is great in all the Baltic countries. A new novel in Estonia is often printed in 30,000 copies, which would correspond to an edition of almost two million copies in Great Britain. An edition of this size is often sold out in a few days after publication. The same thing happens with cultural magazines; they are often difficult to obtain, except on the day of publica-tion.

The attempts to create a truly popular culture have been rather successful. Estonia and Latvia today are the two countries in the world with the highest number of theater visits per head of population. In 1967 the theatergoing share of the total population in Estonia was about three times as large as, for in-stance, in Stockholm. But even in Soviet Estonia workers visit the theater only half as often as other citizens, though the definition of a worker is wider than in Sweden. Only 8% of the audience of a theater studied in the Latvian capital Riga, were workers, according to a survey published in 1972.

Why is culture so popular?
That literature and other forms of culture are so popular depends mainly on the high educational level of Baltic Republics. The low ticket prices to theater performances are also important. Literary magazines, novels and poetry volumes cost much less than in the Western countries. (One has to bear in mind, however, that earnings are considerably lower too.) Popular illustrated weeklies hardly exist. The daily papers are as miserably boring in the Baltic countries, as in most other Communist countries. What remains for those who want to read is, by and large, novels, collections of short stories, and poetry.

We must also remember that the Baltic peoples are young as cultural nations. Perhaps there are remains of national inferiority complexes from colonial times, when cultural life was mostly for the German or Polish speaking upper classes. However, such a firm and solid foundation was laid for Baltic cultures during the time of independence between the two World Wars, that the Baltic nations could resist even Stalin's attempts at cultural genocide. Before the Second World War no other European country, except Denmark, published more new books per head of population than Latvia, and Estonia and Lithuania were not far behind.

The Baltic nations are not large numerically, and think perhaps, like other small nations, that they can be competitive only in the cultural field, where mere numbers count less than in the sphere of economics. Interest in their own culture is one way of showing patriotism under Russian pressure. A similar reaction is found among exiled Balts. They often define their national consciousness in cultural terms, for example, by subscribing to books, journals, and newspapers in their respective languages, which are published in order to keep free Estonian, Latvian, and Lithuanian literatures alive in the West.

Books in Large Numbers
More books are published now in Estonia, Latvia, and Lithuania in relation to the size of population than in any other country, according to Soviet statistics. Most of the published material consists of text books and non-fiction, mostly translations from Russian. About 60% of all literature in the Estonian language is translated from the Russian.

Nine books a year per inhabitant were printed in the Estonian Republic in 1971, seven in the Latvian Republic and five in the Lithuanian Republic. But what of the quality as regards to this quantity? These impressive figures are not good indicators of the development of Baltic cultural life. In the first place more than half are Russian translations. These books are not the result of Baltic creativity. Among them are large editions of Marxist–Leninist classics, anti-religious propaganda, publications of political speeches by Soviet leaders, etc.

Take, for example, the production of books in Estonia according to the national bibliography, in which all publications printed in the Republic are printed. For 1971, it lists 2,981 new titles, including pamphlets. Only 59 of these are literary works in the Estonian language, 38 of which are first editions. Eight of these books are novels, the main branch of fiction, and this was a good year for the novel. During the time of independence twice as many novels were published every year, and for many years after the war there were more novels published by exile Estonians than in the homeland. But the main difference between the exile literature and the books published in the homeland lies in the freedom of the writer, which is far less in the Soviet-occupied homeland.

Exile Literature

The refugees from the Baltic States continued their literary and cultural activities in exile. They published their books in Germany, Sweden, Great Britain, Australia, the United States, Canada, and other countries. In a short time they built up a lively press and flourishing publishing enterprises abroad. At the same time they organized choirs, art exhibitions, and theater companies.

This book does not deal with the cultural activities of the exile Balts, but a comparison between book publishing in the Soviet occupied homelands and by the exile communities in the West should be of interest.

There were 353 new literary works of altogether 59,000 pages published in Estonia in the years 1945–1964. During the same period 366 works of altogether 90,000 pages were published abroad. A far greater number of novels were published abroad, but more volumes of poetry in the homeland. In poetry it is easier to evade the dictates of the Party than in the novel.

The development of Latvian and Lithuanian exile literature has been just as impressive and the number of books published even larger, because there are more Latvians and Lithuanians than Estonians in the West. Since the war, exile Latvian authors have published 766 new literary works in their mother tongue (up to and including 1972). The corresponding figure for Estonians is 575 and for Lithuanians over 500.[1]

[1] Ivar Ivask, "Baltic Literatures in Exile: Balance of a Quarter Century", *Journal of Baltic Studies*, Vol III, No 1, 1972.

Exile literature plays an important although in-direct role in the cultural life of the Baltic Republics. It exerts some pressure on the Soviet authorities. State publishing houses in the Baltic homelands can obtain larger quotas of paper, and authors greater artistic and thematic freedom, in order to compete with exile publications. As an example, in 1953–69, a Lithuanian encyclopedia was published in 36 vol-umes in Boston. Twenty copies were sent to the Vilnius University Library. The Academy of Sciences in Lithuania applied in 1965 for permission to publish an encyclopedia in Lithuanian. The application was refused on the grounds that there were already Russian encyclopedias in the Soviet Union. Only when the academy referred to this exile publication did they receive permission to publish a Lithuanian encyclopedia of their own in three volumes.

Sarunas Zukauskas, born in 1950, was arrested in 1973 for making two copies of volume 15 of the exile Lithuanian encyclopedia, and with collecting and distributing other materials on Lithuania, includ-ing Lithuanian Independence Day proclamations. Zukauskas was also accused of complicity in the theft of typewriters and folk sculptures and was accused of creating an underground organization and inducting members. He was sentenced in 1974 to six years in a strict regime labor camp on charges of anti-Soviet agitation and propaganda. In the same trial four more Lithuanians – A. Sakalauskas, born in 1938, V. Po-vilonis, born in 1947, A. Matskevicius, born in 1949, and I. Rudaitis, born in 1911, were sentenced to between 2 and 5 years of hard labor. They were among the one hundred members of the now defunct Society for Local History in Lithuania, arrested in March, 1973.

When a history of Tartu University was published by Estonian exiles in Sweden, a similar Soviet

Estonian work was quickly started in Tartu. The manuscript was completed, but was then stopped by the authorities, and has not come out. Several other exile publications have inspired, and made it possible, for similar works to be published in the Baltic Republics.

By their activities and contacts with their homelands, the exile authors help and inspire their respective national cultures back home. The scholars and authors at home, however, find it difficult to keep up with what is published in the West, because of a foreign exchange shortage, and postal censorship.

There are strict rules for receiving books from abroad. No western books are available in bookstores, including those in Baltic languages published abroad. No Soviet citizen can order books from the West. When scholars, authors or acquaintances in the Western countries mail books to their colleagues or friends in the Baltic Republics, then only politically harmless works reach their destination safely. There are no restrictions, however, for sending books from the Baltic countries to the West. This is a typical example of the unbalanced state of affairs that still exists in the field of scientific and cultural exchange, even if a "free flow of people and ideas across the borders" was agreed upon at the European Security Conference in Helsinki.

The cultural contacts between Balts living abroad and their Baltic homelands have been limited, and are of a personal nature, rather than organized. People in the Baltic countries who tried to keep up personal contacts with colleagues in the West risked being sent to prison and labor camps during the Stalin era. Such harsh measures are no longer in use, but unofficial contacts with their countrymen living in the West are still precarious. On the other hand, those Balts in the West who initiated cultural contacts with their homelands, and made visits there in order to open up lines of communication, came under attack from the exile establishment and were branded as a kind of "collaborators". Some dogmatic exile leaders still maintain that every form of contact with the homeland is a compromise with the occupiers. Nevertheless, contacts on a personal basis have become more common in recent years.

Some Baltic scientists from the West have appeared before closed groups of colleagues in the homelands. Let me give a few examples. In 1966, a Latvian historian in Sweden, Uldis Germanis, gave a lecture in Riga about the revolution of 1917. A Latvian economist from Canada gave a talk in Riga in 1971 on the international gold crisis. Heino Susi and Lauri Vaska, two Estonian-American chemistry professors, have given guest lectures under the auspices of the Soviet Estonian Academy of Sciences. Two exile Latvian poets, Olafs Sumbra and Valdis Kraslavietis, have recited their poems to members of the Latvian Writers' Union in Riga, but they were not allowed to do it publicly. Several Estonian scholars from the United States and Sweden attended the Third Congress of Finno–Ugric Studies in Tallinn, 1970.

Several Baltic artists now living in the West have in recent years shown their works at exhibitions in their homeland, for example, the two eminent Estonian artists in Sweden, Eerik Haamer and Herman Talvik. One Estonian writer from abroad, Elmar Õun, has sent a manuscript to Estonia and had it accepted for publication there. Selected short stories and poems by several Latvian emigré writers have been published in Soviet–Latvian magazines. The same thing has happened in Estonia and Lithuania without the author's permission (only in 1973 did the Soviet Union ratify the Geneva Copyright Convention).

Two or three Estonian writers at home have sent their manuscripts to the West for publication. The internationally known Estonian composer Eduard Tubin, living as an exile in Sweden since 1944, wrote the opera "Barbara von Tisenhusen" on a commission from the Tallinn Opera, where it was performed with great success and remained in the repertory. Choirs, ballet troupes, and folk dance ensembles from the Baltic Republics have been on tour in the West, etc.

The Classic Heritage
The classics are as much of a headache to the Soviet censors as the exile works. In principle the problem is the same one Soviet Russia faced after the Revolution. The Russian classics have gradually been published in large new editions, even those considered reactionaries and some who opposed the Soviet regime. New editions of such literary works in the Baltic Republics were after World War II far less numerous. A Soviet Russian critic wrote, for example, during the Stalin era that literature in "bourgeois" Latvia was "just the same as in other capitalist countries, only even more shabby and provincial," and that it consisted of "decadent novels and poetry as well as of rubbish and pornography of the cheapest kind."[2]

According to an expert on Latvian Literature, Rolfs Ekmanis, the authorities in the Baltic Republics, as in the entire Soviet Union, regard

---

[2] M. Justsov, "Bard of the Latvian People", *Soviet Literature*, No 4 (April 1953), p. 117, quoted by Rolf Ekmanis in "Soviet Attitudes Towards Pro-Soviet Latvian Writers", in *Journal of Baltic Studies*, No 1, pp. 44–71. Ekmanis has also published Latvian Literature under the Soviets 1940–1975, Nordland Publications, Inc., Belmont, Mass., USA.

. . . literature primarily as a social weapon, involved in the process of history and capable of exerting a powerful influence on the course of public affairs. Therefore, the most "useful" among the classics are those works which would inform the reader that life before the Soviet rule was characterised by misery, superstition and social injustice; works which indirectly would suggest that conditions of life now in the USSR are far superior to those in pre-Soviet Latvia; works which would tell about the spiritual poverty and doom of man in bourgeois society; works which would make the reader form an opinion that capitalism is evil in nature, that future happiness and prosperity justify temporary hardships; in general, works which would somehow contribute to the strengthening of the reader's allegiance to the Soviet Union.[3]

New editions of pre-Soviet Baltic writers have in principle been limited to works by ideologically safe authors. In cases when so-called reactionary writers have been re-issued, only their ideologically acceptable works have been chosen, and to be on the safe side, these have been provided with orthodox introductions and comments. Phrases or passages that are found unacceptable have sometimes been deleted or "improved". In literary criticism every possible opportunity is used to declare that the most eminent of the classic Baltic writers were influenced by Russian literature.

The treatment of the general Latvian writer, Janis Rainis (1865–1929), is an example of this. He was a socialist, and because of this some of his works were released already during the Stalin era. In 1940, Rainis was posthumously awarded the honorary title of People's Writer and a newly founded literary institute was named after him. Some of his plays and

[3] R. Ekmanis, *op. cit.*, pp. 65–66.

collections of poems were published by the new authorities. "Cosmopolitan and aesthetic" features in his poetry were toned down in favor of the "realistic and revolutionary". "Improper" features of the writer's own personal life were no longer mentioned. Thus silence was maintained about the fact that Rainis and his wife, Aspasija, an eminent poetess in her own right, refused to settle in the Soviet Union during the period between the wars, although they had been awarded a pension for life there. Rainis and his wife preferred to stay in independent Latvia as long as they lived, and for a time Rainis was Minister of Education.

An edition of Rainis's collected works has been promised since the beginning of the sixties, but it has not yet appeared. Some of Rainis's writings cannot be fitted to the officially desirable picture of a pro-Russian Marxist. Such works are: *Sveika, briva Latvija!* (I Bless You, Free Latvia!), published 1919; *Daugava* (1919), written in honor of the Latvian Declaration of Independence; and his play *Rigas Ragana* (The Witch of Riga), published 1928, which symbolically warns against the Russian threat.

Ekmanis mentions that the struggle for the classic literary heritage in Latvia began when the leading cultural magazine *Literatura un Maksla* (Literature and Art) printed in 1956 an article which had first appeared in its Estonian counterpart *Sirp ja Vasar* (Hammer and Sickle). The writer of the article deprecated the officially accepted demand that the progress of non-Russian cultures should be described as only a consequence of Russian developments. He demanded that non-Russian cultures should be studied in their own right and be considered equal to Russian culture. This is one example in which the cultural climate in Estonia has been less Stalinist than in Latvia.

Material Conditions for Writers and Artists

Authors receive their remuneration independently of how many copies their books sell. Authors are generally well-compensated. Those who have been awarded by the state the honorary title of a People's Writer get higher fees than others. The same goes for artists. Those painters and sculptors whose work has been judged ideologically satisfactory reap the high monetary rewards for state commissioned paintings, statues, and memorial monuments.

Leading writers and artists are privileged members of Soviet society. Their earnings can be twenty times as high as those of an ordinary worker. But the livelihood of these artists and writers depends on adherence to Party policies and membership in the official Artists' or Writers' Unions, which presupposes a basic loyalty to the system.

The fate of Lithuanian poet and architect Mindaugas Tamonis can illustrate what may happen to "unloyal elements". He refused to restore a monument to the Soviet army and then turned to the Central Committee of the Lithuanian Communist Party, demanding greater freedom and observance of human rights. After this he was subjected to treatment in a psychiatric hospital. On November 5, 1975, upon leaving the hospital, he died under the wheels of a train in mysterious circumstances.

The attitude of Baltic communist officials to the question of artistic liberty was also illustrated by the Foreign Minister of the Latvian Socialist Republic, Viktors Krumins, born in Leningrad in 1923. When he joined the Soviet UN delegation in New York in 1972, a Latvian American journalist asked him about the conditions for Soviet–Latvian writers. Krumins answered:

Here in the West you have quite peculiar ideas of the

duties of a writer. You seem to think that a writer or poet can say anything that pleases him or her. This is not the case in the Soviet Union, where quite clear directions are given. In any case, the fact is that the state pays the writers and pays them well. Surely, then, the state also has the right to demand the writers write the right things?[4]

The Case of Maija Silmale

Maija Silmale was one of the foremost translators of French literature in Latvia. In February, 1971 she was arrested and a month later sent to a psychiatric clinic. No reason for this was given. A short time before her arrest she had been a witness for the defense at a trial of Lidiya Doronina, who was accused of having illegally distributed prohibited literature. It is possible that Silmale had committed a similar act.

Maija Silmale spent the years between 1949 and 1958 in Siberian exile (or labor camp), because she had translated contemporary French writers, mainly Antoine de Saint-Exupery. During the sixties he became something of a literary idol in Latvia, partly thanks to the translations by Silmale.

The most important part of Maija Silmale's literary contribution is an anthology of modern French poetry, *Es tevi turpinu* (I Continue You). She selected the poems, translated a third of them herself, as well as wrote the introduction. The first edition of 16,000 copies was quickly sold out.

When Maija Silmale was arrested in 1971 many people were afraid that this would finish the 46-year old translator, who was suffering from cancer. It was all the more pleasing that she was soon set free again – as far as it is possible for a contemporary Soviet intellectual to be free.

[4] Interview by Dagmar Vallens, published in *Latvija America*, 13 December 1972.

Maija Silmale was, however, struck by bans on both publishing and travelling. She was not allowed to visit France. Neither was she able to find permanent employment after her release.

Silmale's French anthology was included in an official bibliography published in Latvia in 1966–70.[5] Every anthology listed has the name of the compiler, but Silmale's name was nowhere mentioned.

Visitors from the West visiting the Latvian capital were dissuaded or forbidden by the authorities to contact Silmale and given the explanation that "she is crazy". Was she released from the mental hospital only to become what George Orwell called an "unperson", somebody whose very existence the authorities seek to deny? She died in 1973.

The Cases of Sven Kreek and Others

Maija Silmale in Latvia and Mindaugas Tamonis in Lithuania are not the only Baltic cultural personalities driven to death or locked up in psychiatric institutions by the Soviet authorities. Similar cases can be quoted from Estonia.

Poet, and an official of the *Endla* Theater in Pärnu, Sven Kreek was arrested in January, 1975. He was accused of distributing his poetry in leaflet form. He had reportedly also distributed a socialist manifesto which demanded democratic reforms of Soviet society.

The court found Sven Kreek "not responsible" for his acts. He was placed in a mental hospital for compulsory treatment. There he died. The Soviet authorities declared that Kreek hanged himself "by his own free will". This is denied in a letter from "representatives of Estonian democrats" in Pärnu, Estonia, on October 21, 1976. The letter was ad-

---

[5] Valdemars Ancitis, *Piecos gados* (For five years), Liesma, Riga, 1971.

dressed to the United States Congress, Amnesty International, and the UN Commission for Human Rights, and was smuggled out.

In this letter serious doubts are expressed about the official explanation, Kreek was secretly buried in an unknown place. It is quite possible that the KGB saw the possibility for getting rid of an Estonian patriot. In any case the tragic death of Sven Kreek was a result of his political convictions and activities. It was a result of the violation by Soviet authorities of his elementary human rights, say the representatives of Estonian democrats.

Arrests and enforced psychiatric care are extreme measures for dealing with recalcitrant writers. More commonly they are refused membership of the Writers' Union, and dissident members are expelled from it. Editors of cultural magazines who are too liberal can be dismissed on demand by the Party's higher authorities, as were, for example, both the editors of the Latvian cultural weekly *Literatura un Maksla* at the end of 1969.

In a number of cases the censors have rewritten controversial passages of the works of contemporary writers also.

The Latvian poet Aleksandrs Čaks had his works mutilated in this fashion several times. Some of his books have been completely forbidden. Čaks is considered to be the father of modern Latvian poetry and a Latvian counterpart to Mayakovsky and other experimental poets of revolutionary Russia. Čaks survived the Nazi occupation during the Second World War in a kind of internal exile in his home in Riga. He wrote a volume of verse that the Nazis did not allow to be published, as Čaks was generally considered a leftist poet. These poems were not permitted to be published after the war by the Soviet censorship either, there was a demand for this by a number of younger writers. The constant encroachments on Čaks' artistic freedom broke him. He died in 1950.

If the censors do not think that they ought or could rewrite ideologically "weak" passages, they can tell the author himself to do so. The question of publication is in the meantime held in abeyance. In this way the writer is pressurized into censoring himself.

If this mild form of pressure does not achieve the desired result, the censor can refuse permission to publish under the pretext of insufficient literary quality, or because of "paper shortage". Or the authorities can, as was done, for example, in Franco's Spain, publish less desirable writers or works in such small editions that their circulation does not reach most of the population.

If a writer is convinced that his work would not pass the scrutiny of the censors, he probably lets the manuscript remain in his desk drawer, so as not to attract unnecessary attention from the censoring authorities. The manuscript is then only circulated within a narrow circle of friends, but can nevertheless reach a considerable audience. Sometimes enthusiastic readers type several copies of the work. Many Baltic writers write some things for their desk drawer; some are forced to write for it alone.

The Strait Jacket of Socialist Realism
Socialist realism was accepted as a literary program as early as 1934 by the First All-Union Writers' Congress in the Soviet Union. Writers were enjoined to honor the heroes of the socialist construction of society. Writers had to abandon their "aestheticism" and "contemplation" and instead write about ordinary people in factories and on collective farms. The happy tractor driver became the symbol for this interpretation of the purpose of art.

77

Socialist realism and the Party line became the norm also for Baltic writers after the Soviet take-over. Successful writers were forced to become "literary eunuchs", to quote the Russian revolutionary poet Mayakovsky.

Not all Baltic writers have survived this castration. Some of them never had a chance. Three of the leading Latvian poets before the Second World War remained in their native country, others fled to the West. One of them, Janis Medenis, was deported, then rehabilitated during the fifties and returned to publish a volume of poetry. He died soon afterwards – his health had been destroyed during the time spent in labor camp. Aleksandrs Čak's fate has already been told. The third, Eriks Adamsons, died in 1946 without having been able to publish anything after the Soviet take-over. The promising young poet Vilis Cedrins died in the same year, in the notorious forced labor camp Vorkuta. He was sent there after an unsuccessful attempt to flee to Sweden.

The great Estonian poet Heiti Talvik, spiritual leader of the Logomancers, a literary group in the thirties, was arrested, and up to this day his exact fate is unknown. According to some information he was shot, others say that he died in a forced labor camp near the Ob River in Siberia, some say that he died in a Russian prison. The leading Estonian playwright, Hugo Raudsepp, perished in a Russian forced labor camp in 1952.

During the fifties and sixties Baltic writers and artists tried to fight the Stalinists in the Party and state machinery as well as in the Party-controlled Writers' and Artists' Unions. A similar struggle took place in Russia and the other Republics within the Union. Two Swedish scholars, Lars-Erik Blomquist and Magnus Ljunggren, summarize the arguments from both sides:

The older writers and cultural politicians have come to be associated with the demand for the *great truth* of the time, the truth of the century. The historial perspective is upheld. Warning is given that irregularities in the past should not obscure the hopes of the future. The question is asked what kind of reality will be passed on to future generations . . . Against this, the supporters of *the little truth*, the truth about facts, present a different view. They maintain on their side that no truth, however insignificant it might seem, is without interest. All wrongs in the past, all conflicts, all offences against socialist laws and ideas, must be accounted for and dealt with in literature, analysed to see what consequences they have had and will have in the future, so that the "mistakes" of the past will not be repeated.[6]

The attitude of the young Baltic intellectual[5] was expressed by the Latvian poet Ojars Vacietis, who declared that art must retain its social purpose, but at the same time remain art.

The scope for individual interpretation of the thesis of socialist realism was widened during the period of the so-called cultural thaw. Algirdas Antanaitis, a Lithuanian literary critic in the United States, comments on the development of the Lithuanian novel during the sixties:

Perhaps the most important change in the fiction that emerged after the thaw was the disregard for the so-called "no conflict" theory, which had made impossible the conflict between good and evil, since presumably there was no evil in the great socialistic society. The conflict could exist only between good and better. Furthermore, a person acquired some rights in his relationship with the society, no matter how perfect his society might have been in the socialistic establishment.

[6] Lars-Erik Blomqvist and Magnus Ljunggren, *Sovjetprotest. Den nya ryska oppositionen i dokument.* PAN/Norstedt, 1969, p. 10.

Even less desirable characteristics or traits of an individual became more tolerable, since they were gradually recognized as part of his personality. Such a climate apparently was adequate for the emergence of a more serious psychological novel, impossible under the strict and unbending rules of socialist realism.[7]

A number of interesting novels, short stories and collections of poems were published during the later 1960's in the Baltic Republics. Descriptions of people became less black-and-white, as more grey tones were introduced. People in superior positions could now be described without being idealized, and touchy subjects could be referred to a little more openly than before. A typical example is the novel *Senojo miesto amzius* (The Age of an Old Town) by the Lithuanian writer Raimondas Kasauskas, which treats anti-Soviet guerilla fighters, Christian believers and victims of the deportations with much understanding.

Several writers started to seek out and probe the universal human values and the condition of modern man, for example, the Latvian Alberts Bels, in his novels *Izmekletajs* (The Investigator, 1967) and *Buris* (The Cage, 1972), the Lithuanian Alfonsas Bielauskas in a novel called *Kauno romanas* (the Kaunas Romance, 1969), or the young Estonian prose writers Mats Traat, Enn Vetemaa, and Mati Unt.

In 1968, an Estonian author, Eno Raud, published a perceptive novel *Etturid* (The Pawns) about the anti-Soviet guerillas in Estonia during the late forties. The topic of the Estonian anti-Soviet guerillas is treated even more graphically in two novellas by Heino Väli. The first, *Mina, Lauri Pent, künnimees* (I, Lauri Pent, a Plowman) was published in 1965, the

---

[7] Algirdas Antanaitis, "Recent Trends in the Soviet Lithuanian Novel", Lituanus, 1970: 2.

second, *Veri mullal* (Blood on the Soil), appeared in 1974. A similar view of the war period is also to be found in some Latvian novels of recent years. The guerilla fighting is perhaps today regarded by the authorities as history. But it is still forbidden to discuss openly, for example, the mass immigration of Russians and the pressures of Russification. Thus literature is not permitted to deal with what many Balts see as the greatest problem of the present time.

At the end of the sixties and the beginning of the seventies the already limited creative freedom was again reduced. As it had been one decade earlier, the deciding factor was the development in Eastern Europe. After the invasion of Czechoslovakia in 1968 the Soviet authorities thought it necessary to strengthen the home front. The trial of the Russian authors Yury Galanskov and Alexandr Ginzburg was arranged the same year. (Galanskov died in 1972 in a Soviet labor camp, the authorities having refused him the necessary treatment for a bleeding ulcer). Several liberal editors of cultural journals were dismissed in the Baltic Republics. People have been imprisoned for having distributed prohibited literature. The official warnings against Western "ideological diversion" have been increased. There are many signs of a general tightening up of the cultural life of the Baltic Republics.

Protests Against the Lack of Artistic Freedom
On August 16, 1972, Jonas Jurašas, senior director and producer of the Kaunas State Drama Theater in Lithuania, addressed an open letter to the Ministry of Culture of Lithuania, the Kaunas State Drama Theater, and the editors of the cultural magazine *Literaturia ir Menas*. In the letter Jurasas denounced the compromises that an artist has to make because of the arbitrary limitations placed on his creative work by the officialdom:

81

On the road of compromises, the artist is unaware how his spiritual resources are evaporating, how he is approaching degeneration. That road is not for me. I cannot accept truths imposed from the outside. In actualizing alien "truth", the artist becomes a stranger to himself. In isolating himself from his own micro-world, the creator loses ties with the contemporary planet.[8]

By September of the same year Jurašas was out of a job because he had dared to speak his mind. He later wrote an open letter to the world theatrical community along the same lines. This courageous step did not, of course, get him his job back. In December, 1974, he was allowed to emigrate with his family.

Other Baltic artists have also criticized the restrictions placed on creative work by the Soviet system. For example, on May 15, 1975, Tomas Venclova, considered one of the most original young Lithuanian poets, declared in a letter to the Central Committee of the Lithuanian Communist Party:

The Communist ideology is alien to me and, in my view, is largely false. Its absolute reign has brought much misfortune to our land. The information barriers and repressions imposed on those who think differently are pushing our society into stagnation and the entire country into regression . . . I take a serious view of the Communist ideology, and therefore I refuse to repeat its formulas in a mechanical or hypocritical manner. By refusing to echo them, I am only inviting discrimination, which I have experienced in large amounts during my life.[9]

Venclova ended his letter with a request that he

[8] *Lituanus*, no 2, 1973, p. 69.
[9] *Lietuvos Kataliku Baznycios Kronika* (Chronicle of the Lithuanian Catholic Church, a Lithuanian underground or *samizdat* publication), no 19.

and his family be allowed to emigrate. After joining the five-member group to monitor observance of the Helsinki accords in Lithuania, he became an uncomfortable figure for the authorities and was able to get his visa for emigration. Tomas Venclova arrived in the United States on February 16, 1977 and took up a position as Professor at the University of California at Berkeley. He had to leave his family behind.

Vladislovas Zhilius, a Lithuanian painter who had for twelve years been denied permission to exhibit his works, wrote on January 23, 1976 to Petras Grishkevicius, First Secretary of the Lithuanian Communist Party. In his letters Zhilius denounced the tenets of socialist realism and the officials who try to impose them on the artist. In this letter he says:

> A voice of protest is rising from by innermost being. It is a protest against the compulsory, machine-like programming of the creative consciousness in order to reduce it to a primitive pattern. The result of this programming is the destruction of the individual's creative individuality, of his subjective dimension, even though that very subjectivity and individuality constitutes each artist's genuine and fundamental core of worth.[10]

Zhilius joined the growing number of eminent artists exiled from the Soviet Union in recent years; he arrived in the West early in 1976.

Lithuanian Samizdat
The well-known underground literature of Russian dissidents has also inspired Baltic groups to produce and distribute self-printed literature, the *samizdat*. Publications in Estonia and Latvia have been more

[10] AS (=Arkhiv Samizdata) (Samizdat Archive), document no 2555.

sporadic, but in Lithuania the *Lietuvos Kataliku Baznycios Kronika* (Chronicle of the Lithuanian Catholic Church) has appeared regularly since the spring of 1972. It contains valuable information also on cultural affairs in contemporary Lithuania.

In October, 1975 another Lithuanian samizdat journal began to appear. The journal sees itself as a successor to a 19th-century monthly that played an important role in the Lithuanian national awakening. *Aušra* (Dawn) repudiates violence and disclaims political goals, emphasizing instead spiritual values and cultural progress in order to preserve the Lithuanian national identity, which it sees threatened under the Soviet régime.

Parallels between today and the tsarist occupation of the 19th century, as well as the Lithuanian "national awakening" are stressed in the lead article of the new *Aušra*. The picture of contemporary Lithuania is shown as very bleak:

> The tsarist occupation has been replaced by a Soviet one. The existence of the Lithuanian nation is again in danger . . . In a manner both planned and disguised, Lithuania is being spiritually undermined and physically destroyed.[11]

According to the lead article, the Communist régime is attempting "to pull a shroud of silence over the heroic past of Lithuania", by limiting the teaching of Lithuanian history in the schools, reducing the circulation of historic literature to "beggarly" quantities, and then subjecting it to "a merciless massacre by the censors". Simultaneously, "the darker sides of contemporary life" also get the silent treatment, especially "the rising crime rate, the camps, and the

[11] RL (Radio Liberty Research Bulletin) 63/76.

horrible diseases". The attention of the nation is "diverted" instead to the "material" aspects of life, since "a flabby nation gorging its fill of material goods and drinking to excess is an easy target for denationalization and destruction".

The new *samizdat* journal sees the "awakening" of Lithuania from "this spiritual sleep" as its major task, which is to be accomplished by following the program offered by *Aušra* almost 100 years ago: "to show the Lithuanians their own past, to give a proper evaluation of the present, to help them envision the Lithuania of the future".

Aušra disclaims any political goals, such as "fomenting a revolution or restoring the Capitalist system". Neither shall it "incite national hatreds", extending its welcome as it does to all "people of goodwill . . . who wish Lithuania well". The journal invites the support of all "who sincerely love Lithuania", including Party members and prominent officials who "do not stop loving their fatherland and promoting its welfare to the best of their powers". The editors of *Aušra* hope that the journal's ideas will "spread among the young . . . and intensify their love for their native country". Finally, they "salute the *Chronicle of the Lithuanian Catholic Church*", and will "welcome with joy any new publications".

In disclaiming violence and purely political activity, the editors of *Aušra* express the following conviction: "The Lithuanian nation will prevail if it proves to be more cultured than the oppressors. That is why ancient history must repeat itself: the Romans conquered the Greeks by the force of arms, but the Greek culture conquered the Romans."

CHAPTER 6

Faith and Persecution

Before the Second World War 78% of the population of Estonia were Lutheran, 19% Orthodox, 1·5% different Evangelical denominations, and 0·4% Jews. In Latvia 55% were Lutheran, 24% Catholics, 14% Orthodox, 5% Jews, and 1% Free Church. In Lithuania 81% were Catholics, 10% Protestants (Lutherans and Reformists), 7% Jews, and 3% Orthodox. The share of Catholics among the ethnic Lithuanians in Lithuania was as high as 95%. The Protestants were found mainly in the Germanized Klaipeda (Memel) area.

The clergy was one of the groups hardest hit by the terror during the first years of Soviet occupation. This persecution was aimed at destroying the last nation-wide organization which was not under Party control. The mass deportations in June, 1941 included also a number of clergymen. The small Catholic Church in Estonia, with its six congregations and five priests, almost ceased to function. The Catholic Archbishop, Eduard Profittlich, was arrested and has not been heard of since. The Churches in Estonia lost four bishops – one Catholic, one Orthodox, and two Lutherans. The extensive deportation wave of 1949 hit the clergy hard. The number of remaining Lutheran ministers in Estonia was reduced from eighty to fifty.

Eleven Catholic priests were imprisoned in Latvia. Six of them were shot. Thirteen Lutheran ministers were arrested and deported. About a hundred Catho-

lic priests were imprisoned in Lithuania. 180 were
sent to labor camps, among them three bishops.
Archbishop Reinys was arrested in 1947 after having
publicly declared in his cathedral that he had never
put his name to a statement supporting the Soviet
foreign policy which was published in *Pravda* under
his name. The other two bishops were accused of
having supported anti-Soviet "bandits", i.e., the
nationalist guerillas that were very active during and
after the Second World War. Another Lithuanian
bishop, Borisevicius, was sentenced to death at a
secret trial for alleged cooperation with the guerillas.
As a warning to other clergymen and believers not to
oppose the Soviet authorities he was shot.

The clergymen who remained in Lithuania were
forced to pay rent three times higher than other
citizens. Religious instruction in schools was forbidden. The theological faculties of the Baltic universities were closed. At the University of Tartu alone,
70,000 books on religion were confiscated or burned.

From Flirtation to Persecution

A new and more tolerant relationship to religious
believers began after Stalin's death in 1954. The
Lithuanian Party organ *Tiesa* declared that one had to
differentiate between good and bad Christians. Believers who were honest and devoted workers
should not be considered as unreliable simply because of their faith.

About 130 priests who had survived the labor
camps were allowed to return to Lithuania. The
Lithuanian bishops Ramanauskas and Matulionis
were released in 1956. They were allowed to return
to Lithuania, though not to their cathedral cities.
They were held in a form of house arrest in rural
areas until they died.

The period of thaw during the middle 1950's

meant further concessions to the Catholics of Lithuania:[1]

1. For the first time since the Second World War the regime allowed a prayer book and a religious calendar to be published.
2. Bishops were allowed, for the first time since the war, to visit their congregations and to confirm thousands of young people.
3. The authorities in Moscow agreed to the appointment of three new bishops.
4. Even more remarkable was the permission to build a new Church in the seaport of Klaipeda. Many of the faithful took the opportunity to repair churches which they had not been allowed to maintain for years.

The concessions to the believers turned out to be temporary. The newly built church in Klaipeda was never opened for services. The priests who had built the church were put on trial in 1962, accused of illegal construction and "currency speculation". (They had received donations from religious compatriots in the United States.) The priests received sentences of four to eight years of imprisonment.

The purely physical persecution of clergymen and believers became less common. Instead of this, antireligious propaganda was intensified. No denomination in the Baltic countries was allowed to print new religious literature during the rest of the Khrushchev period, which lasted until 1964.

Lenin's Heritage
Those in power have been influenced by the attitude of the "fathers of Communism" to religion. Marx said that religion is the opium of the people. Lenin went even further. He said that Communism will never be victorious until the myth of God is eradi-

cated from man's mind. Any idea about God was according to him an indescribable ignobleness of the most dangerous kind, an infection of the most abominable sort. Millions of sins, base acts, acts of violence and physical sources of contagion are far less dangerous than the ingenious idea of a God decked out in the most splendid of ideological comments.[2]

How could people who have been educated along such lines be genuinely tolerant of religious activities and beliefs?

Church and State
The relationship between the State and the Church is officially based on the 1918 decree, which separated the State and education from the Church.

According to the 1929 law on religious associations, amended in 1975, the official Council for Religious Affairs decides which congregations shall be allowed, which persons can hold religious offices, which clergymen can get work permits and permission to study, which churches can be rented by the believers, how high the rent for a church should be, if any new church should be built or any old one demolished or closed, etc.

The decisions of the Council are often communicated orally and not in writing. The arbitrariness is increased by the diffuse limits between what religious practices are permitted and are not permitted.

A clergyman is allowed to preach at a service in church. However, if he wants to visit someone who is dying, for example, outside the church, he must

[1] See "Vin in Lithuania", in *Lithuania under the Soviets* (ed. V. Stanley Vardys), Praeger, New York, 1965, pp. 215–237; J. Savasis, *The War against God in Lithuania*, Manyland Books, New York, 1966; Vincentas Brizgys, *Religious Conditions in Lithuania under Soviet Russian Occupation*, Chicago, 1968.
[2] Lenin, *Collected Works*, Moscow, 1941–1950. Vol 35, English edition.

apply for permission from the local Soviet (administrative council). Believers may themselves attend church; if, however, someone brings a friend, he is, in principle, guilty of religious propaganda. It is the same for religious literature: in principle a believer is allowed to possess religious works and read them himself, but if he lends them to others he can be punished for religious propaganda. You are also allowed to be baptized and to have your children baptized, if they are at least 18 years old. On the other hand, priests who give children a religious education can be punished.

Practicing one's faith on special premises, assigned by the authorities, is tolerated, while "religious propaganda" is unlawful. The latter prohibition can be interpreted in different ways by different authorities, and be applied in different ways from case to case. It affords great opportunities for arbitrariness, and those subjected to it have hardly any chance of influencing or criticizing the decisions reached.

Some paragraphs in the Soviet Criminal Code contribute to the confusion. It is, for example, a crime "to prevent the performance of religious rites, if these do not disturb the peace and are not contrary to civil rights". Over and above these very general limitations there is another paragraph forbidding "deceitful actions aimed at fostering religious superstitions". The question is then: What is acceptable religious faith and what is forbidden superstition? The atheist authorities provide the answer.

Atheistic Propaganda
There are a number of atheistic associations in the Baltic Republics as well as all over the Soviet Union. They are very active, they give lectures, hold discussion meetings, and also publish books and tracts.

The atheistic propaganda has been especially intensive in Lithuania. This is because the Church and religion is stronger there than in any other Union Republic. This is also confirmed by Soviet sources; for example, the Soviet journal *Nauka i religia* (Science and Religion). The Lithuanian Catholics have carried out a number of protest actions against "religious discrimination". (Examples are given later on in this chapter.)

Atheism in the Baltic Republics, and especially in Lithuania, is not only directed against religion but also against Baltic nationalism and western influences. Catholicism in Lithuania has historically been a westernizing influence. Since the 19th century the Church has been very closely connected with Lithuanian nationalism.

Those clergymen who are working as such today are described in the Soviet mass media not only as "bourgeois nationalists" and "counter-revolutionaries", but also as generally immoral people. Stanley Vardys comments:

> Clergymen are according to this type of literature "drunkards" if alcohol is served at religious festivals; the clergy are "immoral" if they ask young boys to participate in religious ceremonials or ask young girls to sing in the choir; they are "speculators" if they distribute home-made religious objects; "embezzlers" if they build a church hall and register it in their own name (it cannot be registered in the name of the congregation as it has no legal rights).[3]

The atheist upbringing of children and young people is considered very important. All Soviet children ought to join "The October Children" at a tender age and then "The Pioneers", between the

[3] V. Stanley Vardys, "Catholicism in Lithuania" in *Aspects of Religion in the Soviet Union, 1917–1967*, University of Chicago Press, 1971. (Ed. Richard H. Marshall), p. 391.

age of nine to fourteen. The activities of these organizations are somewhat similar to those of the Scout movement in the West, but the collectivistic and anti-religious education of the young takes up most of the time. Atheist courses and lectures are then regularly arranged by the young Communists' organization, Komsomol. Atheism is continuously preached at school and through the state controlled media. One of the tasks of all teachers is to expose "religious superstition" to their pupils. This propaganda is so intensive that a lot of people have grown tired of it and do not take it seriously. Violent anti-religious propaganda has in some quarters created an indifference to all ideology.

Many students and young people in the Baltic Republics, as in many other parts of the Soviet Union, seem to think that religion is a private matter. There has been open criticism in Baltic newspapers of Young Communists attending Church services or getting married in church. Young people have headed religious demonstrations in Lithuania in recent years.

The atheist propaganda has been directed especially towards the church confirmation. Secular summer-camps have been introduced as a substitute. Religious customs are opposed. Father Christmas is now called Father Frost in the Baltic Republics, as well as in the Soviet Union. The New Year is celebrated instead of Christmas, and Easter has become the spring holiday. A survey in Estonia at the end of the sixties showed that every third family still went to church at Christmas and that every fifth family sang Christmas songs at home. A good atheist should only celebrate his birthday and not the originally Christian name days or Saints' Days. Civil marriages are encouraged, especially by the introduction of official lay ceremonies conducted in special houses or "palaces".

According to official Soviet statistics, 10·4% of newborn children were baptized and 2·9% of weddings, and 38·6% of burials were officiated by the Church in Estonia in 1974.

Religious Life Today
All Church property in the Baltic Republics became the property of the state after the Soviet occupation of 1940. A number of churches have been closed or are today used for non-religious purposes. This is so for more than 80 Lutheran churches in Latvia alone. The church of St. Casimir in Vilnius is now a museum of atheism, whose importance is only surpassed by the Central Museum of Atheism in Leningrad. The Lutheran Archbishop's Cathedral in Riga has been made into a concert hall and the Orthodox Cathedral in Riga is now used as a movie house and café.

Churches that are still allowed to be used for their original purpose can be rented by the faithful with permission from the Council for Religious Affairs. The rents are high, as churches are placed on par with places of entertainment. In 1970, the congregation of one of the largest churches in Tallinn paid about 3,200 roubles a year in rent. The rent of the Cathedral in Kaunas was twice the amount in the same year.

The State received, in 1970, some 100,000 roubles in rent for 125 Lutheran churches in use in Estonia, according to the Swedish Lutheran Bishop Ragnar Askmark.[4] The number of Lutheran churches in Latvia was in early 1970's about one hundred, while the Catholics in Lithuania had more than 600 usable churches. It sometimes happens that the members of several congregations join in renting a church in order to save money.

The number of Protestant congregations is about 150 in Estonia and 240 in Latvia. In Lithuania there are several hundred Catholic congregations and 25

[4] *Östgöta Correspondenten*, August 7, 1970.

Protestant ones. In the Baltic Republics there are also Orthodox, Jewish, Baptist, Pentecostal, and other evangelical congregations. The ecumenical movement has grown between the Protestant, the Catholic and the Orthodox in recent years, and Baltic Christians have also established links with fellow believers in other parts of the Soviet Union.

Communist writers always maintain that the number of Christians has decreased. The two largest of the five Lutheran congregations in Tallinn have at present only one-tenth of the number of members they had during the time of independence. The comparison is somewhat misleading, as many of the members during the period between the two World Wars were passive ones. In reality, it is the number of registered Church members that has gone down, while the number of believers does not seem to have changed so much. The Lutheran Church in Estonia in the middle 1970's had about 300,000 baptized members.

The number of Lutherans is a little larger in Latvia than in Estonia. The position of religion and the Church is undoubtedly the strongest in Lithuania. One reason for this is probably that the Catholic faith, with its colorful rites, is in greater contrast to the dull everyday life.

Youth and the Church
When you visit a Baltic church during a service, you notice immediately that most of those present are elderly people. Young people who openly show their faith risk being expelled from the university, or they may lose their jobs, or find it very hard to advance in their profession. Believers seldom, if ever, reach any high positions. Retired people are not as much affected by this kind of pressure.

Young Christians often practice their faith in private. Sometimes Young Communists and ardent members of atheistic associations go to church to spy on believers who are their school mates. It probably also happens that some "spies" go there in order to taste for themselves of the forbidden fruit that religion has become.

Names and photographs of children who go to church are sometimes put up on the school notice boards or published in mass media as something to make fun of. Such pressure can certainly be effective on sensitive young people, but it hardly leads to any lasting or deep solidarity with the norms enforced by society.

Free Churches, Jews and Orthodox
Several Free Churches are active in the Baltic Republics. The Baptists, including the Pentecostals, who have not been permitted to organize nationwide, are comparatively numerous. They have today some eighty congregations in Estonia alone and over 8,000 registered members. The Methodists have increased their membership in Estonia in recent years. They are still a small group of a couple of thousand people, the only Methodist Church permitted in the whole of the Soviet Union. There are some fifteen congregations in Estonia, the largest of them in Tallinn, with over a thousand members. At least half regularly attend services several times a week. The leader of Estonian Methodists, A. Kuum, was able to participate in the World Conference of the Methodist Church in 1971. The Salvation Army no longer exists in any of the Baltic countries. The Jehovah's Witnesses are forbidden. The Jews still have one congregation in Tallinn, two in Latvia (in Riga and Daugavpils), and also a few in Lithuania.

The relatively large number of Orthodox believers in Estonia and Latvia is a heritage from the Tsarist era. The Orthodox Church was then encouraged by the authorities as a means of Russification. A large number of peasants in the northern parts of the Baltic provinces voluntarily became Orthodox, hoping for Tsarist protection against the landowners, who were mostly German Protestants. Almost one-fifth of the faithful in Estonia before World War II were Orthodox believers, this including the Russian minority. Most of the Russians in the Baltic countries were Orthodox. The increase in the numbers of the Orthodox during the Soviet period depends mainly on Russian immigration.

The Orthodox have been less persecuted than other Churches in the Baltic countries. The Orthodox Church in Estonia was permitted to publish a calendar in 1948. At the middle of the sixties, the Church also received permission to publish a collection of ten religious songs.

There are several reasons why the Orthodox Church is somewhat less persecuted than other denominations. The Orthodox Church is considered to be, originally, a Russian community. The Estonian and Latvian Orthodox Churches previously came under the Patriarchate of Constantinople but were forcibly merged, in 1941, with the Moscow Patriarchate. The Orthodox Church is the largest in the Soviet Union with an estimated 50 million members – almost one-fifth of the entire of the Soviet population. There are more than three times as many Orthodox believers in the Soviet Union as there are members and candidate members of the Communist Party.

The Orthodox are not suspected of hidden loyalties, as are Jews and Catholics, nor of "nationalism", as are the Baltic Christians. In addition, the Baltic Protestants have contacts with the West, with the Lutheran World Federation, and their Nordic brother churches. In 1978, the Finnish Archbishop installed his Estonian colleague Edgar Hark, and the Latvian Archbishop Janis Matulis was installed by the Swedish Bishop Emeritus, Sven Danell.

The Shortage of Clergymen
The training of young clergymen is essential for the future of the Church. Most clergymen today are elderly or middle-aged. Although they do not retire willingly, the shortage of clergymen is great. In Estonia there are about 125 Protestant ministers, in Latvia there are less than 90. The Catholic Church in Latvia has about 170 priests, almost as many as there are congregations. The small Baptist congregations in Latvia have some 60 ministers.

The number of active clergymen is considerably larger in Lithuania. There were more than 700 in the early 1980's. (In 1939 there were about 1,650.) Even if the actual number of priests is high in Lithuania, the shortage is probably more felt there, as the number of faithful and their part of the population is considerably larger than in Estonia and Latvia.

The education and training of clergymen on a small scale is still permitted in the Baltic Republics. The number of students is decided by the Council for Religious Affairs, which also decides who will be allowed to attend. In Estonia, the Lutherans have a Theological Examination Board which conducts correspondence courses. In 1976, twenty-two candidates were enrolled. In Lithuania, the seminaries are kept under strict control by the authorities. Four heads of the Lithuanian seminary were arrested and deported during the first decade after the war. Lithuanian believers have repeatedly protested against official infiltration of KGB agents among students. When the Lithuanian bishop Steponavicius, in 1961, refused to ordain three alleged agents, he was deposed by the secular authorities.

Theology students must have "an honest job", in addition to studies, which is done mainly by correspondence. The theology students meet once a month for a discussion session, which lasts for a couple of days. The four-year course is paid for by voluntary contributions from the members of the congregation. The salaries of the clergy are paid for in the same way. They are considered as unearned income by the tax authorities and are more heavily taxed than regular salaries and wages. Only recently has the clergy been given the right to have the old age pension.

In Latvia, one Catholic seminary is operating now, although it was forbidden during most of the sixties. Catholic priests are trained there for other parts of the Soviet Union also; ten Latvian priests are working today in thirteen small communities in Ukraine and in Byelorussia. Only ten Lutheran ministers were trained in Latvia between 1955 and 1966.

In Lithuania, there were, before the war, four Catholic seminaries with more than 400 students. After the war only one seminary was allowed to continue; at first it had 150 students. Since then the number of students has been cut and is now ten per year. Not all of them finish their course of studies. Even if they did, the recruitment of new clergymen in the Baltic countries would not at all cover the natural attrition.

Shortage of Bibles
The lack of religious literature is felt strongly. The Protestant Church in Estonia, during the whole of the post-war period, has been allowed to publish only one item, a religious "yearbook" (1956). It did

not contain much religious text, but still it was not allowed to appear more than once.

Bibles are treasures in the Baltic Republics today. The songsheets I saw in Tallinn churches were so well-thumbed that you could hardly read the text. I tried to take one sheet with me as a souvenir. An old woman ran after me in the street outside the church and reproached me for my thoughtlessness. The congregation had so few songsheets that they couldn't spare any for curious tourists.

Visitors from the West sometimes try to smuggle Bibles for their compatriots in the homeland. The new Estonian translation of the Bible, which was published in Sweden in 1968, is in high demand by believers in Estonia. There is no formal ban on entering with Bibles, as the Bible as such is not prohibited in the Soviet Union; it has even been printed, although in extremely small quantities (about 200,000 Bibles in Russian since 1917). When two Swedish women tried to take in a substantial number of Bibles in December, 1976, they were caught by the Soviet customs officials in Tallinn and immediately sent back.

The only religious publication permitted in Latvia is a Church Calendar. The 1970 edition, which I have seen, contained a daily biblical quotation, three short articles on Church and community affairs, and for each month a picture of an old Latvian altar with an explanatory caption. The official edition was as small as that of the 1954 hymn book and the 1960 New Testament, i.e., 5,000 copies.

Printers of Gospel Arrested
On October 24, 1974, at seven o'clock in the morning, at the signal of a siren, an enormous detachment of KGB and militia surrounded a forest farmstead in Latvia, where one of the printing presses of the pub-

lishing house was located. (Before this operation, for several days in a row a helicopter had circled the house.) As a result the following workers of the publishing house were arrested: two brothers and five sisters; a hand-made printing machine was confiscated, along with over nine tons of paper acquired by the voluntary contributions of all the people of God, and also about 15,000 printed Gospels and other materials.[5]

In connection with the arrest of the workers of the printing plant of the underground Christian publishing house Khristianin, the leaders of the Reform Baptist movement in the Soviet Union protested to the then Head of State, Nikolai Podgorny, and Prime Minister Aleksei Kosygin. In the document, it is stated that "this incident is viewed by Christians as an act of blatant injustice, and it evokes a feeling of profound grief among all believing citizens, who, only because of the extremely unjust position in which the church and believers of our country are placed, have been forced to seek the means and possibility of securing for themselves the necessary religious literature".[6]

Priests at Trial
The shortage of priests and religious literature is felt also in Catholic Lithuania. On January 8, 1969, Fr. Juozas Zdebskis and Fr. Petras Dumbliauskas declared in an appeal to the authorities that there are "repeated violations of the freedom of conscience

[5] *Bratsky Listok* (Fraternal Leaflet), No. 5, 1974, quoted in *Religion in Communist Dominated Areas (RCDA)* No. 4–6, 1975. *Bratsky Listok* is a leaflet of the illegal Reform Baptist movement in the Soviet Union, that broke away from the officially recognized All-Union Evangelical Christian-Baptist Union in the early 1960's because of excessive official control of the latter.
[6] Op cit.

guaranteed by the USSR Constitution, especially in regard to the theological seminary in Kaunas".[7] The two fathers continued:

> Because of the shortage of priests, it is already impossible to serve the faithful. Some of the priests are old and some are already taking care of several parishes. Since some 30 priests die each year in Lithuania, it is obvious that some government officials are using administrative measures to achieve their goal: the destruction of the Catholic Church in Lithuania . . .

> The rector of the seminary is obliged each year to send the list of candidates to the Lithuanian representative of the Council for Religious Affairs, so that he can determine their loyalty to the Soviet government. He has the power to eliminate any candidate, without any explanation, despite the fact that the candidate for admission is a full citizen of the Soviet Union, has never been tried and has committed no crimes against the Soviet Government. We do not understand why young men who have graduated from higher and special schools are not entitled to enroll in the seminary. Why do candidates, once removed from the list, lose their right to apply for entry to the seminary again? Why are candidatures sometimes rejected for quite insignificant reason? We know that other educational institutions are not treated this way. Is this not a violation of the Soviet Constitution?

One of the signatories of this appeal, Fr. Juozas Zdebskis, was arrested in August, 1971, accused of having taught children the Ten Commandments. Two thousand Roman Catholics in Zdebskis' home town, Prienai, demanded in a protest letter that their priest should be released and in future be allowed to freely carry out his religious work without persecu-

[7] *Religion in Communist Lands* (RCDA), July–October, 1973, p. 50–51.

tion and fear. The congregation also demanded that the constitutional freedom of religion should not be denied them.

Prienai is a small town in an agricultural area thirty kilometres south of Kaunas, with just under 10,000 inhabitants. One fifth of the inhabitants signed the petition. About forty of them were arrested and others were persecuted in various ways. The faithful were, however, not dismayed. On November 11, 1971, the day of the trial, more than six hundred people gathered outside the court building in Kaunas and demonstrated against the trial. The demonstrators were only dispersed when police arrived and used force.

The trial took place as planned. The authorities had by persuasion and torture tried to get them to sign the bill of indictment, as at earlier actions against priests. Zdebskis refused and was so badly treated that his mother, having visited him in prison, maintained that she could hardly recognize her son because of ill-treatment.

Zdebskis refused to give in, even before the court. He gave a speech in his own defense, in which he accused the Soviet authorities of violating the Constitution and the United Nations Declaration of Human Rights.[8] He criticized the legal actions taken against priests, and pointed out that no legal action had ever been taken against atheists who violated the human rights of believers. Zdebskis did not hide his bitterness and his disappointment that believers had to be loyal to the atheist regime, but that the regime never has to be loyal to the believer.

Fr. Zdebskis also declared: "I am being tried for fulfilling my rightful duties . . . If the courts do not judge us priests now, then our nation will judge us!

[8] *Lituanus*, No. 2, 1972, and RCDA, Jan–March 1972, p. 7–11, gives Zdebskis' defense speech, unabridged, in English.

And finally will come the hour for the true judgment by the Supreme Being. May God help us priests to fear this more than your judgment".[9]

Fr. Zdebskis noted that (1) the clergy of the Catholic Church in Lithuania had been infiltrated by atheists who try to "level the Catholic Church to the same condition in which the Orthodox Church finds itself"; (2) only four or five priests were being ordained, while each year 20 or 30 priests died in Lithuania, and capable and spiritually minded students are discouraged to study theology; (3) it was deceitful to permit children to receive of their first Holy Communion, but to require that each child be instructed separately.

In his courageous speech, Fr. Zdebskis concluded that under these circumstances there were two possibilities open for a priest: (1) either to be a priest in accordance with the mind of Christ and to perform his duties accordingly, no matter what the cost, or (2) to choose the path of "peaceful collaboration" with the atheists, to serve two masters and to enter into conflict with one's own conscience and "just worry about what you'll have for lunch; forget about the fact that children will be told about God, but of that type of god that doesn't exist. Even I myself have no faith in the gods depicted for us by the press and radio".[10]

Fr. Zdebskis was sentenced to one year in prison. He was again arrested on March 10, 1976, charged with drunken driving and deprived of his driving licence. 308 members of his parish wrote a protest letter to the head of the KGB in Lithuania demanding that he investigate the charge. Five priests of the Lazdijai area also denounced the incident as a provocation, in a letter to Bishop Povilonis.

At the same time that Fr. Zdebskis was prosecuted, another trial took place agsinst Fr. Prosberas Bubnys

[9] RCL, Jan.–February 1973, p. 10.
[10] RCDA, Jan.–March 1972, page 7.

in the town of Rassinai. He was also charged with giving children religious instruction. Fr. Bubnys ended his defense speech with the words: "If today I must publicly state whether I taught religion or not, then I cannot defend myself or repent of it, since this would signify going against my conscience . . .. At this solemn hour allotted to me, dust of the earth, I cannot renounce our beloved Jesus who urged that little children should not be stopped from coming to Him. I want to say: 'Praise be to Jesus Christ!' "[11]

Fr. Bubnys was also sentenced to one year in prison, as was Fr. Zdebskis and one year earlier Fr. Antanas Seskevicius.[12] A group of 1,344 believers protested in vain against the sentence against Fr. Bubnys to President Podgorny.

17,054 Catholics Protest
With the memory of these trials fresh in their mind, a group of believers set about organizing a "Memorandum of Lithuanian Catholics", dated December, 1971. It was addressed to Mr. Brezhnev and appealed again for religious liberty in Lithuania. 17,054 believers signed the petition and many more might have signed, if the KGB would not have acted against those collecting signatures. Anyhow, the "Memorandum of Lithuanian Catholics" became the most impressive protest manifestation ever carried out openly in the Soviet Union. Only the Crimean Tartars and the Uniates in western Ukraine have been able to collect a similar number of signatures on political or religious appeals. The Lithuanian document was also sent to the Secretary

[11] RCL, January–February 1973, p. 10.
[12] For an English version of the defense speech of Fr. A. Seskevicius, see RCDA, Vol X (1971) Nos. 19–24, p. 157–163.

General of the United Nations, Kurt Waldheim, as previous appeals to the Soviet authorities had not been answered.

The petition from the 17,054 believers repeated some of the accusations made in the earlier documents, namely that priests had been imprisoned or deported for preparing Catholic children for their first communion; that Catholic children have to study atheism in Soviet schools and are forced to speak, write, and act against their conscience; that the Soviet authorities have complete control over the one Catholic seminary in Lithuania and only allow ten students a year to enter, which increases the shortage of priests; that Catholics have been dismissed from their jobs because of their faith and have not been able to get another job; that the authorities have not allowed Catholics to restore churches which have burned or fallen into disrepair, not even if the repairs would have been carried out and paid for by the believers themselves.

"The Memorandum of Lithuanian Catholics" ends as follows:

> We could point out many more cases of discrimination which have embittered our life and sown dissillusionment with the Soviet Constitution and laws. We therefore ask the Soviet Government to grant us the freedom of conscience, which has been guaranteed by the Constitution of the USSR, but which has not been put into practice heretofore. What we want is not pretty words in the press and on the radio, but serious government efforts that would help us Catholics to feel citizens of the Soviet Union with equal rights.[13]

Protests Continue
The mood of discontent must have been very strong indeed among Lithuanian Catholics, because the

[13] *RCL*, July–October 1973, p. 49.

Lithuanian representative of the government controlled Council for Religious Affairs presented a "pastoral letter" for the bishops and administrators of the Catholic Church in Lithuania to sign. The letter was to be read in all parishes on April 30, 1972. It condemned the organized circulation of "irresponsible documents".[14]

The following month there came a reply to this "pastoral letter" by an unknown number of priests. They refuted charges of "falsification" in the Memorandum and continued:

The "Letter" was packed with familiar quotations from the Gospel. Many people think that two more should have been quoted: "The Good Shepherd lays down his life for his sheep" (John 10:11); "Verily, verily, I say unto you, he that entereth not by the door into the sheepfold, but climbeth up some other way, the same is a thief and a robber" (John 10:1). It is scandalous that the Bible should be used to gloss over matters that are far from holy.[15]

Referring to the sentence in the "Letter": "We must not forget that a signature placed below an irresponsible document affects the relationship between Church and State," the priests continue:

What kind of relations are they talking about here? About the relations between cat and mouse? Can we be happy about good relations? Lithuania's Catholics have no catechisms, prayer books, church press or literature. The children of believing parents are in atheist schools. The seminary produces four to six priests every year, whereas 20–30 die each year. Priests are jailed merely because they dare to teach the truths of the faith at the request of parents. Priests are

[14] Op. cit, p. 49.   [15] Op. cit, p. 49–50.

punished merely because children serve at Mass and participate in processions. Without trials, two bishops have been banished for over 10 years. Very active priests are hustled off to small parishes and elderly priests are sent to large ones. Catholic intellectuals are fired from their jobs for attending church. Representatives of the atheist state convene bishops' conferences and dictate "pastoral letters". What more do we have to lose that we have not already lost? A little personal well-being and limited personal freedom. "Blessed are they which are persecuted for righteousness' sake; for theirs is the kingdom of heaven" (Matthew 5:10).[16]

Later in the same year, another petition, this time bearing 1,709 signatures, was addressed to Brezhnev. In it the writers complain about the damage inflicted by the local authorities on their recently repaired church. In March, 1973, as many as 14,284 Lithuanian students and their parents objected to the compulsory instruction of atheism in school, and no fewer than 16,498 persons complained about the lack of religious books.

All these courageous actions taken by Lithuanian Catholics culminated in the publication of an underground *samizdat* journal called the *Chronicle of the Lithuanian Catholic Church* (in Lithuanian: *Lietuvos Kataliku Baznycios Kronika*). Its first issue came out in 1972, and up to the beginning of 1980 thirty-nine issues of this underground publication had arrived in the West.

This unique periodical provides detailed information not only on the religious situation in Lithuania but also on certain political, social, and cultural developments in Lithuania, especially those related to the human rights movement and the Soviet efforts to suppress it.

---

[16] *Keston News Service*, June 30, 1977.

The KGB has repeatedly taken steps to stop the publication of the Lithuanian *Chronicle*. In December, 1974, five Lithuanians were tried in Vilnius for producing and distributing religious literature. That they had reproduced 20,000 prayer-books was also seen as a crime, but the main attack of the prosecution was on the publication of the "anti-Soviet" *Chronicle*. The defendants constantly tried to emphasize that they had acted from purely religious motives, that they had no anti-Soviet aims, and that they did not consider the *Chronicle of the Lithuanian Catholic Church* to be anti-Soviet.

All the defendants were, however, found guilty on December 24, 1974. Petras Plumpa received the most severe sentence: eight years in a strict regime labor camp. Povilas Petronis was sentenced to four years in a strict regime camp, Virgilius Jaugelis to two years in an ordinary regime camp. Jonas Stasaitis and A. Petrubavicius, both of whom cooperated with the authorities during the trial, received suspended sentences.

This and later trials could, however, not stop the *Chronicle* from appearing regularly and reporting on the plight of religious and patriotic Lithuanians under the Soviet rule. The stiff sentences and life in the strict regime camps could not even break the resistance of Petras Plumpa and the others. *Chronicle* No. 24 includes part of a letter from Plumpa:

> Wherever we live the most important problem . . . is the salvation of souls. It's not always easy to know where we can benefit others most, what field is most suitable for us. Only the King of souls knows that, while we are left to bloom where He has sown us. If He has sown us in the field of sorrows, let us bloom in sorrow; if in that of solitude – let it be in solitude, for the Creator sows the most beautiful of flowers in inaccessible places among mountain tracks, and they

have their own value, though no man sees them . . .
The anguish of the soul can be unseen and can be
plucked and offered, like a flower, to the Saviour. This is
the most beautiful decoration for the altar of Jesus.
Without such decorations, even the finest churches are
sad places . . .[17]

"No Greater Love . . .", the Case of Nijole Sadunaite

Nijole Sadunaite was born in 1938, in independent
Lithuania. Her father was an instructor at the Institute
of Agronomy, her mother a housewife. Both of
Nijole's parents were deeply religious people and
Nijole shared their faith.

In 1955, Nijole completed high school. By that time,
she had made a name for herself. Students who
showed signs of religious belief were discriminated
against in the school, but Nijole never missed Mass
on Sundays. During field trips, when the students
were taken to see Catholic churches as relics of a
bygone era, Nijole would always genuflect before the
Blessed Sacrament, no matter what her friends or
teachers might think.

For five years she nursed her sick mother, who
died in 1970. Her father had died in 1963, so that she
and her brother Jonas are now the only living members of the family.

After her mother's death, apart from her normal
everyday duties, Nijole nursed a sick priest for
several years. Any person in need found a helping
hand at Nijole's door. She began to practice what
might be called a radical Christianity. She tried to
keep her personal needs to the barest minimum in
order that she could help others, and she often gave
away her necessities if anyone seemed to be in need.

On November 14, 1973, a decision was made by the
State Security Committee, (the Soviet secret police in

[17] *Lithuanian Chronicle*, no 12, quoted by Keston News Service.

Lithuania), to organize large-scale searches to find out how and where the *Chronicle* was being published, in order, of course, to stop it. Since then, several persons have been arrested, tried, and sentenced for their involvement with the *Chronicle*. Nijole Sadunaite was one of them.

Nijole Sadunaite was arrested in August, 1974, for typing copies of issue No. 11 of *The Chronicle of the Lithuanian Catholic Church*. During the investigation she was threatened with incarceration in psychiatric hospital because she refused to make any statements. On 16 and 17 June 1975, she was tried for "anti-Soviet agitation and propaganda" in the Supreme Court of the Lithuanian SSR.

Sadunaite refused to be defended by a lawyer, as she did not want anyone else to get into trouble. She refused to give evidence, as she did not consider herself a criminal; the judges themselves, she said, were "criminals who are violating the most elementary human rights . . . and torturing innocent people in prisons and camps". In her defense speech she stated:

> Truth does not need to be defended, it is all-powerful and invincible. Only treachery and lies need weapons, soldiers and prisons, for they are weak . . . There is no greater joy than of suffering for the truth and for other people . . .[17]

In her final statement, Sadunaite compared *The Chronicle of the Lithuanian Catholic Church* to a mirror, which reflected atheist crimes against believers.

> This is the reason why you hate all who tear off your lying, hypocritical mask . . . A thief steals money from people, but you rob and deprive them of the most precious thing they possess – loyalty to their convictions and the possibility of handing down these trea-

sures to their children . . . In Lithuania, the Church is not separated from the State, but enslaved by it. The state authorities interfere, in the most blatant way, in the internal affairs of the Church. . . . Everyone's sacred duty is to fight for human rights. . . . This is the happiest day of my life. I am being tried because of the *Chronicle of the Lithuanian Catholic Church*, which fights spiritual and physical tyranny. It is my enviable lot not only to fight for the peoples' rights and for truth, but also to be condemned for it . . . I am sorry that I was only able to work for a short time on behalf of others. . . . I shall go joyfully to slavery, so that others may have freedom, and I am willing to die, so that others may live.

Nijole Sadunaite was sentenced to three years forced labor in a strict regime camp followed by three years exile within the Soviet Union.

Summary
Religious believers are discriminated against in Baltic Republics as well as in the rest of the Soviet Union. Both religion and Church have, however, managed to survive, in spite of the difficult conditions.

Why do Soviet authorities not openly fight the various religious groups? Why are the small theological colleges allowed to carry on when the authorities cut down their intake so dramatically? Why is not all training of clergymen forbidden? Why are some churches still permitted to be open for religious purposes?

Basically, the authorities have lacked the strength and daring rather than the will to wipe out religion, Church and Believers. The religious communities have four times as many members as the Communist Party. If they try to crush the Church too quickly, the Communists risk activating these forces. The authorities are probably aware that martyrdom and

111

outright persecution has never been able to break the Church or suppress the faithful. On the contrary, it has stimulated the interest in religion, and given the faithful strength.

The authorities have, in the present situation, fairly good general control over the believers, mainly because of the system of registered membership and collaborators on the Church committees. The Soviet "powers that be" do least of all want to encourage the growth of a strong underground opposition, which is difficult to control, either secular or religious. There are already strong underground communities, e.g., the dissident Baptists, Pentecostals, and the Old Believers. These "catacomb Churches" encourage their members to actively resist the ungodly regime. The authorities want to prevent such groups from growing stronger. The worldly "powers that be" hope that the constant atheist propaganda and the religious discrimination will gradually undermine the Church.

The Constitution promises freedom of religion. Paragraph 18 in the United Nations Declaration of Human Rights guarantees:

> Everyone has the right to freedom of thought, conscience and religion; this right includes freedom to change his religion or belief, and freedom, either alone or in community with others and in public or private, to manifest his religion or belief in teaching, practice, worship and observance.

The Soviet Baltic Churches also send representatives to the World Council of Churches and the Lutheran World Federation, where they demand the expulsion of the Baltic exile Churches from these organizations. For these reasons the Soviet authorities want to show at least a facade of living churches.

Many of those in power will remember Khrushchev's guiding rule: "Peaceful coexistence with the Churches abroad but unrelenting struggle against religion in our own country." The renowned dialogue between Marxists and Christians seems to be directed exclusively toward the Christians in the West. It has also been sporadically permitted in East Europe, mainly during the short Dubcek period in Czechoslovakia, but never in the Soviet Union.

CHAPTER 7

Rich republics?

Industrialization was underway in the Baltic countries already before the First World War, especially
in Estonia and Latvia. This early industrialization
was planned with the Russian market in mind.
Two-thirds of the industrial production in Latvia was
exported to the rest of Tsarist Russia before the First
World War. When the Baltic countries became independent after this war, the Soviet Russian market
was closed to their export industries, which, therefore, declined. During the period between the
World Wars, Estonia, Latvia, and Lithuania became
instead relatively prosperous agricultural countries.
Today they are industrial countries with a modern
and highly developed technology.

Baltic industry was quickly rebuilt from the ra-
vages suffered in the war. As during tsarist times,
Baltic industry was integrated with the enormous
Russian market. After 1945, the Soviet authorities
invested heavily in the Baltic Republics as a processing area for the whole Soviet Union.

Several factors contributed to this.[1] The Baltic
Republics already had a considerable manufacturing
capacity. Factories which had previously been used
for one shift could now be used for work in two or

[1] See Benedict V. Maciuika, "The Role of the Baltic Republics in the
Economy of the USSR", in *Journal of Baltic Studies*, Vol. III, No. 1,
1972, pp. 18–26.

three shifts in order to rapidly increase production. Energy resources were available and could be exploited further. The average Baltic income before the war was so high, by Soviet standards, that it could be cut considerably in order to make room for increased capital investment and production.

Housing capacity in the towns was large enough, despite bombing and other destruction. With lower Soviet housing norms the population could be doubled by immigration, thereby ensuring labor resources for the new industrial enterprises. The Soviet authorities did not consider the social disadvantages of overcrowding and night work. They found the mass immigration of Russian workers to the Baltic Republics valuable from a political and military point of view, in order to strengthen the Soviet hold on the recently incorporated countries. Baltic industry was made dependent on raw materials from other parts of the Soviet Union. In this way, the Baltic countries were tied more closely to the rest of the Soviet Union.

Production increase has been given the highest priority by the Soviet authorities. Production plans and economic growth figures are worshipped as a new religion. All criticism of the excessively high rate of production is suppressed; the wheels must continue to turn, faster and faster. A spokesman for zero-growth would be silenced and perhaps sentenced to forced labor. Those in power seem to think that a high and every-increasing rate of production is essential, even if achieved at the price of working in three shifts and a piece-rate pay system, or the destruction of the environment.

Highly Industrialized
Estonia, Latvia and Lithuania play an important role within several branches of the all-Union economy.

Estonia plays an important role in the production of electric power, textiles, mineral fertilizers. Also produced in Estonia are electric motors and transformers, excavating and oil processing machinery, as well as 82% of the oil shale in the Soviet Union. Every fourth Soviet railway carriage, every fifth transistor radio, every sixth tram, every seventh diesel engine and washing machine, and every ninth electric light bulb was produced in Latvia at the beginning of the seventies. Since 1940, the year when independent Latvia was turned into a Soviet Republic, the Latvian industrial production rate has increased twice as fast as the average production rate for the whole Soviet Union. The rate of increase has grown less in recent years in relation to that of other Union Republics, but during the last Five-Year Plan it was still higher than the all-Union average.

Lithuania is the least industrialized of the three Baltic Republics, but the rate of increase has been even higher than in her Baltic neighbors over the post-war period. As a matter of fact Lithuania's rate of increase of industrial production is the highest of all the Soviet Republics. Serious attempts are being made to bring Lithuania up to the same level as Estonia and Latvia, which are the most urbanized and industrialized Soviet Republics. Already, Lithuania produces a number of important industrial items, for example, a third of the Soviet Union's electric welding equipment, and large quantities of electronic apparatus and machine tools. There is also ship building, textile and paper industry, etc., in the Baltic Republics.

Centralization Gone too Far
During the whole of the Soviet period the Baltic Communist leaders have tried to criticize the increasing centralization of all economic planning,

large-scale management, and decision making to Moscow. Aleksei Müürisepp, who was then Chairman of the Estonian Council of Ministers, asked, in an article printed in Izvestia in 1956, that there should be more economic self-determination:

1. Estonian raw materials should be used by local industries and not be taken out of the Republic.
2. Estonian manufactured goods should not be exported to the rest of the Soviet Union until the needs of the Estonian population had been met.
3. The enforced brain-drain from Estonia to other parts of the Union should be stopped.

The 20th all-Union Party Congress had discussed the question of decentralization earlier the same year. Khrushchev spoke then of each nation's right to choose its own way to socialism. Baltic Communist leaders hoped that this right may also include their people. Another development which raised hopes for more local autonomy was the establishment of regional Economic Councils in 1957. Each of the three Baltic Republics, Estonia, Latvia and Lithuania, became a separate Economic Region and the power of the central ministries in Moscow was greatly diminished. A couple of years later Khrushchev had second thoughts about decentralization. The administrative power of economic regions was cut back. The Latvian Communist leaders, who at this time advocated ideas similar to those that Müürisepp had put forth a few years earlier, now fell into disfavor and were purged.

Since the end of the sixties, Baltic Communist leaders have again become more critical of Moscow in economic questions. This was because of the strong centralization that had taken place since the middle of the sixties. Economic Regions were liquidated in 1965. Many industries in the Baltic Republics came directly under Moscow.

Baltic Party and government leaders have sometimes publicly criticized the all-Union authorities' decision in budget affairs. They have been permitted to question the relative size of different allocations in the budgets which the all-Union authorities put forward for the Baltic Republics. The head of the Estonian State Planning Committee, Hendrik Allik, complained at the December, 1969, session of the Supreme Soviet that a "strange habit" had been developed by the ministries of the Union Republics – in good years the surplus goes to the central authorities in Moscow, while in bad years Estonia has to cover the deficit.[2]

Should a Baltic Communist leader go one step further and demand that the economic development in, for example, Latvia, ought to be planned according to the interests of the Latvian people, then he would be accused of bourgeois nationalism and chauvinism. In all probability, he would be removed from office on an order from Moscow and may be even sent to a labor camp, or at best, become the head of a power station in Central Asia. His fate would depend on the current political climate in Moscow.

Management Reforms
The discussion on economic management reforms was lively in the Soviet Union during the sixties. Several innovations were carried out in the Baltic Republics on a trial basis. These aimed at giving the local management more say in the running of their enterprises. The local management was given more latitude in the disposing of profits and wages. They

[2] See the Soviet Estonian newspaper *Rahva Hääl*, Dec. 20, 1969.

118

were, for example, given greater opportunity to decide on the number of workers, and a way of paying them according to their actual work contribution.

These kinds of innovations have been most extensive in Estonia and Latvia. Their industry is highly developed and these Republics are small enough to act as laboratories for management reform for the rest of the Soviet Union.

The reforms began in industrial enterprises in the middle of the sixties, and were then extended to agriculture. Local control was introduced in the summer of 1967 on Estonian state farms. These demonstrated their efficiency by making a profit for a period of several years. Edgar Tõnurist, the Estonian Minister of Agriculture, stated the following year that the increase in production had been greater than ever. He therefore asked that autonomy be made more extensive. At the beginning of 1970, the Chairman of the Estonian Council of Ministers, Viktor Klauson, stated that 96% of all enterprises in the Republic came under the new economic system. The reforms seem to have been quite successful in Estonia and Latvia. The technocrats, the "Communist professionals", seem to be more successful than their predecessors, the "professional Communists".

Decentralization and Freedom
Some people, both in the Baltic countries and abroad, hope that these reforms in the economy will also bring about a liberalization of cultural and political life. If economists and the managerial staff have more say in their fields, would it not also be more difficult for the authorities to refuse the corresponding demand for greater freedom from, for example, writers and journalists?

In my opinion, these hopes are based on a semantic confusion. Economists and technocrats would certainly like more and more important decisions to be transferred from the central authorities in Moscow to the Republican level, and then to the individual enterprises. This should not be called liberalization, but decentralization. This freedom is different and much less dangerous to the authorities than the freedom of expression that the artists and journalists are asking. Those in power regard an increased freedom of expression as a much more serious threat to the system than economic reforms. This could be seen in Czechoslovakia in 1968.

As I have already mentioned, cultural freedom is somewhat wider in the Baltic Republics than in the rest of the Soviet Union. Is it only a coincidence that the Baltic Republics happen to be that part of the Soviet Union where cultural freedom is the greatest, as well as where economic reforms have reached the furthest? Or is there a connection? If so, it is not a case of cause and effect. This is illustrated by situations elsewhere in Eastern Europe. The German Democratic Republic (East Germany) is perhaps the best example that far-reaching economic, managerial, and technological reforms can be carried out without any corresponding reforms in the political and cultural life.

Impressive Statistics

If we restrict ourselves merely to looking at the impressive economic growth statistics in the Baltic Republics without discussing its effects on other facts of life, then we have to admit that industrialization and economic capacity have indeed advanced very rapidly. According to official statistics, Estonian industrial production today is as great in a week as it was in the entire year of 1939, the last year Estonia was independent.

The Baltic Republics have an extensive trade with foreign countries. But all exports and imports are strictly controlled by all-Union authorities in Moscow. Baltic industrial goods and agricultural products are exported to some eighty countries in the world. Estonian exports to countries outside the Soviet Union grew more than four times in size during the sixties and in 1974 made up 12% of all exports. (88% of Estonian exports went to other parts of the Soviet Union.) Foreign trade could be considerably larger and its benefits to Baltic Republics much greater if it were not subordinated to the all-Union authorities and their restrictions and regulations.

The Soviet central government in Moscow keeps 80 to 90% of the revenue from the Baltic foreign exports. During the sixties, Baltic Republics were allowed to export certain goods directly and keep all the inflow of foreign exchange for their own imports. These privileges have now been withdrawn.

Four Reservations
The first time I went to Estonia I was impressed by the rapid industrialization since the war. Many Baltic Communist leaders, as well as other people are proud of the material riches that have been created in their countries in the post-war period. But if you look closer at the economic situation and the industrial development, dark spots appear in a bright picture. The four most important are:

1. The unreliable statistics.
2. The unfavourable effects on the environment.
3. The difference between what is being produced in the Baltic countries and what is being consumed by the local population.

4. The enormous immigration from other parts of the Soviet Union, which is a consequence of the rapid industrialization and which threatens the very existence of Baltic peoples.

Some Western observers, as well as some people in Estonia and the other two Baltic Republics, regard the official Soviet statistics as a great bluff. According to them, there is one kind of official statistics for external use as propaganda, while the true figures are only for internal use. Conspiratory theories of this kind should be dismissed. Such double book-keeping, had it existed, would certainly have been mentioned to me by some of the patriotic officials that I spoke to in Estonia.

The Soviet statistics are, however, difficult to interpret. Index figures and base years are often chosen to show the greatest possible percentage increase. For example, current production figures are often compared with the figures for 1940. A misleading device which occurs now and then in the published propaganda figures is the taking into account of only half the production for the year 1940, i.e., only the period after the Soviet take-over in June, 1940. Even if based on the statistics for the whole year, 1940 would be a very doubtful basis for any comparison. You can hardly expect a normal level of production in a year of war and occupation.

It is also easy to draw misleading comparisons between the Baltic grain production before and after the Second World War. The grain is nowadays weighed at a certain moisture content level, not when dry. It is a kind of gross weight, without deduction for moisture and the weight of chaff. In this way, the production results can be "improved" by one-fifth, if compared with the pre-war method of calculation. The record harvest of grain in Soviet

Estonia was 1,105,300 tons in 1974, according to the official statistics. This record figure is reduced to 884,240 tons if measured in dry weight, which can then be compared with the record figure for the time of independence, that of 1939, of 706,000 tons.

The Environment in Latvia
The impressive Soviet statistics do not consider the unfavorable effects on the environment. As Estonia and Latvia are the most highly industrialized Republics in the Soviet Union, and Lithuania is catching up with her Baltic neighbors, the environmental problems in the Baltic Republics are among the greatest in the Soviet Union.

The Latvian Party organ *Cina* has, for example, from 1957 on criticized the large paper-mill in Sloka. It discharges its non-purified waste into the River Lielupe, which runs into the Riga Bay. The problem of the Sloka mill's pollution has not been dealt with, 20 years after the first alarming reports.

A booklet, published by the Latvian National Foundation in Sweden, in connection with the UN Environment Conference held in Stockholm in the summer of 1972, gives more examples of Baltic environmental problems, mainly in Latvia.[3] The Director of the Institute of Biology of the Latvian Academy of Sciences, Gunars Andrusaitis, complained in a radio lecture in 1967:

> With few exceptions the waste water in our Republic is not purified at all before being discharged. Only four industrial enterprises have purification plants.

But the Latvian authorities are not completely ignor-

[3] *Pollution in Soviet Russia and Countries Occupied and Exploited by Russia, Especially in Latvia and Ukraine*; Latvian National Foundation, Stockholm, 1972.

ing the problem. The superphosphate factory in Riga, for example, built in tsarist times, was closed at the end of the sixties, when it had been proven that its polluted air had killed the trees in a nearby park. This is one of the few instances of a Soviet industrial plant being shut down for environmental reasons. The factory's share of the Soviet production of phosphate fertilizers at the time of the closure had been reduced from 10% to a very insignificant amount.

Estonian Environmental Problems
The above-mentioned Andrusaitis stated in another radio lecture that Tallinn Bay is far more polluted than Riga Bay. The Pirita Beach in Tallinn was an expensive and popular holiday resort before the Second World War. People still bathe at Pirita today, but at the risk of infections. The industrial waste has killed most of the fish in the bay.

One serious problem concerns the intensive exploitation of oil shale, Estonia's most important natural resource. Those who visit Estonia's main industrial region, the oil shale basin between Rakvere and Narva, will be surprised by the moon-like landscape that has been created by the shale mining and processing. This environmental problem is particularly difficult to solve, as the Estonian government and the planning authorities have hardly any influence over the oil shale mining and processing industry. It comes directly under the all-Union ministry in Moscow. The same problem is faced by the Estonian authorities when they try to alleviate the environmental pollution caused by heavy industry, which is also to a large extent directed from Moscow.

The dilemma faced by the local Baltic authorities as far as protection of the environment is concerned is made clear by the following situation. During the years 1971 and 1972, under the initiative of the

Estonian Ministry of Forest Economy and Nature Protection, the Ministry of Justice and the Estonian Academy of Sciences, a draft of the Environment Protection Act was prepared. This act, however, has remained on paper only. Since there is no such act or law for the Soviet Union as a whole, the Estonian authorities have been reluctant to upstage the Soviet central government in Moscow, and the Estonian Environment Protection Draft Law has not been presented for legislative action.

Letter of 18 Estonian Natural Scientists

> . . . forced building of still more quarries, mines and thermal power plants (as is officially forseen by the 10th Five Year Plan) will inevitably bring about drama-tic changes in environmental balance not only in Nor-thern Estonia but also in the Baltic Sea basin . . . In our opinion, the actual dramatic environmental situation in Northern Estonia is a direct result of a bureaucratic, short-sighted extensive colonial administration. As such it must serve as a warning example for the neighboring nations, demonstrating how one must not utilize one's natural resources.

These statements are taken from a letter of 18 Estonian naturalists and scientists from the Nature Conservation Society of the Estonian SSR, the Academy of Sciences of the Estonian SSR, Tallinn Polytechnic Institute, and Tartu State University. The letter was written in May, 1977, and smuggled out the same year. The Estonian naturalists asked colleagues and mass media in Western countries to publicize their appeal. They want to inform the world about the dangerous situation that is rapidly developing in Northern Estonia as a result of the devastating exhaustion of local natural resources and general pollution of water, air and soil.

Because of her oil shale reserves, Estonia is the only country at the Baltic Sea, and one of the few in Europe, which is fully self-reliant in her energy needs. Estonian oil is furthermore cheap due to the fact that large high-quality deposits of shale lie very close to the surface. In addition, Estonian oil shale industry is favored by its long traditions. (The first oil shale distilleries in Estonia, and in the world, were founded there in the 1920's.) In a time of world-wide oil shortage, the importance of Estonian oil shale resources is easy to realize.

Unfortunately, the major part of Estonian oil shale is simply burned up in two gigantic thermal power plants. Such a waste of highly valuable raw material, which could be used for the production of a wide variety of chemical products, is being officially justified by the scarcity of other natural energy resources in the Northwestern Economic Region of the Soviet Union. As the energy crisis is growing more acute in the Soviet Union also, the authorities are planning a third gigantic thermal plant in Estonia, working on oil shale. The letter of the 18 Estonian naturalists opposes such a plant for its waste of scarce natural resources, and its destruction of the environment:

In result of large-scale extensive oil-shale mining a considerable part of the Northeastern Estonia has been turned into a moon landscape: huge terricones of ash and barren rock are towering above grey and nearly dead landscape, fertile soil and vegetation has been destroyed over large areas, air has been polluted with dust, smoke, compounds of sulphur, nitrogen, phenols and other toxic substances, rivers like Purtse and Pühajõgi (once swarming with trout and salmon) are now without a trace of life, poisoning even waters of the sea many kilometres from their mouths, ground waters dangerously polluted – such is a "natural"

126

scenery of the oil shale mining regions of the northeast Estonia.

The letter continues:

A further item of major concern is Moscow's directive about founding a gigantic phosphorite quarry at Toolse, on the shore of the Finnish Gulf (estimated production capability 5 million tons a year). The phosphorite mined will be enriched in a new refinery to be built nearby and then transported to the Soviet Union or exported abroad (lately the price of phosphorite on the world market is steeply rising). Competent Estonian scientists, scientific organizations and even some local administrative bodies have raised serious objections against such schemes of Moscow central planners. A state of alarm has spread also among the wider Estonian public in view of the prospect that on vast areas, nature, soil and water would be contaminated by extensive methods of production, which are too well known from Maardu and Kohtla-Järve experience. Building of the Toolse quarry also means that the two already existing industrial "desert" zones (Maardu and Kohtla-Järve oil-share mining area) would be linked together by a similar area in the central part of Northern Estonia. Today the word "Toolse" has for Estonians an alarming and gloomy sound. It means to them further devastated landscape on the vast scale, and also the introduction of thousands of Russian immigrants who will only further upset precarious national balance of the Northeastern Estonia.

The letter writers admit that some measures have already been taken in Estonia to protect and conserve the natural environment. Several government officials are said to have been awakened from their bureaucratic indifference and they are now backing measures to protect nature and its resources. At the beginning of 1977 some 4% of the entire area of Estonia has been set under state protection, notably the first national park of the Soviet Union, the

Lahemaa area in the North Estonia. As for other measures, electric filters have been introduced in the thermal power plants, building of a sewage purification installation was started in the oil shale area and some deserted oil shale opencasts are being restored. It could be added that a large collector is under construction in Tallinn which will take the city's human and industrial waste out into the sea after purification. Also DDT is completely banned.

The basic problem, however, remains, and is valid for the Soviet economy as a whole. "Under the present system the central, as well as local party and government organs, are interested almost exclusively in meeting their current production targets and getting their premium notwithstanding any long term costs or harm done to the nature". This was also admitted by the journal *Eesti Loodus* (Estonian Nature):

> "So producers are often regarding nature as a treasury, from which every possible raw material can be taken for nothing, planning the utilization of nature only from the angle of the most simple and economical availability of its resources. Certainly, such a purely consumptive mentality does not take into consideration possible changes that may take place in nature as a result of industrial production; frequently these changes directly worsen our living conditions (unhealthy compounds in the environment, spoiled landscapes, etc.)".

> And further: "Generally results of the production are being accounted only on the basis of overall economic figures . . . i.e., so far there exist no material stimuli for more rational utilization of the natural resources"[4]

Development Assistance
It happened to me several times in Estonia when discussing the economy with "ordinary" people and

[4] *Eesti Loodus*, no. 5, 1977. pp. 280–81.

referring to the impressive statistics of production, that they angrily raised the objection: "Yes, but being an economist you ought to understand that you have to differentiate between production and consumption. What use is it to us producing a large amount of goods which are then exported to Russia."

Trade with other parts of the Soviet Union is not altogether to the disadvantage of the Baltic Republics. The industrialization of the Baltic Republics could not have taken place as rapidly and have been so diversified without the deliveries of metals from Russia and the Ukraine to the Baltic engineering and machine-building industry, of cotton from the Central Asian Republics to the Baltic textile industry and oil from the Caucasus for fuel.

The Baltic Republics are forced to give a large part of their economic surpluses to other, poorer regions within the Soviet Union, and also for certain all-Union purposes, such as defense, Soviet foreign aid, military assistance programs abroad and space research. This reminds me of an Estonian worker who said: "What's so difficult about sending up sputniks when you enslave other people and let them produce food and other things for you?"

The largest part of the Soviet state revenue comes from a turnover or sales tax. Some of this revenue is given back to the Union Republics for their own investments. The amounts refunded are not directly related and do not correspond to the taxes received. During the first half of the sixties, Latvia, for example, was refunded via the state budget only between one tenth and one fifth of the taxes paid. The large all-Union capital investments in the Baltic Republics are more than offset by the sums taken out every year in the form of tax payments to Moscow.

Estonia, Latvia, and Lithuania furthermore receive no share of the income from their ocean fishing industry, the use of their harbors, or from their shipping on the high seas, as these branches of the economy come directly under Moscow. The Baltic Republics also get very little from those enterprises in heavy industry that are directly subordinated to all-Union ministries. Moscow has considerable "invisible" revenue from the exploitation of Baltic agriculture through the device of setting artificially low prices for agricultural products. As a matter of fact, all prices of Baltic products are set in Moscow. This gives the Soviet central government all the leverage it needs for dominating the Baltic economies.

Some of the surplus from the Baltic production is thus used to redistribute income and production between different parts of the Soviet Union. From the points of view of the all-Union administration this may be right and reasonable. The Balts, however, have little sympathy for such enforced "development aid". It is easy for them to see it as a kind of Russian or Soviet exploitation, especially when they notice that the food they produce is sent on a priority basis to Moscow and Leningrad and their taxes are being invested for the development of the Russian hinterland in Siberia or the Central Asia Soviet Republics. There is no solution to this conflict within the Soviet system as it now stands.

It is not surprising that the Balts react as they do. Few peoples are enthusiastic about aid to developing countries, even if such aid is freely decided upon by Parliament. You can hardly expect a more generous attitude from the oppressed Baltic peoples. They do not wish to give up their relative prosperity for Russians or for Central Asians any more than they did for the Germans during the Second World War.

Many Balts consider their Republics wrongfully exploited by the Soviets. But the nature of the planned economy makes it theoretically impossible to analyse objectively whether or not the Baltic countries are in fact subjected to a Soviet exploitation. Statistics available in the West do not permit the necessary analysis of investment activities, tax payments and the exchange of goods. If such data have been worked out in the Baltic Republics they are perhaps too sensitive to be published.

The Soviet authorities maintain that the large Soviet investments in Baltic industry since the war and the access to the all-Union market were necessary for the rapid economic growth. Baltic industry is now able to produce in large series. This makes it possible to produce goods at competitive unit-cost in special fields. But no one knows how things would have developed if private initiative and national interests had been given greater scope.

Many Balts are convinced that Russian exploitation lies behind the shortage of consumer goods and food stuffs which still occurs in the Baltic Republics. Sometimes they cite the example of Baltic electric power. Estonia produces more electric power per capita than all the other countries in the world except Canada and Norway. But two-thirds of the electric power is exported to other parts of the Soviet Union, mainly to the Leningrad area. This export is decided in Moscow, where prices and other conditions for export are also set. Estonia also exports to other regions of the Soviet Union about nine-tenths of all instruments, the radio-electronic and electro-technical equipment made in the Republic, as well as two-thirds of the chemical products and of the fish catch. About a third of Estonia's meat, butter, and milk goes to feed Russians, mostly in Moscow and Leningrad. Roughly the same proportion of industrial and consumer goods produced in Latvia and Lithuania is going to other parts of the Soviet Union, mostly to the Russian Federation.

131

Many Balts would prefer to reduce the rate of industrial production in order to escape the mass immigration of Russian labor which is required for the rapid increase in production. This immigration is seen as a grave threat against the future of the Baltic peoples. Many Balts also feel that the immigrants lower the native population's standard of living, by appropriating new housing and making the consumer goods and food items more scarce than these already are.

There is an Estonian ditty which succinctly expresses this popular objection:

Välja, välja vabariigi seest,
kes joovad eesti viina ja ei räägi eesti keelt!

Välja, välja vabariigi seest,
kes söövad eesti leiba ja ei räägi eesti keelt!

(Out, out from our Republic you
who drink Estonian whisky, but don't speak Estonian tongue!

Out, out from our Republic you
who eat Estonian bread, but don't speak the Estonian tongue!)

Shortage of Consumer Goods

The growth figures say little about how production fulfills consumer demand. The Soviet planning authorities need not bother too much about the consumers. The norms of production are in principle based on the planners' ideas of what the economy needs and what therefore the consumers ought to want.

The prices of many consumer goods are higher and wages considerably lower than in the West. It is difficult to understand how Baltic families manage to balance their budgets even if both parents work and often have two jobs each. But still the greatest problem for many families is not how to manage on what money they have, but how to get hold of desirable goods.

I heard innumerable complaints from Estonians trying to find simple but essential things. To search for something and then to stand in line for it is irritating and time-consuming. In Soviet shops you first have to queue at a certain counter, then you have to join another queue in order to pay before you return to receive whatever you paid for. There are often different queues for different kinds of food.

Better quality goods are often imported from East European countries, such as Czechoslovakia, but they are depleted as soon as they reach the shops and stores. In Tallinn I saw a long line suddenly forming outside a shop. It had just received some Czechoslovak shoes. These are considered to be of a much better quality than the Soviet ones. The assistants in the shoe shop had therefore telephoned their friends to spread the good news. Obviously, the friends had not been long in telling others and so, in a very short time, a queue several hundred metres long formed outside the shop.

Jokes and Dissatisfaction

These long queues lend themselves to an excellent environment for making up and spreading jokes about all sorts of things, mainly about the way the economic system works (or rather, does not work). The first such joke I was told concerned the difference between socialist fairy tales and capitalist ones. According to the story the capitalist ones begin with the words: "Once upon a time there was . . .", while the socialist ones begin: "Once upon a time there will be . . ."

Another standard joke was: "Which is the best place after death, the socialist hell or the capitalist hell?" – "The socialist hell, of course. There you can always hope that they are short of tar or coal for the fires".

Another one is popular all over Eastern Europe: "What is the difference between capitalism and socialism?" – "Capitalism makes social mistakes, but socialism makes capital ones."

Another story goes like this. Freshly scrubbed, well-fed Estonian pigs stand in line in a slaughter-house waiting to be killed. "What is your last wish?", they are asked. "We want our bones to be buried in Estonian soil!", respond the pigs in chorus. This joke is of course directed against the obligatory export of meat to Russia while the needs of the local population are not met.

The meat shortage creates other forms of protest as well. "Riga dockers end up in labor camps after fish-day strike," reported *The London Times* from Moscow on November 1, 1976. Four dockers from the Latvian capital had been sent to labor camps after a protest strike in May. The disastrous Soviet grain harvests of recent years have created a shortage of animal foodstuffs, so one or more "fish-days" have been introduced in Soviet restaurants. On such days no meat dishes are available.

Sergei Frolov, 30, and Janis Varna, 28, had each been sentenced to three years in a labor camp for their part in the strike of the Riga dockers, reported *The London Times*. Andris Goldbergs, 40, and Mikhail Larchenkov, 37, had received two-year sentences at the trial before the Latvian Supreme Court in August, 1972.

If we can believe the Baltic storytellers, it is not so certain that even "once upon a time there will be" consumer goods and foodstuffs in sufficient quantities. One joke, set in the future, when the Communist society has been realized, is scathing about both

134

the present and the future: "Daddy, what is money?" – "Well, you see, my lad, in the old days you had to use money to pay for things you wanted. It wasn't like it is now, when everybody can eat as much as they like without paying. Then you had to pay for all the food you had, even for rye bread". – "Daddy, what is rye bread?".

Jokes of this kind are often exaggerated and misleading. The Baltic Republics today enjoy the highest standard of living that exists within the framework of the Soviet Union, and the extreme shortages of the Stalin era are only a memory. The picture of living standards is strongly dependent on the choice of perspective. The impression is gloomy if you compare the situation with that in the West, but much brighter if you compare it with the situation in the Baltic countries in the forties and fifties or with the situation in less developed parts of the Soviet Union.

That there is all the same a shortage of consumer goods, and that the quality of the goods available is often low, is partly the result of a deliberate policy which can be seen in all Communist countries. Private consumption is held back, heavy industry and collective needs are encouraged. The shortage of consumer goods is also partly a result of low efficiency, due to bureaucratization, over-centralized decision making and the workers' feelings of alienation. The quantitative bias of the Soviet planned economy contributes to the low quality of goods. Goods are brought on the market which in the West would have been rejected as being of inferior quality. The management does everything to meet the planning norms. Norms reached are rewarded, but norms not met cause complaints and a lower bonus for the management.

A similar consequence of the state economy is extensive pilfering. Many people who think it im-

135

moral to steal from private individuals can gladly cheat the de-personalized state and its enterprises. This is the same "philosophy" which in the West lies behind tax evasion and similar things, but in the Soviet Union it has reached vast proportions. Bribes are much more common in the Soviet Union as in the West, being sometimes necessary for the strongly centralized and bureaucratized planned economy to function tolerably.

Alcoholism
Heavy drinking contributes to the extensive absenteeism and the low work productivity and through this to considerable production losses. Estonia and Latvia are the two Republics in the Union that have the greatest consumption of alcohol per head of population. Many tourists visiting restaurants in Tallinn and Riga have been amazed at the large quantities of spirits consumed by people during the long wait for meals to be served.

The alcohol consumption in Estonia rose by a half during the second half of the sixties. The inhabitants of Estonia drink one and a half times as much as the population in the rest of the Soviet Union or in the United States. One example of the damaging effects this had on the economy: in 1968 every fourteenth "happy" tractor driver lost his driving licence because of drunken driving. The frequency was almost as high during the first half of 1972. In Lithuania the consumption of spirits per inhabitant was doubled in the sixties and the consumption of wine rose by four times. Alcoholism in the Soviet Union has become a social evil of such magnitude that it is becoming the target of open discussion. In 1972 the sale of vodka was restricted to shops that are not situated in the vicinity of working-places, schools or railway stations, the sales hours were cut down and the strongest brands were prohibited. Also the right to sick allowance for absence from work due to misuse of alcohol was abolished. But still vodka is one of the few daily consumption goods that is never lacking in Soviet shops. Alcohol, that is nowadays registered as "other foods" in Soviet trade statistics, reached 1/3 of total turnover in Soviet food shops already some years ago. Vodka was sold as much as meat, fish, canned food, bread, vegetables and fruit altogether. People on official level try to explain away the large and growing excessive use of alcohol in the Soviet Union as a "remnant of capitalism" although it was, after all, abolished more than sixty years ago. Soviet leaders have begun to speak openly about the heavy production losses and social problems created by too much drinking.

Shortage of Housing

A considerable part of the housing in the large Baltic cities was destroyed by Nazi and Soviet warfare during the Second World War. In Tallinn the pre-war housing level was not reached until the end of the sixties. It will be 1980 before housing space per capita in all Estonian towns reaches the same level as before the war. The shortage of housing today is mainly the result of the mass immigration since the war, but also of insufficient housing construction. Usually you must have been resident in a community for at least eight years before you can be placed on the housing queue. Russian immigrants are, however, often housed immediately.

Every inhabitant of the Baltic Republics today has an average living space of eight square metres. This is a standard prescribed by law. The standard when building new housing is twice this size. This rule is often broken and many people do not even achieve the average. Often a whole family lives in one room,

137

or two families in a flat of more than one room. If you have four square meters or more per member of the family you are not placed in the most favored part of the housing queue. The figures mentioned corresponds to sixteen square meters for a family with two children.

Comparing Living Standards

Tourists from the West who go to the Baltic Republics usually notice that more and better consumer goods are available there than, for example, in Leningrad or Moscow, but they are fewer and of worse quality than, for example, in Helsinki. Such observations are difficult to prove statistically, but the impression is probably correct.

It is even more difficult to make a comparison with the living standards before World War II. You have to take many things into consideration, such as the average income, the range of wages and salaries, the burden of taxation, the expenditure for education, health services, and rent. People in the Baltic countries today have a greater proportion of their needs covered by collective consumption than do people in many Western countries. Certain costs are covered by the State budget instead of the family budget. Comparisons of the living standards, "then and now", are made much more difficult by the radical changes in the economic system and by the fact that both habits and the quality of consumer goods change over long periods of time.

A Swedish journalist, Jan Leijonhielm, stated after a visit to the Baltic Republics that, "Those who maintain that you eat, live and dress better in the Baltic countries today than you did in the thirties are few and far between.[5] If his impression is typical of

[5] Jan Leijonhielm, *Industria*, Nov. 1969.

what most **Balts** think, this is rather remarkable if you consider the enormous increases in living standards in the Western world since the Second World War.

In this context a most interesting comparison can be drawn between Estonia and Finland, a country which had a similar economic and cultural starting-point at the end of the thirties. The gap in the living standards of Finland and Estonia, which was small in 1939, has, according to both the consumer statistics available and the evidence of travellers, widened considerably to Finland's advantage. Finland was almost as hard hit as Estonia by the Second World War and has had no Soviet help in rebuilding. As far as I can see there are only two possible explanations for the widening gap between Finland and Estonia. Either Estonia has been exploited or has had an inefficient economic system forced upon her – or both.

The comparison with living standards in the West is perhaps unrealistic for most Balts at home. For them it is more close at hand to see that life has become better during the sixties and seventies (and that the living standard is also higher than in other parts of the Soviet Union).

The huge Russian Soviet Republic, or Russia proper, contains areas of very different levels of development. Some areas in central Russia have a higher proportion of town dwellers, greater industrial output, and may also have a higher average income per capita than both Estonia and Latvia. This is an important but often ignored factor in drawing comparisons between the Russian SFSR and the Baltic Republics.

In 1968 the gross national income per capita in Estonia and Latvia was more than 1,400 roubles as against an average of 1,000 for the whole of the

Soviet Union. It is difficult to convert this to Western circumstances because of the great differences in the Soviet and Western economies. The official rate of exchange does not indicate the true difference in buying power between Western currencies and the rouble.

The Baltic share of the total national income of the Soviet Union increased somewhat during the sixties. In Estonia the share increased from 0·7% in 1958 to 0·8% in 1968; in Latvia from 1·3% to 1·4%, and in Lithuania from 1·2% to 1·5%. Thus the total Baltic share grew from 3·2% to 3·7% during the same time.[6]

The Soviet Republic which during this period increased its average income most rapidly was Lithuania. Lithuania and Byelorussia were the only Republics which succeeded in doubling their income. Estonia and Latvia came in third and fourth place. The average increase for the Baltic Republics was about 97%, almost doubling, while the all-Union average was increased by two-thirds.

During the sixties, the Baltic Republics thus increased their economic lead over the other Soviet Republics. The only Republic which since the war has achieved an economic development as rapid as the Baltic Republics is Moldavia (which like the Baltic countries, was incorporated during the Second World War).

But the central problem remains – the Balts themselves have very little to say about how this relatively high gross national income, or income per capita, is to be used and where is it going to be invested – locally or all over the Soviet Union.

[6] These percentages are taken from H. J. Wagener, "Regional Output Levels in the Soviet Union", Radio Liberty Research Paper No. 41, 1971, reported in *Estonian Events*, Dec. 1971, p. 2.

Working Class Power?

In the Baltic Republics, as in the rest of the Soviet Union, the trade unions are, like commerce and industry, an inseparable part of the Party and state machinery. The non-Communist independent Baltic trade unions were completely crushed at the beginning of the Soviet period. Social democrat politicians and trade union leaders were condemned as "social fascists", and belonged to the groups hardest hit by the purges and mass deportations.

Today's Soviet (and Baltic) trade unions differ in a number of ways from their Western counterparts. A trade union in the Soviet Union combines the functions of a government department, social security administration, local council, and personnel department of a big firm. It looks after social and cultural institutions, such as hospitals, holiday homes, cultural facilities, libraries, club activities, and sports facilities.

The trade unions have, however, very little say in matters regarding wages and working conditions. Strikes and other forms of militancy are prohibited. It is hardly remarkable that a trade union robbed of its main weapon finds it hard to hold its own against the authorities and management.

The only trade unions allowed are those approved of by the government. The trade union movement, like other organizations in the Soviet Union, has been developed according to the principle of "democratic centralism". Lower, subordinated bodies must obey orders from higher levels. The trade union leaders are also supervised by parallel Party committees according to "the principle of double responsibility".

Wages in different branches of the economy are fixed by the authorities, without the workers being able to make themselves heard. The piece-rate system is more widespread in the Soviet Union than in any other country in the world. Already in 1918 Lenin demanded that piece-work should be introduced in order to improve discipline and increase the productivity of the workers. Time and motion studies are common. Competitions between workers, departments and plants are a common way of raising the level of production. Especially productive workers get their picture pinned on a notice-board with an honorary mention, just like successful schoolchildren.

Every Soviet worker has an employment book which follows him from job to job. The employer writes his comments on the employee in it. The obligation to work is statutory and according to the 1970 Employment Law those who do not work shall not eat. Those who lack permanent work and do not study can be sentenced for vagrancy.

The following statement about the conditions for the working class in Latvia is taken from the 1970 Latvian Social Democratic Party program in exile. It seems equally applicable to conditions in Estonia and Lithuania:

> A new class society has been established in Latvia according to the Russian model, with a wealthy elite and Party bureaucracy as its main social force. The working class is being heavily exploited, wages are low, and prices of consumer goods very high. The State, controlled by the Russian Communist Party, appropriates the bulk of the value of output produced by Latvian workers and uses it for the purposes of Russian imperialism and militarism. The trade unions are totally bureaucratized. They are not free organizations, but are controlled by the Communist Party. They do not protect the workers' interest, but aid management in the exploitation of the workers.[7]

[7] The whole program is printed in *Briviba*, no. 8, 1970, the organ of the Latvian Social Democrats in Exile.

Wages and Equality

Differences in wages and salaries after tax are higher in the Baltic Republics and the rest of the Soviet Union than in the West. These differences are increased by productivity-related bonuses, that are normally proportional to the nominal wages. Bonuses are paid out when production plans have been exceeded. The highest salaries go to leading artists and writers, high-ranking military officers, Party and Government leaders. High-ranking officers received at the end of the sixties 800 to 1,000 roubles a month, some ten times as much as an unskilled worker; local Party secretaries got 1,500 roubles, fifteen times as much as the unskilled worker; and the "deserving few" among the cultural personalities up to 2,000 roubles a month, twenty times as much as an unskilled worker.

Leading Party members, favored as they are as regards salaries, also have access to special shops with more and better goods at lower prices – where ordinary people cannot buy. Leading Party men and other members of the Soviet upper class do not have to wait years to obtain desirable consumer goods like, for example, cars. They also have their own hospitals, pharmacies, holiday homes and nightclubs. Sometimes the highest political leaders live in secluded houses surrounded by high walls and armed guards. In short, a privileged class like the nobility in the Middle Ages.

From Starvation to Well-being

When Baltic agriculture was collectivized at the end of the forties, hundreds of thousands of reluctant farmers were sent to Siberian exile or to labor camps. (At the same time the Soviet delegates voted in the UN to ban genocide.) "The kulaks as a class were liquidated," state the Baltic Communist historians.

All farmers who used hired labor, including relatives who were paid to help with the harvest, were classed as kulaks. The authorities also demanded forced deliveries to the state and drastically increased the taxes on income and farming. In this way the "voluntary" change to collective farming was facilitated.

Agriculture was for a long time after collectivization a thorn in the flesh for the economy of the Baltic Republics (as in the whole of the Soviet Union). The farmers became the black sheep in the "workers' paradise". The Soviet authorities are still, most recently in 1974 and 1979, forced to buy enormous quantities of grain from abroad in order to manage the food supplies. Baltic farmers like to tell the joke: "Which are the latest improvements in Russian agriculture?" – "That they sow the wheat in Central Asia and reap the harvest in Canada and Australia."

Not until the middle sixties did the grain production reach the same level as during the time of independence. Compared to the thirties the area of arable land has been reduced by a quarter in Estonia and by almost the same in Latvia. The yield per unit area has been increased, however, mainly through mechanization, improved plant breeding, and increased use of mineral fertilizers. This is of course a common development all over the world, at least in the industrial countries.

The yield of grain per hectare has been doubled as compared with the average for the pre-war period in the thirties, and averaged in 1971–1974, 2·33 tons in Estonia. The figure for Lithuania is higher, 2·6 tons. This is also twice the figure for the thirties. The yield is still, however, lower than, for example, in Sweden. The harvest per hectare in the Swedish county of Södermanland, which lies on the same latitude as the northern parts of the Baltic countries, averaged in 1971–74 more than 3·5 tons for all grain crops per hectare.

The Flight from the Countryside
In Estonia agriculture still employs one-fifth of the working population. This is twice as high a figure as that for Sweden, and five times that for the United States. There are thus still great possibilities of increasing productivity through increased mechanization and modernization.

The flight from the Baltic rural areas has been extensive since the war but has recently become less. 1969 was the first year in which the rural population in Estonia did not decrease. One contributing factor is the increasing environmental problems in the capital cities.

The Baltic rural areas have on the whole more native character than the large industrial towns and the romantic notions of the rural areas have, therefore, patriotic undertones. Last but not least, the gap in living standards between rural and urban areas has diminished with the growing prosperity of collective farmers. The collective farmers also obtained a government retirement pension in the middle sixties. Before that time, it was only the richest collective farms, about one-fifth of the total in Latvia, that looked after their members in old age, through voluntary retirement funds. On other collective farms elderly people were forced to work to the bitter end; otherwise they risked being excluded.

During the whole of this century the population in rural areas has been better fed than in the towns. The average intake of calories in Estonia per person per day was at the beginning of the seventies about 2,800 in urban areas and 3,600 in rural areas. The increase in production from Baltic agriculture and the greater concentration on animal produce has made it possible to change from a fattening bread and potato diet to a healthier fare.

The forced deliveries of produce to the state have stopped and state purchase prices have increased considerably since the fall of Khrushchev. The collective farmers' wages have been partly decontrolled in the Baltic Republics. Cash payments have been doubled since the middle of the sixties. The freer setting of wage rates is a result of the pioneering economic reforms. Should the experiments with Baltic agriculture be successful the reforms will probably be instituted elsewhere in the Soviet Union also.

The Private Plot

Every collective farmer in the Baltic Republics, as in the whole of the Soviet Union, has the right to cultivate a plot of his own of not more than 0·6 hectares (1·5 acres). The corresponding figure for employees at the state farms (sovkhozes) is 0·4 hectares (about 1 acre). The farmers are also allowed to pasture their domestic animals. They can have, at the most, one cow and one calf, two pigs, five sheep, and an unlimited number of chickens.

These private allotments are most important for the agricultural production in the Baltic Republics and in the rest of the Soviet Union. The produce that is not used by the farmer himself and his family is given to friends and relations or sold at the so-called farmers' or kolkhoz markets in the towns. There is no price control at these markets. Apart from the black market this is the only market in Soviet society where prices are set according to supply and demand alone.

The private sector was even more important in the fifties. Today some collective and state farmers cultivate their allotments more as a hobby. Many think it is too much trouble to keep a cow and content themselves with the smaller animals or the land allotment only. In 1969 one third of the cash income of the Estonian collective farmers came from the private sector. In 1970 more than a third of the meat, egg, and milk production and over half of the potatoes and vegetables in Latvia came from this private sector.

Table 1

The private sector's percentage of the yearly production in Estonia

	1950	1960	1971
Potatoes		34	41
Eggs	88	70	35
Beef	72	43	23
Milk	56	45	30
Pork			29

Sources: *Eesti NSV rahvamajandus, 1971* (The National Economy of the Estonian SSR in 1971), op. cit., for 1969, and an interview with the Deputy Minister for Agriculture, Ilmar Aamisepp, in Tallinn, summer, 1970. The figures in the table should be considered against the background that 17% of all cattle, 4·2% of all hens and 2·5% of all cultivated land was used privately at the beginning of 1969.

Table 2

The private sector's percentage of the yearly production in Latvia

	1950	1960	1971
Potatoes	64	63	60
Eggs	93	71	34
Beef	73	49	35
Milk	60	49	39
Vegetables	84	66	58
Wool	76	75	82

Source: The statistical yearbook, *Latvijas PSR tautas simnieciba 1971.* (Statistical data for the Latvian SSR 1971).
   In Latvia 4·6% of all cultivated land was privately used.

The yield per unit area is very high on the privately cultivated allotments. The farmers put much more care into cultivating their own patches rather than the collective's fields. In Estonia the privately owned cows gave, in 1968, on the average, almost 450 kg. more milk per year than the communally owned cows. And a decade later it is still officially stressed that the private plots are necessary both for their vital contribution to agrarian production and for their contribution to the cash and nature income of those employed in agriculture.[8] The same points of view were stressed for the Soviet economy as a whole by Brezhnev, for example, at the XVIth All-Union Trades Union Congress in 1977.

Three Reservations
Baltic collective and state farming can be evaluated in different ways. Yields are higher than in the rest of the Soviet Union, apart from in the very fertile belt of black earth in southern Russia and the Ukraine. The Baltic soils are not at all as good. Therefore they must be worked far more intensively to give as high or higher yields. The high yields of Baltic agriculture, high according to Soviet standards, are not due to collectivization or Sovietization. The Baltic countries have been among the first in the world as regards nutritional standards ever since the turn of this century when modern methods began to be practiced in Baltic farming. Today the yields are lower than they are at the corresponding latitude in neighboring Sweden. A large part of the Baltic farm produce comes from the small private allotments and the stock of privately owned animals.

Another question in this connection can be formu-

[8] See for instance the *Eesti Pollumehe teatmik* (Agrarian Almanac) Tallinn, 1978, p. 163.

lated as follows: how should you balance today's high standard of nutrition and rising income for the collective and state farmers against the hundreds of thousands of people who were deported to make it possible to carry out the collectivization – a collectivization which furthermore has not been all to the good? How long should the fate of those deported be considered when discussing the development of Baltic agriculture today? Should they be excluded from the economic accounts and be left only to the history books?

Bread and Freedom

The material shortcomings that still exist in the Baltic societies, as in all other societies, are not the most important. The basic dilemma remains, independent of how high the living standards might grow in the future. It becomes increasingly important with the rising material standards. The problem was summarized in the title of a novel by the Russian author Dudintsev, which appeared already in 1956, during the period of a political and literary thaw. The book was called *Not by Bread Alone*. The present and future problems in the Baltic countries can hardly be better summarized than by this biblical quotation. The lack of vital human rights is felt even more with the increasing material standard of living.

CHAPTER 8

The Communist Party – Nationalism or Centralism?

The Communist Party is the most important center of power in the Baltic Republics as well as in other constituent republics in the Soviet Union. The Estonian, Latvian and Lithuanian Parties are not independent. They are only regional subdivisions of the all-Union Party.

The all-Union Party's most important organ, the Politburo, consisted in 1980 of ten Russians, one Ukrainian, one Kazakh and one Latvian. The Latvian member has since 1966 been Arvids Pelshe, an old Stalinist, whom many Latvians regard as more Russian than Latvian. Pelshe has advised communists in Latvia to "let the Russians fight the Great Russian chauvinism and let us fight our own nationalists!" The advice might seem sound, but the problem is to get Russian officials to see Russian chauvinistic nationalism as a threat. Pelshe's seemingly double-edged sword was therefore raised against the Latvian patriots only. Pelshe's attitude reminds us of Stalin – the Georgian who became the greatest Russian chauvinist of them all.

Pelshe is the first, and so far the only Balt to become a member of the Politburo in Moscow. His position is a reward for long and faithful service as Moscow's watch-dog in Latvia.

All members of the Secretariat of the Central Committee in Moscow, headed by Leonid Brezhnev,

150

are Russians. The Russians also dominate among the Party membership. The Russian share was over 60% in 1970, although the Russian share of the total population in the Soviet Union was barely more than half. Russians are in the majority among the Party members in five non-Russian Union Republics, including Latvia. Nine out of ten employees in the all-Union Party machinery in Moscow are Russian by nationality, most of the remainder are Ukrainians.

Moscow's Watchdogs
The post of Second Secretary of the Party's Central Committee is in all-Union Republics filled by a reliable man, usually a Russian. They are Moscow's special watchdogs and therefore more powerful than one could guess from their formally subordinate position. They seldom speak the local language. Discussions in the Party Secretariats and Politburos of the non-Russian Union Republics are therefore held in Russian. Because the Second Secretary is a trusted Moscow emissary, the local communists can be allowed to fill the formally highest posts, such as the Chairman of the Republican Council of Ministers, Chairman of the Presidium of the Republican Supreme Soviet, and First Secretary of the Central Committee of the local Party organization. The local nationalists are thus pacified, and the risk for foreign criticism of Russian domination and colonialism is decreased.

The Second Secretaries in the Baltic Republics are named Konstantin Lebedev (a Russian born in 1918, and sent to Tallinn in 1971 from Moscow), Nikolai Beluha (a Russian born in 1920, and sent to Riga from Leningrad) and Nikolai Dybenko (a Russian sent from Moscow to Vilnius in 1978). The Russian commander-in-chief for the Baltic Military District serves also as a member of the Latvian Party executive.

The Three Top Men

The Party machinery is far more important than the State bureaucracy. The First Secretaries of the respective Communist Parties in the three Baltic Republics have for many years been Johannes Käbin in Estonia, Augusts Voss in Latvia, and, until his death in 1974, Antanas Snieckus in Lithuania. The personal background of these three men, the composition of their Party executives, as well as historical reasons and the demographic situation, may explain some of the differences in the political and cultural climate between the three Baltic countries today.

Augusts Voss, although of Latvian descent, was born and educated in Russia and has no sympathy for Latvian national communists. As a Russified Latvian, he is strictly a Soviet and comes down on everything which slows up the Sovietization of Latvia. Russians, and Latvians born in Russia, also have a stronger position in the Latvian Communist Party than their counterparts in the Estonian and Lithuanian Parties. The Party leadership in Latvia is the most Stalinist and also the least nationally oriented.

Latvia was in the late 1950's subjected to an extensive purge of nationally-minded Communists. These "national communists" tried to oppose Russification and centralization in a number of ways. They also demanded that those in power in the local Republican Party and state machinery, as well as in trade and industry, should be able to speak both Russian and Latvian. This meant in practice that Russian officials sent to Latvia should learn Latvian. National communists, under the leadership of the deputy prime minister Eduards Berklavs, gained in 1958–59 the majority in the Central Committee of the Latvian Communist Party. Nikita Khrushchev then rushed to the Latvian capital and brought them to task with the help of the Moscow-oriented veteran

Latvian communist Arvids Pelshe, who was appointed First Secretary of the Latvian Communist Party.

Berklavs was deported from Latvia. Hundreds of leading communists were purged, among them the Chairman of the Presidium, two Party Secretaries, six ministers or deputy ministers, and several leaders of the Communist Youth Organization. This purge was a telling proof of the strength of the national opposition in Latvia – even among leading communists.

The top man in Estonia, Johannes Käbin, was born in Estonia but grew up in Russia. During the four decades that he has been back in his native land he has gone through an interesting process of re-Estonianization. He started off as a faithful Stalinist when Stalin was still alive. Käbin stated that knowledge of the Estonian language was not necessary for Party officials or civil servants in the Republic. Perhaps Käbin made a virtue of necessity. At that time it was difficult to get Estonians to join the Party, which was generally seen as the mouthpiece for the occupying power. Käbin's personal attitude was at that time probably strongly pro-Russian. He chose, for example, to write his name in the Russian way, Ivan Kebin.

The early 1950's were a black time for Estonian communists, as well as non-communists. Extensive purges took place within the Communist Party of Estonia in 1950. Nikolai Karotamm, First Secretary of the Central Committee of the Estonian Communist Party; Arnold Veimer, Chairman of the Council of Ministers; Eduard Päll, Chairman of the Presidium of the Supreme Soviet; and well-known Estonian Communists such as Hans Kruus, Nigol Andresen, Aleksander Jõeäär and Oskar Sepre were all accused of holding bourgeois-nationalist views and of putting republican interests before Soviet interests. They were specifically charged with opposing Russian mass immigration, encouraging national traditions and trying to place the local leadership in native hands. Instrumental in helping Moscow to purge the Communist Party of Estonia from these alleged nationalists was Johannes Käbin. He became the First Secretary of the Central Committee of the Estonian Communist Party in March, 1950.

Käbin's hard-line policy during the next few years was perhaps not entirely self-chosen. Käbin knew that Stalin was pathologically suspicious of every form of opposition, and not only of the non-Russian communist leaders. The tense international situation during the cold war also contributed to the tightening up of the political situation within the Soviet Union.

Käbin's attitude towards native and national-minded communists has gradually softened with the years. He reportedly also takes pride in being in Moscow's eyes the top representative of Estonia's considerable contributions to the Soviet economy. In recent years he seems to be functioning more and more as a buffer between the Moscow-oriented centralists and the advocates for Russification on the one hand, and the Estonian regionalists and the native population on the other. It has been suggested that Käbin has reached a silent understanding with the local communists, after having started off as a Moscow puppet. In 1978 Käbin became Chairman of the Estonian Supreme Soviet and was replaced as 1st Party Secretary by Karl Vaino, another Russified Estonian Communist.

Antanas Snieckus, the Lithuanian communist leader, hardly came from a proletarian background. Born in Lithuania in 1903, his father was a well-to-do farmer and his mother a devout Catholic. Both his parents, as well as his brother and sisters, fled to the West during World War II. Snieckus was trained in Russia and became a trusted revolutionary. He was a member of the Lithuanian Communist Party's Secretariat since the middle of the twenties and First Secretary since 1936. He was the Communist politician in the Baltic region – and probably also in all Europe and the Soviet Union – who had been the leader of his party and his country longest, until his death in January, 1974.

Snieckus had achieved considerable prestige also among those in power in Moscow. His position was strengthened by the fact that he always avoided getting mixed up in the power struggles in Moscow, and never was under the protection of anyone in particular. Snieckus preferred to be number one in his own country instead of trying to be number two in the Kremlin. He was the only one of the three Baltic leaders who was firmly rooted in the native soil.

Only in the strongly nationalistic Union Republics of Armenia and Georgia are there more native communists in the leading organs of the Party than in Lithuania. Like his colleagues in the Lithuanian Party executive, Snieckus was genuinely proud of his own people's past, remembering the time that Lithuania was a great power in Europe. Rein Taagepera notes that:

> those Republics with the most autonomy (Lithuania and Estonia) have the least impact on central Soviet decision-making; Latvia (and Byelorussia) on the other hand have served as stepping-stones for several present members of the Moscow politburo and government.[1]

Snieckus was succeeded as First Secretary of the

[1] Rein Taagepera, "Dissimilarities Among the Northwestern Soviet Republics", in "Problems of Mini-Nations". *Baltic Perspectives*, AABS, New York 1973, p. 81.

Communist Party of Lithuania by 48-year-old Petras Griskevicius. Insiders regard him as a compromise choice between the Moscow-oriented and nationally-oriented communists in Lithuania.

Griskevicius was born in the village of Kraiaunos in 1924, the son of a tailor. He was a student in Lithuania when the Soviet Army invaded his native land in 1940. Griskevicius joined the Communist Youth League. He fled with the retreating Soviet troops and fought in their ranks. Later he was parachuted back into German-occupied Lithuania to join the communist partisans. He joined the Communist Party and became a Party activist. He rose rapidly through the Party hierarchy and was First Secretary of the Party Committee in Vilnius before he was picked to succeed Snieckus.

The Baltic Communist leaders have little opportunity counteract to the Russification and centralization in any decisive way. Firstly, their freedom of action is severely limited by the principle of democratic centralism within the all-Union Party machinery. Decisions made in Moscow become orders that the leaders of the Union Republics must follow. Secondly, Russians or Moscow-oriented non-Russians play an important role in the leadership of the Baltic and other non-Russian Union Republics. Thirdly, many local leaders are Russified or have a basically positive attitude to the demands of centralization and of promoting the Russian language and culture.

The "national communist" opposition within the Baltic branches of the Party has been of a wholly cultural and economic nature. No communist has openly asked for the secession of Estonia, Latvia or Lithuania from the Soviet Union.

Historical Flashback
A group of young intellectuals in Latvia had already during the 1890's dissociated themselves from the

national struggle of the Latvians. Their slogan was "Proletarians have no fatherland". A large part of the Latvian Social Democratic Party agreed with this.

Riga and Tallinn were both important in the revolutionary struggle against Tsarism. The revolutionaries of 1905 were relatively stronger in the Baltic countries than in Russia. The Tsarist persecution of the revolutionaries made even more people join the ranks, especially in Latvia where the oppression was hardest after 1905.

In 1906, the Latvian Social Democratic Party became an autonomous unit within the Russian Social Democratic Workers Party and was drawn into its internal struggles. The Bolsheviks took power at the Latvian Party's congress in Brussels in 1914. Lenin himself traveled to the Belgian capital. He was indefatigable in trying to influence the delegates. The take-over was sealed with a majority of only one vote – that of an infiltrated agent for the Tsar's secret police. The Bolshevik take-over in the Latvian Social Democratic Party was of great importance for the political development of Latvia and also of Russia during the First World War and the Russian Revolution.

During the First World War the German–Russian front line went for a long time straight across Latvia. Because of that 800,000 Latvians were dispersed as refugees all over Tsarist Russia. In the homeland the famous Latvian rifle regiments were organized. These had been formed after the Russian forces suffered severe losses on the German front at the beginning of the war. The main task of the Latvian rifle regiments was to hold the Riga front and also to defend the access towards the then Russian capital, Petrograd (today's Leningrad). The Latvian Social Democracy was a strong influence among the Latvian Rifles. After the October Revolution of 1917, the

Latvian Rifles fought on the side of the Reds in the Russian Civil War. They were given the task of guarding the headquarters of the October Revolution at Smolnyi, and they also formed the bodyguard of the new Soviet government as well as of Lenin himself.

At the 1917 elections the Latvian Rifles voted almost unanimously for the Bolsheviks. The first commander-in-chief of the Red Army was a previously liberal-minded Latvian colonel, Jukums Vacietis. One important reason for Vacietis and the Latvian Rifles choosing the side of the Bolsheviks was that a White Russian counter-revolutionary victory over Lenin and the Bolsheviks could have meant the reinstatement of Tsarist Russia. Latvia and both the other Baltic countries would then probably have been reincorporated into the Russian empire.

The contribution by the Latvian Rifles to the Soviet side came to be of decisive and finally of world historical importance. Lenin later openly admitted that the Bolsheviks would never have gained victory without them. Latvians were important on the military scene later also. During the period between the two World Wars, Jekabs Alksnis was the chief of the Soviet Air Force and Deputy Minister for Defense. Robert Eidemanis was the head of the military college, the Frunze Academy. A number of Lenin's civil advisors were also Latvian, such as the first People's Commissar for Legal Affairs, Peteris Stucka.

The Estonian Bolsheviks asked for the formation of an Estonian Soviet Republic immediately in 1917, while the Latvian Bolsheviks did not at this time want to separate their country from revolutionary Russia. The Latvian Social Democrats, on the other hand, demanded categorically that an independent non-Soviet Latvia should be established. The Social

Democrats co-operated with the Liberals and other non-socialist groups for this purpose. This split between the Latvian socialists became impossible to bridge. Two parties were formed, one of Social Democrats and one of Communists.

The Estonian Workers' Commune
The question of centralism or nationalism is as old within the Baltic Communist Parties as the organizations themselves. Nationalistic considerations caused conflict with those who were for centralization and Russification. Estonian Bolsheviks demanded during the short-lived Estonian Workers' Commune of 1919, though without success, control over the units of the Red Army on whose bayonets they had been brought to power. The Estonian Bolsheviks set up a completely Estonian-speaking administration in the border town of Narva which had a large Russian population. Teaching in schools was to be carried out in the native language. When most of the leaders of the Estonian Workers' Commune were executed by Stalin twenty years later, one accusation against them was "nationalistic deviation" during the days of the Commune and later. A large number of Latvian officials in the Soviet Russian Communist Party were liquidated at the same time and for the same reason. Sixteen of twenty-one previous members of the 1919 Latvian Soviet government and Central Committee were executed. The same fate befell seven out of eight previous members of the 1918–1919 Lithuanian Soviet government.

The parties represented in the Estonian Soviets received in the indirect elections to the Estonian Diet in July, 1919, 24% of the vote. A large number of the voters in Estonia at that time were Russian soldiers, sailors, workers, and bureaucrats. The Bolsheviks were at this time seen as democrats, friends of peace, and supporters of Estonia's independence. The workers' councils would probably have gotten more votes if they had not been seen as Russian, and thus alien, institutions. They used Russian in their written communications, as the authorities had done in Tsarist times.[2]

The Lithuanian Communist Party was one of the youngest and weakest in the whole Soviet Union. The Party was forbidden between the two World Wars and never succeeded in getting more than a couple of thousand members. Most of them were Russians, Jews, and Poles. The Central Committee was situated in Moscow and was controlled by the Russian Communist Party and the Communist International, Komintern. In 1922 almost 1,500 members of the Lithuanian Party lived in Russia and only 241 in Lithuania. The number of members in Lithuania had doubled a decade later but was still only 480.

Several leading Lithuanian Communists were executed in connection with the Moscow trials of 1936–1938. Many Party members were purged during the first Soviet occupation. In spring of 1941 only half of the pre-war Communists were left in the Party. The native Communists were replaced by Party men sent from Moscow. Stalin did not trust the few surviving Lithuanian Communist leaders and the recruitment of new members went badly.

After the Second World War, the Republic was not even governed by the local Communists, but by a special bureau under the Russian Communist Party. This special organ was led by Mikhail Suslov between 1944 and 1946. Even when the Lithuanian Communist Party took over the reins again, half the members of the Central Committee were non-

---

[2] Martna, Mihkel, *Estland, die Esten und die estnische Frage*, Olten, 1920, p. 175.

Lithuanian. This situation existed almost up to Stalin's death in 1953. The share of Lithuanians in the Party and government leadership increased during the following decade, for example in the Council of Ministers from 55 to 90%. The share of native Party members increased from 32% in 1945 to 38% in 1953, 56% in 1956 and 66% in 1968.

A purge within the Party took place at the end of the fifties. It was less extensive than the one in Latvia. The Minister for Education, the Rector of Vilnius University, and several professors were dismissed. They were charged with having removed in 1956 a number of Russian lecturers from their posts at Lithuanian universities. A few years earlier legal proceedings, attracting much attention, had been instituted against some Russian officials who were accused of corruption. These proceedings had nationalist overtones, as Lithuanian civil servants could equally well have been accused of taking bribes. These purges of Russian civil servants and Party officials were defended by reference to the 1953 resolution from the Central Committee of the Soviet Communist Party, accepted after Stalin's death. The resolution admitted that serious mistakes had been made as regards the national question. When the "corrections" went too far, as in Lithuania and Latvia, the leadership in Moscow found countermeasures necessary, hence the purge of homegrown communists in Latvia and Lithuania at the end of the fifties.

Lenin and the Question of Nationalities
The nationalities question has always been a difficult problem for Russian and non-Russian Bolsheviks, both before and after the revolution.

Lenin and the first Bolshevik government in Russia declared that the non-Russian peoples had the right to leave the Russian empire. Because of this Lenin is sometimes misleadingly depicted as an advocate for national self-determination. Lenin was a convinced internationalist and thought that all forms of nationalism should be opposed on principle.

But he considered it good tactics to exploit national sentiments. Lenin therefore called Tsarist Russia a "prison of peoples" where the rights of non-Russians were suppressed. As he and the Bolsheviks fought against the Tsarist regime, they of course welcomed everything that weakened Tsarist power. Nationalism among the non-Russian peoples was such a factor. As long as it was directed against the Tsarist regime all was well, but after the revolution nationalism must not become an obstacle to the building of a socialist empire.

The nationalities question had no prominent place in Lenin's thoughts or writings. He wrote, for example, ten times as much on the peasant question, as on the problem of nationalities.

The demand for national self-determination had low priority for the Bolsheviks. It finally became only a means of realizing their central aim, the world revolution and the dictatorship of the proletariat. Lenin and the Bolsheviks provided the principle of national self-determination with a number of reservations. No national self-determination whatever was allowed in the most important organ of power, the Communist Party.

It is often said that Lenin condemned the Russification of non-Russian peoples. Towards the end of his life he warned against military intervention in the affairs of non-Russian peoples. Lenin warned his colleagues against letting the constitutional right to secede from the Soviet Union become an empty and meaningless paragraph. But in the prime of his power Lenin – despite his internationalist convictions – for all practical purposes acted like a Russian chauvinist and an enemy of non-Russian nationalism.

When several peoples who had come under Tsarist Russian declared their independence at the end of the First World War, he sent the Red Army to subdue them and to bring them back to the fold. Georgia, Armenia, the Ukraine, Byelorussia, and Turkmenistan were in this manner incorporated into the Soviet Union. Lenin did not intervene as a Russian chauvinist to establish a "Russian dictatorship" over the non-Russians, but as a Communist internationalist to accomplish the "dictatorship of the proletariat" in these countries. The Soviet Russian military intervention was, however, incompatible with the non-Russian peoples' national aspirations and thus was seen by them as a drive for Russian dominance. The main enemy of the Soviet nationalities policy gradually came to be not the chauvinism of the largest people, the Russians, but the "bourgeois nationalism" of the smaller nations.

Lenin encouraged Bolshevik puppet governments to take over power in the Baltic countries at the end of the First World War. These attempts did not succeed, but Soviet infiltration continued. A Moscow-directed coup in Estonia on December 1, 1924, failed completely. A large contingent of the Estonian communists who attempted the uprising were trained in Russia. They received no support from the population. The Soviet leaders were, therefore, forced to wait until the outbreak of the Second World War before Estonia could be occupied – and then together with Latvia and Lithuania.

During Stalin's time the principle of the absolute power of the Communist Party was supplemented by the non-Marxist, anti-Leninist dogma of Russian dominance. The leading theorists of the Soviet nationalities policy was Joseph Stalin, who, amongst other things, wrote *Marxism and the National and Colonial Questions*. Stalin's ideas on this subject are still generally prevalent in the Soviet Union, though much of his other teachings have been discredited. Stalin's ideas on national self-determination are, however, more difficult for Communists to criticize. The central essay in the above-mentioned book was written before the revolution and was approved by Lenin. Furthermore Lenin chose Stalin as the People's Commissar for Nationality Policy in the first revolutionary government in 1917.

A statement which illustrates Stalin's attitude to the nationalities question is:

> There are cases when the right of self-determination conflicts with another, a higher right – the right of the working class that has come to power to consolidate that power. In such cases – this must be said bluntly – the right of self-determination cannot and must not serve as an obstacle to the working class in exercising its right to dictatorship.[3]

Centralization or Decentralization?

The rights of the Union Republics were set forth in the 1936 Constitution. Article 17 of this Constitution ruled that the independence of the Union Republics could only be limited according to article 14. This article is the longest in the whole constitution. It gave the central government in Moscow powers to decide questions of defense, foreign policy, foreign trade, state security, territorial changes, economic planning, foreign credit and exchange, education,

[3] "Stalin on Lenin's Theories", quoted in: Robert Conquest, *Nation Killers*, Macmillan, London, 1970, p. 117.

etc. The Soviet government has far greater powers than any other federal government. The autonomy of the Union Republics is extremely limited. There were only three provisions in the constitution that could make the Soviet Union a truly federal state:

1. The right of the Union Republics to secession.
2. The right to have diplomatic relations with foreign countries.
3. The right to have national units within the armed forces.

These three provisions were left out of the new constitution, adopted in 1978.

The constitutionally limited autonomy of the Union Republics is further undermined by the leading role of the Party. This principle has also become established in article 126 of the Constitution. The decisions of the central Party organs are binding for Party organizations on the Republic and local levels. The pre-eminence of the Party over the state administration, together with "democratic centralism" in the Party makes the limited formal autonomy of the Union Republics even more illusory.

Native officials in the Baltic and other non-Russian Union Republics have on several occasions tried to increase their autonomy. The response to their demands has been dependent on current leadership patterns in Moscow.

During the first years after the Second World War, and at the beginning of the fifties, there was no room at all for Baltic autonomy. Moscow then needed to establish communism and Russian influence in the newly annexed areas. The native communist leaders in the Baltic countries gained a greater freedom of action in cultural and economic affairs after the death of Stalin.

The 20th all-Union Party Congress of 1956 stated in a resolution:

> Socialism does not at all obliterate national differences and special characteristics; on the contrary, it secures the all-around development and prosperity of the economic and cultural life of all nations and nationalities. The Party should also in future pay great regard to these national characteristics in all their practical activities.

After the Congress the leaders of most of the non-Russian Republics tried to follow the new trends. More attention was given to the language, literature, and history of their own peoples. The teaching of Estonia's geography and history dates from 1957. The first textbook on Lithuanian history was published the same year, and on Latvian history a year later. Attempts were made to stop or at least decrease the immigration of Russians to the Baltic Republics. Light industry was encouraged at the expense of heavy industry in order to increase the supplies of consumer goods.

Khrushchev deliberately plucked at national strings during his climb to power after Stalin's death. The non-Russian peoples' cultures were encouraged. The Union Republics became more autonomous. Soviet economic life was decentralized by the establishment of regional economic councils. However, the control of the central Party never ceased.

The development changed direction in 1957, after Khrushchev had purged the so-called anti-Party group within the Politburo and became the supreme leader. Before his fall, in 1964, the authorities in Moscow had regained most of the power that a few years earlier had been transferred to the Union Republics.

The balance of power between Moscow and the Union Republics has on the whole remained unchanged during the period of Leonid Brezhnev. The budgets of the different Republics are still laid down by the central planning authority, Gosplan, in Moscow. The rate of economic development in the Baltic Republics and the ensuing higher level of development might possibly increase the sphere of local influence and experimentation in the future. Management from Moscow seems to become less efficient the more complicated the production becomes in the outlying areas.

Disappointed Fellow-travelers
The first Premier of Soviet Estonia, the poet and physician Johannes Vares-Barbarus, committed suicide in 1946. He was disappointed when Estonia did not get even the limited autonomy that was granted, for example, to Mongolia. Both he and many Estonian communists with him had counted on such a solution to the national question. Some vague promises to the effect were made to them by Moscow.

The native Party leaders in Estonia were purged in 1950 and replaced by the so-called Yestonians. These descendants of Estonian emigrants have grown up in Russia and often speak Estonian badly. They are called Yestonians because their Russian accent makes it hard for them to pronounce the Estonian letter "e" so they say "ye" as in Russian.

The first Foreign Minister of Soviet Lithuania, the popular author Vincas Kreve-Mickevicius, became just as disappointed as his Estonian colleague, but much sooner. He visited the Soviet Foreign Minister in Moscow, Molotov, in July, 1940, to complain about the repeated Soviet breaches of promise. As he had no positive response from Molotov to his complaints, Kreve-Mickevicius decided to resign, as did also the

Minister of Finance, Professor Galvanauskas. Kreve-Mickevicius fled to the United States at the end of the war, where he worked until his death as a lecturer at the University of Pennsylvania.

Dissatisfaction with the Party
Stories making fun of "Yestonian" pronunciation are common in Estonia. One concerns a speech of welcome which First Secretary Käbin is said to have given on a certain occasion. He started by exclaiming *Kallid sõbrad!* (Dear friends), which pronounced by him sounded like *Kallid seebrad!* (Dear zebras). A similar story concerns another occasion when Käbin tried to give a speech in Estonian. All went well as long as he followed his written script, even if his pronunciation was not the best. It became worse when he recklessly improvised and called: *Elagu üks Mai!* (Long live one May!) instead of *Elagu esimene mai!* (Long live the First of May!).

The Party, its leaders, and even ordinary members, are still disliked by many Balts. Some young people are afraid to join the Party because they don't want to be ostracized by their nationalist friends. Collaboration with a foreign occupant has always created a moral dilemma. But experience shows the importance of native Party leaders and cadres, who would be prepared as much as possible to counteract Russification and centralization.

The ratio of Party members is smaller in the Baltic Republics than the all-Union average. In 1971, Lithuania was the Union Republic with the lowest percentage of Party members (together with Turkmenistan and Uzbekistan), only 5·5% of the total adult population. The recruitment of new Party members had, however, during the previous five years been more extensive in Lithuania than in any other Union Republic. The new recruitment in Lithuania was, percentage-wise, twice as large as the all-Union average.

The dissatisfaction with the Party and its members is twofold. People are often outraged by the privileges leading Party members have, such as access to their own shops, pharmacies, holiday facilities, medical services, and hospitals. Patriotic Balts are also dissatisfied that their local officials do not more whole-heartedly oppose the mass immigration of Russians.

The Letter from the 17 Latvian Communists

We, 17 Communists of Latvia, are turning to you. We are writing to you because we see no other means of influencing action and events which are doing grave harm to the Communist movement, to Marxism–Leninism, to us, and to other small nations.[4]

This is the beginning of a letter from a group of Communists in Latvia smuggled out to their fellow Communists in Europe and to world opinion. The letter became known in the West at the beginning of 1972 and attracted much attention.

The writers of the letter preferred to remain anonymous. They only stated that most of them had been members of the Communist Party for 25 to 35 years, or even longer. They were all born in Latvia and have spent all their lives there. Many of them were put in prison or labor camps during the time of the Ulmanis dictatorship in the thirties. They fought against the Nazis during the Second World War, in the Red Army, or as partisans. They write:

[4] The letter is quoted here in the translation made by the Latvian Social Democratic Party in exile. Abbreviations used in the letter are: CPSU = The Communist Party of the Soviet Union, LCP = the Latvian Communist Party, CC = Central Committee (within LCP or CPSU).

The struggle for Soviet power, for the socialist system was the goal and content of our lives.

The 17 sharply criticize the way the Soviet nationality policy has been carried out, violating the principles of Marxism and Leninism as well as the United Nations Declaration of Human Rights.

With clean consciences we did everything that depended on us to make the teachings of Marx, Engels and Lenin reality; but with aching hearts we saw that with each passing year their ideas were being distorted more and more, that Marxism–Leninism was being used as a cover for Great Russian chauvinism, that words have differed from deeds, that the work of Communists in other countries is being hampered, that instead of aid there is intervention.

Initially we thought that these occurrences were simply the mistakes of individual leaders, their lack of awareness of the evils of such policies. But over time we realized that the Great Russian chauvinism is a policy which has been carefully thought out by the CPSU leadership. Forced assimilation of small nations in the USSR has been set as one of the more important and immediate tasks of internal state policy.

Self-examination in Moscow
In 1953, the same year that Stalin died, the all-Union Party leadership admitted for the first and only time since Stalin's death that grave mistakes had been made as regards nationality policy. Mass deportation of Balts to Siberia had been carried out and the organized Jewish cultural life had been crushed. Other national minorities had also been persecuted. After Stalin's death, the all-Union Party leadership seemed prepared to rethink their nationality policy, and to begin to respect and encourage the distinctive national characteristics of the non-Russian peoples.

170

The First Secretary of the Central Committee of the Latvian Communist Party, Janis Kalnberzins, gave a speech on June 22, 1953, before the Central Committee. In this speech he told of a decree which had been adopted by the all-Union Party Presidium ten days earlier:

The Presidium of the Soviet Union Communist Party Central Committee has adopted a decree which states: 1) to charge all Party and State organs to fundamentally correct the situation existing in the national Republics, *to end the distortion of Soviet nationality policy*; 2) to organize the preparation, training and broad promotion of people of the local nationality for leading work; to end the practice of promoting local cadres who do not belong to the local nationality; to recall and place at the disposal of the CPSU CC those nomenclature officials who do not speak the local language; 3) to conduct business in the national Republics in the local, native language . . .

The distortions of the nationality policy were openly discussed in Estonia and Latvia at the meetings of their respective Central Committees in the summer of 1953. In Lithuania, purges of Russian officials were launched.

The 17 letter-writers continue:

At this plenum Latvian CP CC First Secretary Kalnberzins described what had been bitterly, but truthfully, said about the Latvian SSR at the CPSU CC plenum. In the decree it was stated that the Latvian CP CC and Council of Ministers (of course, as forced by Moscow) until this time had *grossly violated the Leninist principles of nationality policy*. Many Party, government, and economic officials, expressing an unwarranted mistrust of local cadres and lying about a need for security, had promoted mostly non-Latvians to leading work. The result of this attitude towards local cadres was that only

171

42% of all district and city Party committee secretaries were Latvians. Moreover, many of them were Latvians in name only, because they had spent long years or all their lives in Russia, and could not speak Latvian.

Because this policy was given "from above", Kalnberzins, who was extremely subservient to Moscow, at that time correctly said that the situation with national cadres was particularly unsatisfactory in the Riga city Party organization. In the apparatus of the city committees not a single section head was Latvian, and out of 31 instructors only 2 were Latvians.

Cadre policy and the growth of Party ranks is determined by officials of organizational sections of district Party committees and secretaries of Party primary organizations. Among these officials there were even fewer Latvians. In each district there was but one Latvian per section, and only 17% of Party primary organization secretaries were Latvians.

Such behaviour, full of unwarranted mistrust of Latvian workers, peasants and intelligentsia, and such composition of Party cadres, led to the result that only 18% of all Communists in the city of Riga were Latvians.

Even such a lackey of great power politics as Arvids Pelshe, then the Latvian CP CC Secretary for Propaganda (presently a member of the CPSU CC Politburo and head of the CPSU CC Party Control Committee) admitted that there had been discrimination against Latvians and gross distortions of nationality policy. In his speech at the Latvian CP CC plenum he spoke about the PCSU CC Presidium decree, and said: "This decision gives clear and unmistakable directives – the first task is to fundamentally correct the situation in the Republic, to end the perversion of Soviet nationality policy . . . in the immediate future to prepare, educate and broadly promote Latvian cadres to leading work . . ."

The new course was not put into practice. The measures intended to halt the Russian dominance in the Latvian Communist Party remained on paper only. The Russian mass immigration continued and discontent grew among the national communists and other Balts. One consequence of this was the Berklavs affair, when a group of nationally-minded communists were purged. The authorities in Moscow retained their hold over Latvia and the other two Baltic countries.

The Latvian communist letter-writers give a detailed description of how Russification takes place in various ways. They tell us of the mass immigration of foreign labor, which has made Latvians a minority in their own capital city. They note that immigration has been encouraged by the extensive industrialization which does not seem to be economically motivated. Raw materials, industrial workers, and specialists are brought in – while the output is taken out. The seventeen Latvians state:

> Now the Republic already has a number of large enterprises where there are almost no Latvians among the workers, engineering–technical personnel, or directors ("REZ", the diesel factory, the hydrometric instruments factory, and many others); there are also those where most of the workers are Latvians, but none of the executives understands Latvian (the Popov radio factory, the railroad car plant, the auto-electrical instruments factory, "Rigas audums", etc.)

The local population is subjected to cultural Russification as well as the mass immigration of non-Latvians. All children in Latvian schools learn Russian, while very few children in Russian schools learn Latvian. Though all-Union newspapers and magazines in Russian are distributed in Latvia, about half of the periodicals published in Latvia itself are also in Russian. One television and one radio channel broadcast in Russian only; on the other there are programs in both Russian and Latvian. The letter-writers inform us that the former head of the Riga television service, Elinskis, did not submit to pro-Russian demands and was therefore removed from his post.

Russian is the dominant language in Latvia. As soon as a Russian is present he can demand that the meeting be conducted in Russian. If any Latvian (or Estonian or Lithuanian) opposes this he could be accused of "bourgeois nationalism" or "chauvinism". Members of all the nations in the Soviet Union has been accused of, and sentenced for, bourgeois nationalism – but seldom a Russian. The letter-writers maintain that there are "entire institutions where there are very few Latvians." As an example they give the Ministry of the Interior in Riga, where only one-fifth of the 1,500 employees are said to be Latvians. Various organs who are responsible for internal security and order in the Republic come under the Ministry of the Interior.

The seventeen Latvians accuse their superiors:

Now only foreigners, and those Latvians who have spent all their lives in Russia, and came to Latvia only after World War II, are in leading work. Most of them do not speak Latvian at all, or speak it very badly. This is illustrated by the following facts: at the present time the following are working as Secretaries of the Latvian CP CC: CC First Secretary Voss, a Latvian from Russia, who usually does not speak Latvian in public; CC Second Secretary Beluha, a Russian from Russia, who does not understand Latvian; CC Secretary for Propaganda Drizulis, a Latvian from Russia; Secretary for Agriculture Verro, an Estonian from Russia, who does not understand Latvian; CC Secretary for Industry

Petersons, a Latvian from Russian, who speaks Latvian very badly.

The leadership of the Council of Ministers: Chairman J. Rubenis, a Latvian from Russia, who speaks Latvian very badly; Deputy Chairman Bondaletov, a Russian from Russia, who does not understand Latvian. The Chairman of the Presidium of the Latvian SSR Supreme Soviet, V. Rubenis, a Latvian from Russia, who speaks Latvian very badly, usually does not speak it in public.

The Reaction in Riga

The Soviet reaction to the letter from the seventeen Latvian communists was violent. The letter was branded as an American Central Intelligence Agency provocation. This was a routine statement. The attempts to meet the row of factual accusations were more interesting. The Latvian Communist Party's organ *Cina*, and its counterpart in the Russian language, *Sovetskaya Latviya*, counter-attacked at the end of February, 1972, in an unsigned full-page article.

The writer of the official reply from Riga denied that there has been any forced settlement of Russians into the Baltic Republics. He pointed out that according to the 1970 census, the native population had increased in all the Union Republics, though more rapidly in some than in others. This has also brought about certain changes in the national composition of the population.

It is true, as maintained in *Cina*, that the native population in Latvia has increased in number during the last decade, as it has in other non-Russian Republics. This answer conceals, however, the fact that there are today fewer Latvians in Latvia than there were at the beginning of the Soviet period. The number of Latvians has decreased by over 100,000 during the Soviet period, while there are half a million more Russians in Soviet Latvia than in independent Latvia. Neither is it mentioned that the Latvian share of the population decreased considerably during the sixties. Between the census of 1959 and 1970 it went down from 62% to 57% in the country as a whole, and from 45% to 40% in Riga, the capital.

Cina also produced a whole row of figures to show how flourishing Latvian cultural life is. In 1970, altogether 11·9 million copies of books in the Latvian language were published, compared with only 3·8 million copies in 1939. The same applies to the publication of magazines and journals in Latvian – 15·6 million copies in 1939, and 35·6 million in 1970. Since World War II, an Academy of Science and Letters has been established in the Latvian Republic comprising twelve research institutes, of which one is the Institute for Language and Literature. The academic staff of the Academy has 1,558 members of which 71·5% are Latvian. The rest represent other nationalities who actively participate in the development of the various branches of research of the Academy. There are 411 researches in the Republic engaged in the study of the Latvian language, literature, ethnography, folklore and history.

Cina also says that the letter-writers' reasoning about the Russification of Latvia's cultural life is ridiculous. According to *Cina*, it is generally known that in the small Republic of Latvia there are some 200 Latvian writers, 586 artists, and 65 composers.

"We Latvians are indeed proud of our splendid song festivals, which, every time they are held, turn into grandiose manifestations of Latvian culture, national in form, and socialist in content," writes *Cina*. Eight of the nine professional theaters perform in Latvian. 875 state-employed artists and directors work in these collectives.

Are the Latvians Powerless?

Cina continues by listing more figures in order to show that the Latvians are far from powerless or under-represented on the governing bodies. *Cina*'s figures of the number of Latvians who are members of the Soviets from village to Union level, are of limited interest. The real power rests with the organs of the Communist Party.

The official Party organ is silent on the national composition of the Latvian Communist Party and its leadership. Regardless of this composition, the principle of democratic centralism forces national communists to take orders from the authorities in Moscow.

As long as the authorities in Moscow and their henchmen in the Baltic countries continue to demand a one-sided loyalty from the Baltic communists towards Moscow, the Communist Parties in the Baltic countries can hardly be expected to win the confidence of the Baltic peoples.

CHAPTER 9

Minorities in their own lands?

There were 300,000 Russians in the independent Baltic states before the Second World War. In 1970, the number of Russians had increased to 1,300,000.

There are today twelve times as many Russians in Estonia, fives times as many in Lithuania, and three to four times as many in Latvia as during the thirties. (In calculations the post-war Estonian border adjustments have been taken into account.)

The Russian share of the population has increased since the period between the wars from 4% to 25% in Estonia, from 11% to 30% in Latvia, and from 3% to 9% in Lithuania. Thus the share and number of Russians is greatest in Latvia, followed by Estonia, and then Lithuania.

If you consider not only Russians, but also include Ukrainians, Byelorussians, and other Soviet peoples, the percentages are as follows. The non-Estonian share of the population in Estonia has increased since the middle of the 1930's from 8% to 40%, the non-Latvian share in Latvia from 25% to 43%, and the non-Lithuanian in Lithuania from 16% to 20%.

As seen by this, the position of Latvia is weakest and that of Lithuania the strongest. Estonia occupies an intermediary position, but the share of the native population has decreased most rapidly in this Republic.

Incomparable Quantities
Comparisons with the period between the two World Wars easily underestimate the demographic Russification during the Soviet period.

1. Most Russians in independent Estonia lived in areas which after the war were incorporated in to the Russian Republic (RSFSR). Part of the Estonian province of Petserimaa (Russian: Pechory) in the southeast, as well as the area east of the river Narva, were separated from Estonia in 1945. If we discount the largely Russian population of those areas, then the Russian population of independent Estonia was only 46,100.

   Some parts of independent Latvia at its eastern border, with mostly Russian population, were also separated and turned over to the Russian Republic in 1945. Lithuania instead received an addition of Lithuanians and non-Lithuanians (mostly Poles and Byelorussians) when the ancient Lithuanian capital of Vilnius and its surroundings were turned over to Lithuania from Poland in 1939. In 1945, the Klaipeda (German: Memel) area was reincorporated into Lithuania, having been annexed by Nazi Germany in the spring of 1939.

   Thus population figures from the independent Baltic States and from the Baltic Soviet Republics refer to different territorial units. They must be territorially adjusted to make fair comparisons between the populations now and then. The following factors must also be taken into consideration.
2. The German minority left Estonia and Latvia when the Second World War broke out. The Swedish–Estonians moved to Sweden during the war. Most of the Baltic Jews were exterminated or

fled. For these reasons the non-native share of the population decreased. In Estonia, for example, from 8% to 3% after the war. Comparisons with the pre-war period thus underestimate the share of the native population at the end of the war and the extent of immigration since the war.

3. Political prisoners and those deported are registered as domiciled in their native Baltic Republics, even if they actually are in forced exile, in Russian labor camps or prisons.

4. Baltic conscripts are counted as inhabitants of the Baltic Republics during the two to four years that they are doing their military service, usually far away from their native land.

5. Many Russian military units are stationed in the Baltic Republics, which is one of the most important military districts in the Soviet Union. These Russian soldiers are counted as domiciled in their respective Union Republics, but their presence contributes to the pressure of Russification in the Baltic countries.

The 1970 Census

In 1970 Lithuanians made up 80% of the population in their country, Estonians 60% and the Latvians 57%. But in the Latvian capital, Riga, only two out of every five inhabitants are Latvian. For example, if immigration to Great Britain after World War II had been as extensive as it has been to Latvia, almost 25 of the 55 million people in Britain would now be immigrants of South Asian, African or Caribbean origin. One may wonder what would the attitude of the native British population be in that case?

Kazakhstan is the only non-Russian Republic of the Soviet Union which has a greater proportion of Russians than Latvia. The extent of the Russian colonization of Kazakhstan is indicated by the fact that the European (mostly Russian) population in this Asian Republic is larger than the white population in all Africa.

The Lithuanians succeeded in increasing their share of the population during the sixties, but just barely, about one per cent. Of all the Soviet Union Republics, only Armenia and Russia have a larger native population share than Lithuania. The Lithuanians have also managed to increase their population share in their capital, Vilnius, but in 1970 still made up only 43% of the city's population.

How do the Lithuanians Manage?
Why have the Lithuanians managed to keep their ethnic position demographically so much better than the Estonians and the Latvians? The main reason is that the birth rate in Lithuania is considerably higher than in Estonia and Latvia.

Lithuania is less industrialized and more agricultural than the other two Baltic Republics. There is usually a correlation between high industrialization and low birth rate. The Lithuanians have managed to industrialize by using the native excess labor from agriculture.

The birth rate is usually higher in Catholic than in Protestant countries. Lithuania is from olden times strongly Catholic, while Estonia and Latvia have been mainly Protestant. The position of the Church and of religion today, as we have seen, is much stronger in Lithuania than in its Baltic neighbors.

Another reason for the differences in the population trends is the fact, that a greater number of people left from Estonia and Latvia than from Lithuania. In 1940, there were roughly as many Lithuanians as Estonians and Latvians combined, but only about 75,000 Lithuanians fled to the West during World War II, as compared to 195,000 Estonians and Latvians, taken together.

Another factor is that several age classes of young men in Estonia and Latvia were compulsorily drafted into the German Army, while the Lithuanians managed to prevent the Nazis from creating any large Lithuanian units in the German Army. Therefore far fewer Lithuanian than Estonian and Latvian young men were killed at the front, perished in Soviet prisoner-of-war camps, or ended up as refugees in Germany and other countries.

Why is the Birth Rate so Low?

The declining share of Estonians and Latvians in the populations of their countries depends not only on immigration but also on the low birth rate among the native peoples. Latvia and Estonia are the two union republics in the Soviet Union with the lowest rate of natural increase. Lithuania also belongs to the lower sector, together with the European union republics, with a far lower rate of natural increase than in the Caucasian and Central Asian republics. Latvia actually has the lowest birth rate and the lowest natural population growth rate in the world, closely followed by Estonia and Sweden. The natural population increase in Latvia in 1974 was 0·3% a year. In rural Latvia the number of children born was less than the number of people who died.

In Estonia and Latvia there are relatively few teenagers, the next decade's generation of parents. Estonia and Latvia definitely have the most elderly population in the Soviet Union. Lithuania has fewer pensioners, but comes, even so, in third place in the population "age league" for Soviet Republics.

The low birth rate among Estonians and Latvians occurs for both demographic and socio-economic reasons. The most important are the age distribution of the population, a large proportion of unmarried people, high age at marriage, a shortage of housing, a high divorce rate, a tradition of having few children, high alimonies, the cost of bringing up children, and the shortage of day-nurseries.

Few Marriages

Many people do not get married. According to the census of 1970, 27% of the women in Estonia were single in the child-bearing age group from 20 to 44. The same situation prevails in Latvia. Only a very small part of the unmarried women are unmarried mothers.

Overcrowding

The shortage of housing is one of the greatest social problems and one which also lowers the birth rate. Young couples who want to get married, as well as those newly married, often have to wait for several years before they can move in together. That both partners live with their parents is hardly, either physically or psychologically, conducive to having children. Families with children often have to live in one or two-roomed apartments without modern conveniences. Many people prefer not to have children rather than suffer from extreme overcrowding. Many couples resort to abortion in case of an unwanted pregnancy. One out of six married and five out of six unmarried women in Estonia terminate their pregnancy in this way. The most common reason given is bad housing conditions.

Few Children

Already before the Second World War it was common to have small families in Estonia and Latvia. This tradition is continuing. A sociological survey in 1969 showed that more than half the women in Latvia thought that two children was the ideal. In Estonia most women would have liked three children. The ideal is not the reality. The average family in Estonia and Latvia has only 1·9 children.

Many Divorces
The high divorce rate contributes to the fact that fewer children are born in Estonia and Latvia than could be, even with the current age distribution and marriage frequency. Divorce is more common in the Baltic countries than anywhere else in the world. This is so also in Lithuania, although the population situation there otherwise differs considerably from that prevailing in Latvia and Estonia, and Catholicism forbids divorce.

One out of two marriages entered into in Riga at the end of the sixties was dissolved. In the Latvian capital, the divorce rate is two or three times that in the whole of the Soviet Union and twice that in the United States. In 1970, 24,000 marriages were performed in Latvia, and in the same year 11,000 divorces were registered.

Divorce has become much more common during the Soviet period. In 1950, there were just over six divorces for every hundred marriages in Estonia; today the corresponding figure is more than six times as large.

The most common reasons for divorce in the Baltic countries are over-crowded housing conditions and alcoholism. The consumption of spirits per capita in the Baltic Republics is higher than elsewhere in the Soviet Union. It is easy to see this as a sign of dissatisfaction with Soviet rule. The general lack of faith in the future probably also diminishes the wish to have children.

High Standard of Living, or Children?
The fact that divorce is so common is likely to restrain some couples from having children. The

high alimonies are another factor. Some breadwinners do not want to run the risk of a heavy reduction in living standard in connection with a possible divorce and prefer, therefore, to remain childless.

Many parents refrain from having a larger family because they do not want to lower their own standard of living. Children are an expensive pleasure also in the Soviet Union. According to Soviet information it costs about 50 roubles a month to keep a child (inclusive of clothes, food, and loss of income when the child is ill). This sum corresponds to a third of a Soviet industrial worker's monthly income.

It is difficult to get a place in a day nursery. The shortage of such facilities is severely felt because women in the Baltic countries work outside the home almost to the same extent as men.

Immigration

The nature of the Russian immigration into the Baltic Republics has been often and heatedly discussed. Is this immigration only a consequence of the need for a bigger labor force? Or is there behind it a systematic policy to assimilate and Russify the Baltic peoples?

The issue becomes clearer if we differentiate between the causes and effects of the immigration.

Centrally directed immigration to the Baltic countries was previously the rule. The authorities wanted to mix the unreliable native population in the recently incorporated Baltic countries with more reliable people. The large population losses during the war and during the years immediately after the war also had to be compensated for in order to reduce the shortage of labor.

Government directed immigration seems to take place today to a much smaller extent. The resolve to

185

move, from the Russian Republic to the Baltic Republics for example, is today for most immigrants a personal and voluntary decision. Russian immigrants are attracted to the Baltic countries for a number of reasons. Many come because they have heard that the Baltic Republics have the highest living standard in the Soviet Union and that the Western influences are strong. Some are attracted by the possibility of getting new housing immediately. The shortage of housing is great all over the Soviet Union and the waiting time for new housing is several years.

Russian immigrants to the Baltic countries have priority over the local population in the housing waiting lists. This angers the native population, who feel the housing crisis themselves. They see the favoritism shown to Russian immigrants as a measure calculated to bring more Russian-speaking people into the Baltic Republics.

Russian immigrants do not have to feel isolated. They often have friends or relations who have immigrated earlier. There are plenty of Russian schools and cultural life in the Russian language is abundant, especially in films, as well as radio and television programs.

The Soviet authorities maintain that immigration is necessary to remedy the shortage of labor that is supposed to exist in the Baltic Republics. "Shortage of labor" is an ambiguous term. The shortage is dependent on the economic planning. Many Balts think that the targets are deliberately set so high that they cannot be reached without immigration.

Balts, even Party members, are worried about the extent of this immigration. Latvia's First Secretary, Augusts Voss, complained in the spring of 1971 that some groups within the country took an "anti-Leninist" attitude to the population question. These groups opposed construction of new power plants and other labor-intensive projects. But from the all-Union point of view, it is profitable to use the industrial infrastructure in the Baltic Republics by attracting more labor to the area.

The native share of the population in Estonia and Latvia is decreasing because of immigration and the more rapid natural increase of the non-Baltic population. Immigrants are usually of working, and also of child-bearing age.

The Estonians and Latvians have a lower birth rate and a higher death rate than the immigrants. This is so because of the different age distribution among the immigrants and the native population. In the long term there is therefore a tendency that most pensioners will be Estonian or Latvian while most young people will be immigrants.

Few Mixed Marriages
The frequency of mixed marriages is usually a good indicator of how harmoniously two groups of people live together. It also indicates the rate of assimilation. Marriages between Balts and Russians are much less common than the Russian share of the population would make likely. In 1968, mixed marriages between Russians and Estonians were only one-sixth as many as would have been statistically probable without ethnic prejudice and cultural differences.

Baltic antagonism towards Russification affects the whole Russian population in the Baltic Republics. The language barrier reduces the contacts between Baltic and Russian young people in any case. The Balts do, of course, learn Russian at school, but this does not mean that they like speaking the language.

At the end of the sixties, only 7% of all marriages in Estonia were between Estonians and non-

Estonians. In Estonia nine out of ten Estonians marry within their own ethnic group. In 1968, the Russians in the country entered into about 12,000 marriages; in only 400 of these was the other partner an Estonian male, and in 320 cases an Estonian female. In certain rural areas the mixed marriages have even decreased since the time of independence. There is strong psychological opposition among the Balts against marrying a Russian.

Mixed marriages are most common in the Baltic capitals, as the non-native share of the population is largest there. According to Soviet information, the mixed marriages in Tallinn increased from 21% in 1948 to 22% in 1963, in Riga from 30% to 36%, and in Vilnius from 34% to 38%. These figures are for mixed marriages in all ethnic groups, not only the Estonians', the Latvians' and the Lithuanians' marriages with Russians and other non-native ethnic groups. Figures from the capitals overestimate the frequency of mixed marriages in the Republics as a whole. Mixed marriages occur most commonly in the capitals where the population is unusually diverse.

The native peoples in the Baltic countries marry within their own groups to a greater degree than other population groups there. In 1970, the mixed marriages in Riga had increased to 38%, but only 24% of all Latvian marriages in Riga were with a non-native partner.

The number of mixed marriages will probably increase in the future. The number of non-Baltic young people is growing in both Estonia and Latvia. The growth in the number of non-Balts will, however, also increase Russian young people's possibilities of finding a partner within their own ethnic group. It is therefore possible that mixed marriages will not increase as rapidly as the non-native population.

Children from Mixed Marriages

What is the effect of mixed marriages on the nationality of the children? Because of the general Baltic resistance to Russification, many children of Russian-Baltic marriages do not want to identify with the "wrong" ethnic group. The regime tries to encourage pro-Russian values, but often the anti-Russian attitude of friends and relatives constitutes a greater pressure, both on parents and children.

A number of young people that I talked to in Estonia said that they would break off relations if their best friend married a Russian chauvinist. The displeasure of the friends would probably increase if the children of such a mixed marriage would be identified as Russians. Some of the most ardent Estonian patriots I have met are the children of Estonian–Russian mixed marriages. Their strong patriotism is, perhaps, consciously or unconsciously, a way of "excusing" their background and becoming accepted by their native friends and acquaintances.

All Soviet citizens over 16 must obtain an internal passport. You can be registered as a citizen of the Estonian Soviet Republic, but all the same have the nationality in your passport listed as Russian. This occurs as a matter of course when both parents are Russian. Children of mixed marriages have the right to give the nationality of either parents as their own. A sixteen-year-old youth from, for example, a Russian–Latvian mixed marriage can thus himself choose if he wants to be Russian or Latvian.

A sociological survey of mixed marriages in the three Baltic capitals, based on information from the period 1960–1968, gave some interesting details about the nationality of the children. It was found that 62% of the children of Estonian–Russian mixed marriages in Tallinn declared themselves to be Estonian when they applied for their first internal

189

passport at the age of sixteen. The corresponding figure for Latvian–Russian mixed marriages in Riga was 57%, and for Lithuanian–Russian mixed marriages in Vilnius, 52%.[1]

The investigator states that there are three different assimilation trends among mixed marriages in the Baltic Republics:

1. The tendency to assimilate their Russian partners is weak among the Baltic peoples.
2. The non-Russian minorities are assimilated to a greater extent by Balts in mixed marriages. For example, almost four out of five young people in Riga regard themselves as Latvian in mixed marriages between Latvians and Ukrainians, Byelorussians, or Poles.
3. A strongly pro-Russian assimilation takes place in mixed marriages between Russians and Ukrainians, or other non-Russian and non-Baltic population groups.

Russian-speaking Balts?

The Communist leader have now, as in pre-revolutionary times, their maximum and minimum programs in the nationality question. The maximum goal is that all Soviet peoples in the future should be one, new Soviet people, and speak a common language; that this language should be Russian is seldom openly stated. As long as this maximum program is difficult to realize, a minimum program is applied. Non-Russians are encouraged to learn the Russian language, more Russian schools

[1] L. T. Tereskaya, "How Do Children of Mixed Marriages Choose Nationality?" *Sovietskaja Etnografia*, 1969: 3, published in English translation in the *Bulletin of Baltic Studies*, No. 4 (Dec. 1970).

are being built in the non-Russian Republics, the non-Russian peoples' history is rewritten in a pro-Russian way, etc.

It is good for all non-Russians to learn Russian as long as they can also keep their own languages. As long as the multi-national Union lasts, the different nations and individuals ought to command a common language – whatever their opinion of the Soviet Union as such and its policies.

At the 1970 census, 13 million non-Russians gave the Russian language as their native tongue. This is three million more than at the 1959 census. These three new millions belong mainly to nationalities which live spread out all over the Soviet Union, for example Ukrainians, Byelorussians, Poles, Germans, and Jews, or to a number of small peoples in Siberia and the Far East, where Russian has been introduced as the language for instruction in schools. Those who become Russianized are mostly from other Slavic peoples (Ukrainians, Byelorussians and Poles), or peoples who do not have their own Union Republics (Jews and Germans). It is thus possible that the Baltic horror of Russification is exaggerated; they speak non-Slavic languages and they have their own Union Republics. The Balts have a firm basis for their separate identities.

The great majority of Balts consider the native language of their Republic to be their native tongue. The number of Latvians who gave the Latvian language as their native tongue increased by 0·1% between the two censuses and was in 1970 a solid 95%. The increase is in reality somewhat larger, because the figures for 1970 also include those Latvians who live in Russia, or other Union Republics, and are therefore more Russified. The corresponding figure for the Estonians is just over 95% and for the Lithuanians 98%.

191

In 1970, 42 million out of 100 million non-Russians declared that Russian was their second language, after the native tongue. The majority of the non-Russians can, thus, not yet fluently speak or write Russian. The Latvians are among those in the whole Soviet Union who are most proficient in Russian. According to the 1970 census, 45% of the Latvians speak Russian as their second language, as against only 36% of the Lithuanians, and 29% of the Estonians.

More Children?

What are the Baltic demographic prospects under Soviet rule? One should separate the natural increase of the Balts themselves and the effects of immigration.

The Soviet authorities are responsible for the socio-economic conditions, such as the housing shortage which holds back Baltic population growth. But the same shortage affects the inhabitants of most of the Soviet Union. There is no indication that the authorities in Moscow oppose – or even have the means to oppose – a higher rate of population growth among the Baltic peoples.

Most likely the local Party and government leadership would welcome an increased birthrate among the native Baltic peoples. In 1968, the Estonian Deputy Premier, Edgar Tönurist, openly encouraged his compatriots to have more children. In the autumn of 1972, the biggest Estonian newspaper published an article in honor of a mother of ten children. This was the first article of its kind for many years. Was it a sign of the times?[2]

It is quite likely that the socio-economic conditions for having more children will become better. More

[2] The newspaper *Rahva Hääl*, May 11, 1972, quoted in *Estonian Events*, Dec., 1972.

spacious housing will make for less overcrowding, as long as immigration does not increase faster than new housing. The assistance for families with children was increased according to the latest Five-Year Plan. More day nurseries will be built. A number of demographic conditions and traditions will, however, probably remain and keep the possible number of children down. Such factors are small families, late marrying, many single people, and a high divorce rate.

Is Immigration Decreasing?
The first preliminary results of the 1979 census showed a slowdown of population growth, continuing urbanization, a serious aging of the rural population, and a high ratio of immigration to natural increase in all three Baltic republics. On an annual average basis immigration declined from over 14,000 a year in Latvia and over 8,000 in Estonia 1959–70 to approximately 6,500 and 12,000 respectively in 1970–79. In Lithuania, however, immigration rose from an annual average of 4,600 persons in 1959–70 to 7,300 in 1970–79. As the annual average for natural increase simultaneously declined from 33,400 to 22,800 in Lithuania, this meant a doubling of the ratio of immigration to natural increase in total population growth. The Russian share of population increased in all three republics, but marginally in Lithuania, and to a lesser degree than in 1959–70 in Latvia and Estonia.

Even if the Baltic industrial output could be increased by higher productivity, additional labor from the outside would be needed, especially within the service sector. To stop immigration, the gap in living standards between the Baltic Republics and the other Union Republics would probably have to be closed. The difference in national income per capita between the Baltic Republics and the rest of the

Soviet Union actually increased during the sixties, and this development could continue. In that case the mass immigration will probably not cease, because the higher living standard in the Baltic Republics would continue to attract immigrants.

Will the immigration to the Baltic Republics grow less because of the decreasing Russian birth rate and the need to colonize Siberia? The birth rate in the Russian Republic since 1968 has been lower than in Lithuania and Estonia, and just as low as in Latvia. In the western and northern parts of the Russian Republic, and in Moscow and Leningrad, the birth rate is only 11 per thousand. This is even lower than in Latvia, where the birthrate in 1970 was 14 per thousand. The corresponding figure for Estonia is 14·4 and for Lithuania 17·4 per thousand.

The Russian immigration to the Baltic Republics may slow down because of colonization along the border with China, and the need for more manpower in Russia. But there is no absolute causal relation, assuming that Soviet citizens can freely chose their place of residence. Also, many of the immigrants to the Baltic Republics are non-Russian. Their immigration potential is not affected by the decreasing Russian birth rate.

The Special Case of Karelia
In the protest letter from the seventeen Latvian Communists they say in one place about Russification:

> The fate of the former Karelian Union Republic clearly indicates where this policy is leading. It no longer exists. It was liquidated because the native inhabitants formed less than half of its total population. Karelia now is a part of the Russian Federated Republic. The same fate awaits the Kazakh Union Republic and Latvia.

194

I heard similar fears expressed in Estonia. Many are afraid that the opportunity to keep and develop their native language and culture would be greatly diminished if Estonia's status as a Union Republic were lost.

Karelia is, however, an exception and we should not draw far-fearing conclusions from the development there. Up to 1956, Karelia was one of the sixteen Union Republics of the Soviet Union, but it is today a so-called Autonomous Republic within the Russian Federated Republic.

Administratively, as far as the nationalities are concerned, the Soviet Union is divided according to a fourfold system, with the union Republics at the top of the scale. Then, on a descending scale, there are the autonomous republics, autonomous oblasts, and national districts or okrugs. The division tries to follow ethnic boundaries. In principle the most numerous and most developed peoples have their own union republics.

According to the main rule, Karelia should never have become a union republic at the end of the thirties. This decision to upgrade Karelia was taken in 1940 for special political reasons, just after the Russian–Finnish war. When the Soviet authorities, after Stalin's death, had given up their plans of incorporating Finland, the need for a separate Karelian–Finnish Republic within the Soviet Union had also disappeared.

Karelia is thus an exception to the usual political and population considerations. But the Baltic peoples have a stronger position. There were, according to the 1959 census, only 85,000 Karelians in Karelia. The smallest Baltic people, the Estonians, have today more than ten times as many people. The Karelians' share of the total population in their Republic was in 1959 only 13%. The Latvians, who have the lowest native population share of the three Baltic Republics, are percentagewise more than four times as strong in their union Republic today.

Without attaching too much weight to the case of Karelia, the Estonians and Latvians are still aware that their Republics have the smallest population of all the union republics. And that only in Kazakhstan is the share of the native population smaller than in Latvia. Lithuania, on the other hand, has more inhabitants than four other Union Republics (Armenia, Kirghizia, Tadzkhikistan and Turkmenistan).

Territorial Changes?
Even if the Baltic countries should remain union republics, some Estonians and Latvians fear a repetition of the territorial losses suffered after the Second World War. The areas that were ceded then to the Russian Republic had not been, however, Estonian and Latvian territory before the First World War, and the ceded areas had a largely Russian population.

Several Estonians that I talked to were afraid that a large area in northeastern Estonia might in future be transferred to the Russian Federated Republic. Russian-speaking population there is growing, and forms already a majority. Narva and Sillamäe are today practically Russian towns, and Kohtla-Järve is two-thirds Russian.

The territorial losses of 1945 were not too hard for Estonia, because the areas ceded were the least developed. A further loss of territory today, could, however, prove fatal. The area in question forms Estonia's largest industrial basin. Kohtla-Järve is the center of the biggest oil shale mining and processing region in the world. Narva has two large thermoelectrical power stations which supply electricity

196

to Estonia and to a large area in northwestern Soviet Union.

A transfer of this Estonian territory to the Russian Federated Republic would rob Estonia of her most important economic area. Such a loss could endanger the basis for Estonia's status as union republic. However, the fear of such a development must not be exaggerated, since the main reasons for the territorial losses of 1945 were historical, and not demographical.

Lithuania is an exception as regards the territorial issue. The Lithuanians are not afraid that they would lose territory and population because of territorial changes – but because they would gain! This would be so if the Kaliningrad District (formerly Königsberg area) were incorporated within Lithuania. Kaliningrad is now an *oblast* in the Russian Federated Republic, in spite of having no land frontier with Russia. The Kaliningrad District has about 750,000 inhabitants, mainly Russians, and some Ukrainians and Byelorussians.

The Kaliningrad area, which borders on Poland in the south, and Lithuania in the east, comprises that part of the former German province of East Prussia which up to the First World War was called Lithuania Minor. The originally Lithuanian population was Germanized, especially during the second half of the 19th century, so that there were only about 50,000 Lithuanian-speaking people left by the time the Second World War broke out. After the war the area was rapidly Russified. Almost all Lithuanian place names, which by then had German endings, were now exchanged for Russian ones. Khrushchev suggested that the Kaliningrad area should be incorporated with Lithuania. The suggestion was rejected by the Lithuanians on the formal grounds that the administrative resources of their Republic were not sufficient. The area was, however, placed under the same economic administration as Lithuania. Should the Kaliningrad District be administratively incorporated with Lithuania, the ethnically Lithuanian share of the population of Soviet Lithuania would be reduced at once from 80% to about 70%. This is the reason why Lithuanians do not want to gain this territory.

Some Balts fear that the Baltic Republics might in future be combined into one administrative unit. As the Balts speak quite different languages, such a "Baltic Republic" would have to use Russian as their common contact language. The position of the native languages would be undermined.

An administrative reform of this kind is not likely. The language difficulties would create a chaos which the authorities in Moscow would hardly want. The Baltic industrial and agricultural output is important and must not be disrupted. A reform of this kind would also meet with violent criticism from within the Baltic republics and from abroad. The Soviet authorities have already enough troubles dealing with nationalism in each of the Baltic Republics. An amalgamation of the Baltic Republics might create a united Baltic opposition and even a stronger Baltic nationalism.

The authorities in Moscow often demand that Byelorussian delegations should attend Baltic congresses and other gatherings. This is probably because the Byelorussians are culturally closely related to the Russians and are less nationalistic than the Balts. The Byelorussians are therefore suitable tools in the service of building Soviet patriotism. Another reason given for the Byelorussian attendance is that the area belonged to Lithuania up to 1795. In 1918, the small Lithuanian Communist Party was amalgamated with the Byelorussian Party and up to 1920 they had a joint Central Committee. The United Party was dissolved into its original components when peace had been concluded between Soviet Russian and Lithuania in 1920.

Hope After All
The current population trends in the Baltic Republics could threaten the future of the Baltic peoples. The fact that the native share of the population is decreasing in Estonia and Latvia, is a serious development. The Lithuanians are managing to hold their own and thus constitute a safety factor, and a source of inspiration for the other two Baltic peoples. Latvia seems to be the Baltic Achilles' heel and the development there is of great concern to her Baltic neighbors. If any extensive political or cultural changes are carried out in this middle one of the three Baltic Republics, it cannot fail to affect the other two.

The population of Estonia and Latvia increased during the sixties by 13%. The population of Lithuania increased by 15%. These figures are for the total number of inhabitants, irrespective of their nationality.

During the sixties the native Baltic peoples increased also their total number in their irrespective home Republics. The Estonians increased by 32,000 people, the Latvians by 44,000, and the Lithuanians by 356,000. The number of Estonians and Latvians in their respective homelands has, however, decreased in comparison with the figures for the 1930's, while the number of Lithuanians has remained about the same.

The Baltic peoples' vigorous national cultures and their strong passive resistance to Russification, together with their fairly large and increasing absolute numbers, makes it most unlikely that they would be assimilated and disappear in the Soviet melting pot.

CHAPTER 10

From guerilla war to passive resistance

Dissatisfaction and unrest have grown in the Baltic Republics since the end of the sixties. More reports of unrest and demonstrations have reached the outside world. Individuals and groups now dare send their protests abroad, without risking their lives as in Stalin's time. They also dare now to listen to Western broadcasts, although there are still people like the Latvian Karlis Vetra, who was arrested in 1953 and is still in a forced labor camp in Mordovia. He was sentenced to 25 years for listening to American broadcasts and telling others about it.

The courage of the Baltic and Russian opposition is strengthened by the information received from foreign broadcasts. They can hear that their letters of protest have reached their destination and that they are not alone. Radio Liberty, the Vatican, and the Voice of America all broadcast in one or more of the Baltic languages. The BBC, Deutsche Welle, Radio Sweden, and others broadcast in Russian.

Alexander Solzhenitsyn said of Radio Liberty: "If we ever learn what is happening in this country (meaning the Soviet Union) it is through them." Many East Europeans have said similar things about Radio Free Europe, which in recent years has kept to a factual rather than a propagandistic tone. If these broadcasts were silenced, it would be a severe blow for the opposition in Communist countries. Then it would be even more difficult for them to learn what was going on in their own country, as well as abroad. Why should an open society like the United States help totalitarian societies of the Soviet type to hide the truth from its citizens? The Soviet Union will hardly stop its propaganda broadcasts to the West, so why should Western broadcasts be stopped?

The Guerilla Warfare[1]
The armed resistance of the Baltic peoples lasted until the middle of the fifties. Thus the Baltic guerilla fighting, especially in Lithuania, was one of the most long-lived after the Second World War. The resistance was remarkable, especially as the freedom fighters in Estonia, Latvia, and Lithuania – unlike, for instance, the Vietnamese guerilla – could never find shelter in a neighboring country. The Baltic guerillas received no support from abroad, except on a few occasions when small groups of commandos, trained in the West, were parachuted over Lithuanian territory or set ashore from small boats in Latvia and Estonia. Red Army divisions and units of the Soviet security police did their best to liquidate "the

[1] See Rasma Silde-Karklins, "Formen des Widerstandes im Baltikum 1940–68", in *Ziviler Widerstand* (ed. Theodor Ebert), Bertelsmann, Düsseldorf, 1970; V. Stanley Vardys, "The Partisan Movement in Postwar Lithuania", in *Lithuania under the Soviets* (ed. V. Stanley Vardys), Praeger, New York, 1965; Algirdas Budreckis, "Lithuanian Resistance 1940–52", in *Lithuania 700 Years* (ed. Albert Gerutis), Manyland Books, New York 1969; and K. V. Tauras, *Guerilla Warfare on the Amber Coast*, Voyages Press, New York 1962. All these sources are probably based on the Lithuanian partisan leader Daumantas book *Partizanai* (Partisans), Chicago, 1950. The author came to the West in 1948 as the emissary of the guerillas, wrote his book, returned to Lithuania and was killed there. Soviet Lithuanian sources also contain a great deal of information about the guerilla war, mainly the Soviet Lithuanian encyclopaedia (*Mazoji Tarybine Lietuvos Enciklopedija*), and also the book series *Fektai koltine* (Facts accuse).

forest brethren", as the Baltic resistance groups were called. Mass arrests, house searches, and summary executions were carried out to stop the local population from supporting the guerillas.

The mass deportations and the collectivization of agriculture carried out in the Baltic Republics in the late forties, were fatal for the armed resistance. The guerillas found it difficult to get food and other necessities from the farmers. The fighting had become sporadic and only defensive already in 1953 when Stalin died. The crushing of the 1956 Hungarian uprising finally made the Baltic guerillas lose all hope in the efficacy of armed resistance. They realized that the Western powers would never actively support them.

One of the latest reports of a fallen Lithuanian "bandit" was published in 1965 in the Lithuanian Party publication *Tiesa* and concerned the former partisan leader Antanas Kraujelis. In 1971, the Soviet authorities discovered a Lithuanian guerilla fighter, Henrikas Kajotas, who managed to hide for 26 years. Several Estonian guerillas succeeded in staying in their hide-outs for more than twenty, and even thirty years, as Soviet Estonian press reports show. An Estonian partisan, Kalev Arro, was executed as late as 1976 according to information in the Soviet Estonian press.

The surrounding world knew hardly anything – or did not want to know – about the armed resistance which took place in the Baltic countries during all these years. Western journalists were not allowed to visit the Baltic Republics during the Stalin era. Foreign contact by letter was forbidden. Soviet censorship still tries to suppress information about dissent and disturbances in the Baltic countries and other parts of the Soviet Union, but some information has leaked out all the same.

Resistance

It is always difficult in a totalitarian dictatorship to form underground organizations for armed resistance. It is easier in authoritarian dictatorships of the Latin American kind. Still, even in later years, Balts have been arrested and sentenced for planning armed resistance to the Soviet regime.

In 1960, charges were brought against Vilnis Kruklins and two others for preparing an armed uprising in Latvia. Kruklins was sentenced to ten years in a strict-regime labor camp and released in 1970.

In the spring of 1962, eight Latvians were arrested for forming an organization called the Baltic Federation. At their trial they were found guilty of anti-Soviet agitation and propaganda, participation in an anti-Soviet organization, and treason or plotting, an especially dangerous state crime. They received sentences of eight to fifteen years. The two receiving the severest sentences, Gunars Rode and Viktors Kalnins, later became leading fighters for the human rights of political prisoners in Soviet camps.

Even young Balts, those born or brought up during the Soviet period, have been sentenced for illegal possession of firearms and anti-Soviet activity. On November 7, 1969, Latvians Gunars Berzins (born 1949), Laimonis Markants (born 1951) and Valerijs Luks distributed 8,000 leaflets about Czechoslovakia, Soviet–Chinese relations, and the nationality problem in the Soviet Union. After a secret trial Berzins was sentenced in February, 1970 to three years of hard labor, and his friends to one and a half years at a labor camp with strict regime for anti-Soviet propaganda and possession of weapons.

The *Chronicle* published information about four young Estonians – Raivo Lapp, Enn Paulus, Sven Tamm and Andres Võsu – who in June, 1970, were arrested for illegal possession of firearms. They were also accused of trying to form a secret organization that would, allegedly, side against the Soviet Union in case of an armed conflict between Estonia and the USSR. Three of them were sentenced to between two and a half and five years of hard labor. The fourth was committed to a youth detention center for three years. Three of them were born after the Second World War. One was a technician at Tartu university, the second a taxi driver, and the third a mechanic. The fourth person's background is not known.

Less than a year after this trial, Villem Saarte was tried for attempting to organize an Estonian national party. On November 20, 1970 he was sentenced to four and a half years of hard labor and deported to a Mordovian prison camp.

A Letter in 1968

The Democratic Movement in the Soviet Union has offshoots also in the Baltic Republics. Their main demand is that the Soviet authorities should respect the UN Declaration of Human Rights and their own Constitution. The underground stenciled journal of the Democratic Movement, the *Chronicle of Current Events*, has correspondents in the Baltic capitals.

In the late 1960's, Tallinn became one of the centres for the opposition in the Soviet Union. A leading Western expert on the *Chronicle*, Peter Reddaway, writes:

> The first indication that things were brewing in Tallinn came when two documents reached the West at the end of 1968. The first was signed "Numerous representatives of the technical intelligentsia of Estonia", a formula which left open the possibility – a likely one – that both Estonians and non-Estonians, both civilians and military people, were involved.[2]

[2] Peter Reddaway, *Uncensored Russia. The Human Rights Movement. The annotated text of the Unofficial Moscow Journal 'A Chronicle of Current Events'*, Jonathan Cape, London 1972, pp. 171–172.

The signatories repeatedly warned against the risk of a Stalinist revival. They demanded counter-measures while there was still time:

1. Minority groups must have the legal right to voice dissident views.
2. The administration must be under the control of the people; power should not be considered the private property of the top bureaucracy.
3. The Supreme Soviet must become a forum for discussion, rather than register unanimous decisions.
4. The election procedure must be changed and a multi-party system introduced.
5. The writers Daniel and Sinyavsky, those who demonstrated against the invasion of Czechoslovakia, and all others who lost their freedom because of their courage to voice dissident opinions, must be immediately freed.
6. The non-Russian peoples of the Soviet Union must have the right to become independent.
7. All social strata must have the same rights.[3]

The document continues:

For twelve years already, since the 20th Party congress, we have waited and asked our leadership for liberating reforms. We are prepared to ask and wait for a certain time longer. But eventually we will demand and act! And then tank divisions will have to be sent, not into Prague and Bratislava, but rather into Moscow and Leningrad. . . . Was it not our country which "joined" to itself, in the period 1939–1949, 700,000 square kilometres of territory . . .? We must give up the senseless accumulation of territory, the expansion of our great-

---

[3] *Der Aktuelle Osten*, No. 2, 1969.

power might, and our aggressive policies . . . Since not just half but the greater part of the responsibility for the tension in the world lies with us, it is we who must make the first and biggest move toward reconciliation.[4]

The document demands the creation of a zone of neutral states along the Russian borders under UN supervision. This demand probably refers to the restoration of independence to the Baltic nation.

The Estonian intellectuals' appeal ends with the following:

> It is necessary not only to remove the antagonistic feelings among nations, but also to create direct rapprochment; not only to coexist but also to reconcile; not only to fight against physical hunger but to satisfy moral hunger as well; not only to suppress Stalinism, but also to eradicate it completely; not only to grant amnesty but also to redress the wrong done to those imprisoned and to guarantee that no one will be persecuted in the future because of his political convictions; to carry through not only an insufficient reform system, but also to change the entire economic system.

The second document from Estonia to reach the West in 1968 was an "Open Letter to the citizens of the Soviet Union", signed by "Gennady Alekseyev, Communist". The various points of view expressed in this document were similar to those in the previous one, although made from a more Marxist point of view. This document appeared a month after the invasion of Czechoslovakia and sharply condemned it. Later, it turned out that Gennady Alekseyev was a pseudonym for Gennady Gavrilov, a 31-year-old Baltic Fleet officer who lived, prior to his arrest, with his wife and child in Paldiski, Estonia. Gavrilov was

---

[4] Reddaway, op. cit, p. 172.

sentenced in 1970 by a Leningrad military tribunal to six years in strict-regime labor camps.

The Baltic Fleet

In May, 1969, some naval officers of the Baltic Fleet were arrested. Most of the officers and men of the Soviet Baltic Fleet are not Balts, however. It takes its name from the Baltic Sea. One of the arrested officers was Gennady Gavrilov. Gavrilov and the other officers were accused of founding an "association for the promotion of political rights". This association was to promote the realization in the Soviet Union of the UN Declaration of Human Rights.

Altogether, 31 people were arrested in Estonia in connection with this affair. A quarter of them were Estonians, the rest mainly Russians. They were accused of having connections with civilians of similar persuasion in Tallinn, Riga, Moscow, Leningrad, and elsewhere. One of the civilians suspected of complicity with the accused was an engineer from Tallinn named Sergei Soldatov, later to become better known as one of the "Tallinn Four" who were sentenced for activity in the Estonian Democratic Movement. (See Chapter 1.) Soldatov was an uncooperative witness already at the trial against the Baltic Fleet officers in Tallinn, in September 1969. He was therefore forced to undergo a psychiatric examination and was dismissed from his job.

Then, in October, 1969, *The Chronicle* reported the appearance in underground literature of the "Program of the Democrats in Russia, the Ukraine, and the Baltic countries". According to Reddaway, this program is militant and idealizes the Western type of democracy. Its authors favor the West European or Scandinavian type of mixed economy, whilst most other groups within the democratic movement support a so-called market socialism.

"Estonia for the Estonians!"

In 1971, a leaflet was circulated in Estonia signed RK. This abbreviation probably stands for *Rahvuskomitee* (National Committee). An underground resistance movement bearing this name was active in Estonia during the Nazi occupation of the Second World War.

This leaflet has the heading "Estonia for the Estonians". The text is only one page long, and it begins with a description of the German colonization of the Baltic countries in earlier centuries. The leaflet continues:

> It is nonsense to speak of an Estonian Soviet Socialist Republic when half the population are non-Estonians and where trains from Moscow daily bring a greater number of Russian settlers than there are babies born in Estonia. We already have towns and regions where no Estonian is being heard (Narva, Sillamäe, Kohtla-Järve). The picture is depressing also in Tallinn. Better houses in the centre of the town and new blocks of flats house non-Estonians to 80 per cent of the total. There are administrative centres and large plants where the Estonian language has been ousted long ago and where only 10 per cent of the staff are Estonians. The majority of our militia personnel are non-Estonians who do not know Estonian. Any Estonian who wants a responsible job must know Russian, but a Russian can have any job without knowing the local language.

The leaflet ends with the following appeal:

> We appeal to all Estonians, and more particularly to youth, to struggle for a future real Estonian Soviet Socialist Republic and for the survival of the Estonian nation.

> The Estonian Soviet Socialist Republic shall belong to the Estonians. Estonian RK.[5]

[5] *Newsletter from behind the Iron Curtain*, No. 473, Vol. XXVI, March, 1979, Estonian Information Center, Stockholm, Sweden.

The Estonian Letter of 1972
An anonymous letter from a group of people in
Estonia was smuggled out at about the same time as
The Chronicle reported on the Estonian national front
and the new underground journal. The writers of
the letter protest against Russification, the lack of
freedom and the Russian occupation of the Baltic
countries.

The letter writers say, among other things:

> Let the whole world know that the almost five million
> Estonians, Latvians, and Lithuanians do not want the
> Russian occupation and that they categorically oppose
> the suppression of their culture and the Russification of
> everyday life. We appeal to all Estonians abroad to
> fight, united and with all means, to better our situation
> in Estonia, Latvia, and Lithuania. We also appeal to the
> American people and to other peoples to support this
> fight. The Baltic issue should be taken up by the press
> and discussed in detail, and also be taken before the
> United Nations.

The reference to the American people was made
because the letter was written just before President
Nixon's visit to Moscow in spring 1972. The appeal to
the exile Estonians to stand united was probably
directed to the Estonian World Festival held in
Toronto in the summer of 1972. Some 15,000 Estonians from all over the world took part in this
festival, about one in four of all exile Estonians.

The writers of the letter mention other protest
actions by Balts, e.g., the seventeen Latvian Communists' letter, and the letter from the 17,000
Lithuanian catholics. They stress that a united Baltic
front is needed rather than separate Estonian,
Latvian, and Lithuanian action.

The demand that the Baltic issue be taken up in
the UN is most interesting. An organization called

BATUN (Baltic Appeal to the United Nations) has this as its aim. BATUN was founded in the United States by younger exile Balts, who were not connected with any of the old political central organizations. BATUN's goal is that the Baltic issue should be taken up on the agenda for the UN General Assembly, and that the United Nations should promote the Baltic peoples' right to govern themselves.

Recent Samizdat[6]

The trial against the Estonian Democratic Movement described in Chapter 1 did not silence the Estonian democrats. A new memorandum was written on February 10, 1975, by a group calling itself the "Estonian Patriotic and Democratic Front". Another memorandum was written by "Representatives of Estonian and Latvian Democrats", to all governments participating in the Conference on Security and Co-operation in Europe. The statement was dated: Tallinn–Riga, June 17, 1975.

Then in September, 1975, a joint letter was written and signed by representatives of six underground organizations in the Baltic Republics: the Estonian National Front, the Estonian Democratic Movement, Latvia's Independence Movement, the Latvian Christian Democrats, Latvia's Democratic Youth Committee, and the Lithuanian National Democratic Movement. The letter was addressed to the World Baltic Conference, Mr. Uldis Grava, Chairman of the Latvian Free World Federation, and to the leaders of freedom-loving nations, organizations, and associations throughout the world.

The authors are disappointed that a firm and united stand against the forcible annexation of the

---

[6] See Aina Zarins, *"Dissent in the Baltic Republics: A Survey of Grievances and Hopes"*, RL 496/76, Dec. 14, 1976. (One of the many excellent reports by the research department of Radio Liberty.)

Baltic States by the Soviet Union was not taken by the Western democratic nations participating in the Security Conference. They warn the nations of the West against making agreements that are taken seriously only by one side. The authors also ask for the implementation of human rights in the Soviet Union and propose a program that, under UN supervision, would lead to self-determination in Estonia, Latvia, and Lithuania.

Latvia's Independence Movement was first heard of in the West through a letter from the group dated July 27, 1975, and addressed to all Latvians abroad. Quoting freely from patriotic poems and folk songs, the anonymous authors describe the joy of the Latvian nation when Independence was declared on November 18, 1918. They contrast the hopefulness of the past with the pessimism of the present. If Soviet policies do not change, then the Latvian nation has little hope of survival, warn the authors. Latvians abroad are, therefore, asked to help stop these alarming developments by reminding the world of Latvia's desire for self-determination and independence.

Latvia's Democratic Youth Committee presented itself in a letter of October 5, 1975, to Latvians throughout the world. The four-page typed statement is signed by the Committee's chairman, Janis Briedis, and bears the stamp of the organization. He notes with satisfaction the co-operation between Baltic democratic movements and stresses need for a common program and co-ordinated efforts to achieve the liberation of the Baltic nations.

Later in the year, the Committee prepared a New Year's greeting card. It was printed clandestinely and distributed to the inhabitants of Riga on New Year's Eve, 1975. They are urged to lead a life of integrity and to be aware of and assert their rights, bearing in mind the example of Andrei Sakharov. There are reports of the existence of still another dissident organization, Latvia's Christian Democratic Association. Their ten-page address to Baltic leaders abroad was probably written in December, 1975. The authors praise everyone who has acted morally and condemn those who have, in their opinion, betrayed Christian and Latvian national ideals. They urge all Latvians to lead Christian lives and do everything possible to regain Latvian independence.

The Riots in Kaunas

The national and religious resistance has been even more widespread in Lithuania. One of the most dramatic protests in the whole of the Soviet Union occurred at Whitsun, 1972, in Kaunas, the second largest city in Lithuania. The central character of this event was a 19-year-old worker, Romas Kalanta (incorrectly named Roman Talanta in some foreign mass media). He studied at night school, and was a member of the communist youth organization Komsomol – but at heart he was a Christian believer.

One Sunday in the middle of May, Romas Kalanta went to a park in the center of Kaunas. He poured petrol over himself and set himself on fire, according to his friends "as a political demonstration". The park was full of people out for a Sunday stroll, and thus Kalanta's self-burning was witnessed by a great number of people. He died twelve hours later in a hospital.

The news of Kalanta's immolation traveled fast. Even Estonian and Latvian students went to Kaunas to attend the funeral, but they were stopped on the trains and sent home. Western tourists to Estonia and Latvia in the summer of 1972 reported on returning home that Kalanta's sacrificial suicide seemed to be generally known in both of the other Baltic countries.

Thousands of young Lithuanians demonstrated in the streets of Kaunas after Kalanta's funeral. The demonstration procession stopped in the center of the town, outside the Party headquarters. In chorus they demanded freedom and independence for Lithuania. They continued along Lenin Street to the offices of the Ministry of the Interior, where the KGB headquarters are also. There the demonstrators were dispersed by police and militia.

During the riots the demonstrators set fire to several houses. Molotov cocktails were thrown into the Party headquarters. Windows were broken in a shop which sold political literature. The young people were incensed by a placard in the window with the text, "Long live the Communist Party of the Soviet Union".

When the riots had not ceased after twenty-four hours, paratroop units from Central Asia and the Caucasus were brought into Kaunas in order to quell the demonstrations. The local militia was not considered sufficient or reliable. Two militiamen were killed during the encounters. Eight hundred young people were arrested; six hundred were released after having had their hair cut short, two hundred were jailed. Eight of them were brought to trial in the autumn of 1972, and seven received sentences of imprisonment from one and a half to three years.

The authorities later stated that Kalanta had been "mentally disturbed", and also a drug addict. The demonstrations were attributed to "long-haired, degenerated, perverted hooligans and deformed creatures" described as "having a criminal background".[7] Nobody mentioned that the workers in a textile factory came out on strike in sympathy.

[7] *Kauno Tiesas*, May 22, 1972, quoted in *The Lithuanian Chronicle*, No. 26.

As a consequence of the riots in Kaunas, the Supreme Soviet of the USSR made the punishment for participation in mass demonstrations more severe. This can now be punished by detention for fifteen years.

Other Self-immolations

Romas Kalanta's self-immolation attracted the most attention, but it was neither the first nor the last of its kind in the Baltic Republics. In April, 1969, a young Latvian Jew, Ilya Rips, set fire to himself in the middle of the large Freedom Square in central Riga.

Ilya Rips had at age fourteen been one of the winners of the International Schoolchildren's Mathematics Olympia. While still under sixteen he finished school and enrolled as a student of the Faculty of Mechanics and Mathematics at Riga University. During his studies he held a Lenin scholarship and was the pride of the University. On April 10 he was assigned a very good post at the Physics Institute of the Latvian Academy of Sciences. Three days later he went and stood on Freedom Square with a placard saying: "I PROTEST AGAINST THE OCCUPATION OF CZECHOSLOVAKIA". He then set fire to his clothes, which had been soaked in petrol. Some sailors who happened to pass by managed to put out the flames, but cruelly beat up the young man. Ilya Rips was taken to hospital and survived.

Later Ilya Rips was charged for "anti-Soviet propaganda and agitation". The Latvian Supreme Court examined his case on October 2, 1969. The court resolved to order compulsory treatment for Ilya Rips in a psychiatric hospital. He was released in May, 1971 and deported to Israel.

Several self-immolations took place in Lithuania after Romas Kalanta's martyrdom.

At the beginning of June, 1972, a 60-year-old worker succeeded in burning himself to death. Another attempt was made a few days later by a 62-year-old worker. He was stopped at the last minute by some policemen, just as he had poured easily inflammable acetone over himself.

Then, a few days after that, Kalanta's example was followed by a 23-year-old plumber, Stonis, in the small town of Varena, situated in south-eastern Lithuania.

Stonis had intended to burn himself publicly together with three friends. To begin with, they had hoisted the yellow, green and red flag of independent Lithuania, but the police arrived before they had time to continue. His friends were arrested, but Stonis himself escaped. The following day he climbed a building in the center of the town, set fire to himself and jumped off the roof. He died the next day in a hospital. His funeral took place under the supervision of police and KGB men. Road blocks had been set up on all roads leading into the town.

On August 10, 1976 another young believer, Antanas Kalinauskas, burned himself to death while on military service in Gulbins, Latvia.

Lithuanian Helsinki Group
In late 1976, a five-member group was formed in Lithuania to monitor the observance of the Helsinki agreements. The group was made up of people who differ widely in age, background and experience.[8] They were:

1. Tomas Venclova, a prominent author and poet of the younger generation. (He was later allowed to emigrate to the United States in 1977 where he

[8] RL research bulletin, 12/77, 19 January 1977.

witnessed to a committee of the US Congress on violations of human rights in Lithuania. He is still a member of the Helsinki monitoring group.)

2. Ona Lukaskaite-Poskiene, 70, a poetess known for her verses of social protest already from the days of Lithuanian independence. She has spent nine years in Soviet labor camps, returning to Lithuania in 1955.

3. Fr. Karolis Garuckas, an activist Roman Catholic priest, whose actions have often been recorded in *The Lithuanian Chronicle*. (Died April 10, 1979.)

4. Eitan Finkelstein, a physician and Jewish activist, who moved to Vilnius in the early 1970s, and has in vain requested permission to emigrate.

5. Viktoras Petkus, a religious activist, who has signed numerous protest statements and petitions. He was one of the Lithuanians briefly detained in December, 1975, when he had gone to the Vilnius railway station to greet Nobel Peace prize winner Andrei Sakharov, who had travelled to the Lithuanian capital to attend the trial of one of his closest "collabotrators", Sergei Kovalev. Viktoras Petkus was later arrested in 1977 and sentenced to 10 years in prison and strict-régime camp followed by 5 years of exile.

At their first press conference in Moscow, in December, 1976, the Lithuanian group invoked international law in a specially prepared statement in which they asked the Helsinki signatories to recall that "the modern status of Lithuania, as a Soviet republic, was established as a result of the entry of Soviet troops onto its territory on June 15, 1940." The statement asked the participating countries to pay special attention to the observation of human rights in Lithuania.

The group's charges that the Lithuanian authorities were violating the Helsinki agreement, appeared in two reports and in a document issued during the press conference. The reports described the continuing banishment of two bishops – Julijonas Steponavicius and Vincentas Sladkevicius – to small villages outside their dioceses, and criticized a new law, which subjects religious societies to strict control by the secular authorities. In a third document, the group said that two men – Jonas Matulionis and Vladas Lapienis – were arrested in Vilnius on October 19, 1976, and were charged with duplicating and distributing religious and "slanderous" literature.

The Lithuanian Helsinki group has since published a series of statements about human rights violations in their homeland and has also come to the assistance of other Baltic dissidents.

Jewish Activism
Before the Second World War, the Jews in Estonia and Latvia enjoyed cultural autonomy. They could have their own State-supported schools and cultural institutions. Some Jews whom I interviewed in Israel in 1976, stressed that they never had it so good anywhere in Europe before World War II as in independent Estonia. The cultural autonomy for national minorities further reinforced the strong Jewish identity. Then, however, came the Nazi mass murders and the Soviet occupation. The organized social and cultural life of the Baltic Jews was crushed by Stalin in the 1940's.

The Jews then became for a couple of decades a completely suppressed people. Since the end of the 1960's the Jews in the Baltic Republics have become restive, like elsewhere in the Soviet Union. They were spurred by Israel's victory in the Six-Day War in 1967 and were indignant at the Soviet collaboration with Israel's enemies. The younger generation

217

of Baltic Jews does not seem cowed by the traumatic memories of the Hitler and Stalin period. Jews from Latvia and Lithuania have often spearheaded the Jewish national revival and protest movement in the Soviet Union in recent years.

The struggle of Baltic and other Soviet Jews is mainly concerned with civil rights, such as the right to Jewish education and the right to emigrate. The wish of many Baltic Jews to emigrate was well explained in a letter to Brezhnev from three Latvian Jews, Rivka Aleksandrovich, David Zilberman, and Hirsch Feigin. They analyzed in detail the situation of Soviet Jews and found the conditions detrimental to the preservation of Jewish religious and cultural traditions.

An example of the obstacles in the way of maintaining the Jewish heritage is the arrest and trial of four young Riga Jews, who had in their possession books on the Hebrew language, and information about Israel. In May, 1971, Arkady Shpilberg, Boris Maftser, Mikhail Shepshelovich, and Ruta Aleksandrovich, daughter of Rivka Aleksandrovich, were sentenced from one to three years in prison for fabricating and circulating anti-Soviet propaganda. A large group of Jews held a protest meeting at the Jewish cemetery in Riga. They demanded that the young Jews should be released. There was also widespread protest abroad. And soon the four were set free and deported to Israel.

On June 15, 1970, nine Jews from Latvia – Vulf, Israel and Silva Zalmanson, Silva's husband Eduard Kuznetsov, Mendel Bodnya, Boris Penson, Josif and Meri Mendelevich, and Leib (Arye) Knockh – and one from Odessa, Anatoly Altman, were arrested in Leningrad for an attempt to hijack an airplane. All of them received stiff sentences, ranging from eight to fifteen years. The only exception was Meri Mendelvich, who was released because she was pregnant.

Most attempts of Baltic Jews to leave for Israel have been less dramatic. Many succeed in getting a permit to emigrate after repeated efforts. In the meantime, however, they face great uncertainties as they normally lose their jobs after filing an application to emigrate.

Some Jews and non-Jews have been forced to emigrate against their own will. This confirms what a Baltic Jew is reported to have said: "You never know with the KGB. You are either sent to a labor camp or to Israel – but which it will be the KGB themselves don't know beforehand." The Jewish singer of protest songs, Alexander Galich, for instance, at first was not granted permission to emigrate. The Russian artist Yuri Titov and his wife Elena Stroyeva, on the other hand, were treated as Jews and forced to emigrate to Israel. Those Baltic Jews who have chosen, or been compelled, to stay in the Soviet Union have demanded public assistance for Jewish education. Several Jewish groups in Riga have demanded the right for the city's 30,000 Jewish inhabitants to study the Hebrew language. During the Soviet period, no Hebrew textbooks have been published in Latvia or the other Baltic republics. The Soviet Constitution promises all Soviet citizens the right to study their own language and national culture. The Baltic Jews have never received any official help to exercise this right.

The 17 Latvian Communists in their letter criticized the cultural inequality between Russians and non-Russians. The seventeen concluded: "In all Republics the Russians have everything, the peoples of their own Republics (=Latvians in Latvia, etc.) still have something, and the rest have nothing."

German Demonstrations

There are approximately two million Soviet citizens of German origin. Forty thousand of them have demanded emigration visas to leave for West Germany. After West German Chancellor Willy Brandt initiated his policy of detente with the Soviet Union, 40,000 Soviet Germans have been allowed to emigrate: 1,200 in 1971, 3,500 in 1972, 9,200 in 1977, etc.

Germans from the Baltic Republics have been especially vocal and active. Several groups of Germans from Estonia and Latvia demonstrated in the spring of 1974, because their visa applications had been turned down. Some of them had been waiting for four years without getting any positive answer. Some forty Germans carried placards outside the tourist hotel Viru in the Estonian capital Tallinn. One of them carried the text: "Down with Soviet power!"

Most German demonstrations in Moscow were staged by people coming from Estonia. Four persons were arrested there on February 11, 1974. They were held in prison and interrogated for five months before they were tried in Kehra, Estonia, on August 8, 1974. Peter Bergmann, a father of eight, was sentenced to three years prison for "illegal demonstration" and "slandering the Soviet state". The others – Gerhard Fast, Ludmilla Oldenburg, and Waldemar Schulz, were given two years each in prison.

The Song Festivals

The Baltic peoples have for centuries developed a rich treasure of folksongs. Like the negro slaves of the American South, they could in their songs lament the bitter fate that history seemed to have chosen for them, and dream of a new and better future. A number of Baltic folksongs are about the simple peasant who defies the foreign landowner.

It has been said that the Baltic peoples, like the Irish, sang their way to freedom. This is, of course, an exaggeration, but even today the Estonians, the Latvians and the Lithuanians are fond of singing. The tradition of choral singing is maintained both in the homelands and in exile. Just as folksongs in earlier times, these traditions contain an element of the patriotic "protest song". The large song festivals usually give rise to nationalistic manifestations, even under Soviet conditions. They do not only express national pride, but also dissatisfaction with Russification.

During the Estonian Jubilee Song Festival of 1969 in Tallinn, visiting Russian choirs were met only with a polite applause, while the singers from Finland were greeted heartily, and Estonian classic and patriotic songs were applauded with jubilation and had to be repeated. Most of the works performed during this festival were old, traditional Estonian songs. The demand for communist awareness was met by the inclusion in the program of some Soviet songs such as "Lenin's Party" a few times every day as a matter of form.

How the Estonian audience experienced this huge, open air song festival was made quite clear on the final day. The next to last song was *Mu isamaa on minu arm* (My Fatherland is My Dear Love). The text is a poem by the 19th century patriotic poetess Lydia Koidula, and the music is by Gustav Ernesaks, a conductor and a leading figure in Soviet Estonian cultural life. This song has become an unofficial new national anthem. (Very few people seem to know the words of the official Soviet Estonian national anthem by heart.) The national anthem of independent Estonia has been banned – like the blue, black, and white Estonian flag, and the national coat of arms with its three lions.

221

The organizers of the 1960 and 1965 Song Festivals had been forced by the authorities to exclude "My Fatherland is My Dear Love" from the program, but it was nevertheless, spontaneously, sung at both festivals after the end of the official program. The milita tried in vain to get the audience to sit down or leave.

The same thing happened in 1969. An open-air audience of 200,000 people on the festival grounds stood up in unison and started singing this patriotic song once more after the official end of the program. During my visits to Estonia in 1970, people still talked of what an unforgettable experience the Jubilee Song Festival had been and looked forward to the next one, in 1975. Smaller folk-dance and song festivals take place every year in all three Baltic Republics.

Recordings from the 1970 song festival in Riga showed that the Latvian audience reacted in a similar manner. The classic Latvian choral songs, with patriotic or folkloristic contents, were always the best received. The new communist songs were met with much less enthusiasm and were rarely repeated.

To be Able but Unwilling

Almost all Western journalists who in recent years have been allowed to visit any of the Baltic Soviet Republics have told of the native unwillingness to speak Russian. In Tallinn, I nearly got myself into trouble when addressing an intoxicated native who took me for a Russian. When I asked the way in Russian, several Estonians answered me in Estonian and told me to go to hell – or to Siberia. Others refused to answer.

Being an internationalist and a spokesman for increased immigration to Sweden I was irritated and disappointed during my first visit to Tallinn that some of my compatriots in Estonia were so narrow-minded and nationalistic. I found it difficult to understand how anyone could look down on the Russian language, which is not only the language of Brezhnev but also that of Dostoyevsky, Tolstoy, as well as of Sakharov and Solzhenitsyn today. But when I had been snubbed by Russian shop assistants and drivers in the Estonian capital for speaking the language of the country, and had been told to speak a "civilized" language instead of my "barbarian" native tongue, I began to understand the feelings of the local Estonian population.

The Russians in the Baltic countries are often regarded by the native population merely as symbols of an occupying power and not as ordinary human beings. The attitude of many Balts can be explained, if not always defended, by the mass deportations and the arbitrary terror they have been forced to suffer, and also by the feeling of colonial dependence on Moscow, by the arrogance of resident Russian officials, and the pressure of Russification in schools and in cultural life.

Sometimes the older Russian immigrants, whose parents came to the Baltic countries between the World Wars or even earlier, share the prejudices of the Balts against the new immigrants. These "old Russians" are displeased that the mass immigration of the Soviet period has created a Baltic resentment against local Russians, which did not exist earlier. In the independent Baltic States of the period between the World Wars, the Russian population was well-treated. They enjoyed the legal and cultural rights of a minority in Estonia and Latvia.

Political Anecdotes
All political criticism, especially in any organized form, is forbidden. Only one political party is permitted, and

the legislative body makes only unanimous decisions. The Supreme Soviet meets for a couple of weeks a year, which emphasizes its mainly confirmatory and approving role. A common way for Balts and other Soviet citizens to show their disapproval of things as they are is therefore to tell political anecdotes.

The general lack and the poor quality of consumer goods, the dogmatic views of the political leaders, and the Communist ideology are common targets for jokes and criticism. Such anecdotes are safety valves for all the peoples of East Europe and the Soviet Union, and the same themes occur, often with local variations.

On September 16, 1966, a new Soviet law came into force, according to which a person could be sent to labor camp for three years if sentenced for spreading anti-communist jokes. The former Soviet journalist Leonid Vladimirov, now living in London, comments: "On September 17 the journalists were already busy telling each other their own version of the new law. The KGB, they said, had announced a competition for the best anti-Soviet joke. First prize would be three years of imprisonment."

The leadership cult is one of the things which is most lashed out against. Many people were annoyed by the fact that in connection with the centenary celebrations of Lenin's birth, they had to do even more voluntary and unpaid overtime than usual. They were also irritated by the never-ending slogans in the honor of Lenin. In Estonia, one of these was "Lenin on meiega" (Lenin is with us). This slogan gave rise to a popular joke. "Why do they make double beds for three nowadays?" – "Why, don't you know that Lenin is always with us?"

One manifestation of highly unofficial tribute to the Russian leader of the revolution is to place a pair of galoshes by one of the many busts or statues to the honor of Lenin that are to be found in most Baltic towns. A note is fastened to the galoshes with, for example, the following text: "Put your galoshes on and go away!"

Neither are today's leaders spared. One funny story, which seems to be told all over the Soviet Union, is about the present leaders in Moscow and the Nobel Prize winner Alexander Solzhenitsyn: In the year 2000, a child asks its father, "Daddy, who were Brezhnev and Kosygin?" – "I don't quite remember, but I think they were some kind of politicians in the days of Solzhenitsyn."

This story reminds us of Solzhenitsyn's own words in his novel, *The First Circle*, that a great author is like a second government for his country.

On several occasions, I noticed that the statesmen of the days of Baltic independence have not been forgotten, though they are never officially mentioned. The first President of independent Latvia, Janis Čakste, is buried in a cemetery in Riga. The authorities do nothing about the upkeep of his grave. They have tried to plant trees around it to obscure it completely, but as soon as the trees and the weeds start growing, someone comes along at night and waters them with salt-water.

Every year on All Saints' Day people make pilgrimages to Čakste's resting-place and put flowers on his grave. The KGB have several times arrested visitors to the grave in order to frighten people off. Some students at the Academy of Art were expelled a few years ago for having visited the grave and decorated it with live candles.

The flags of independent Estonia, Latvia, and Lithuania are banned, but they are sometimes hoisted by daring youths on top of official buildings and monuments. Andris Puce, born 1953, was arrested 1972, during an unsuccessful attempt to display a flag of independent Latvia in the center of Riga. He was sentenced to five years in a strict regime labor camp on a charge of anti-Soviet agitation and propaganda. He was deported to a camp in Perm, where he has taken part in actions to gain the official status of a political prisoner for himself and for others. His reputation among fellow political prisoners is reported high. Vladas Maijauskas, born in 1947, was arrested in February, 1972, for putting out a Lithuanian flag. He was put in a mental hospital.

Stories which are directed against the privileges of Party members are very popular. One that I was told during my visit was about the bear, the snail and the monkey who wanted to become Party members. Father Bear came home and told Mother Bear that he had applied for membership in the Party. Mother Bear couldn't understand: "What do you want to do that for – both you and I and the children already have fur coats!" The same thing happened in the Snail family. Mrs. Snail could not see any reason for her husband becoming a Party member. "All of us already have our own houses!", was her reaction. Then Father Monkey came home to his family and said that he was thinking of joining the Party. Mother Monkey was furious: "But why do you hesitate? Can't you see that both you and I and the children walk around with our bottoms bare?"

Members of the Party and others who belong to the "new class", the Soviet upper class, are the only ones who have entered the Communist era. That is to say, they work according to ability and consume according to their needs, quite unlike the ordinary run of people.

Stories that make fun of the Communist ideology are just as common as those directed at the holders of power. One story alludes to the five stages of mankind's history according to historical materialism: primitive society, slave-owning society, feudal society, capitalist society, and communist society. "What is communism?" – "It is the social system which has borrowed its technological standards from the stone age, its social relations from the era of slavery, its social structure from the feudal system, its exploitation of the workers from capitalism, and its name from socialism."

The Baltic peoples' almost colonial dependence on Moscow contributes to the dissatisfaction, and thus also to the collection of jokes. The Estonian version of one story goes like this: "Which is the largest country in the world?" – "Estonia, because her border goes along the Baltic Sea, her capital is Moscow, and her population is in Siberia."

A Latvian variation on the same theme is: "Which country is the most neutral in the world?" – "Latvia, because here we don't even interfere with our own affairs." That this story reflects reality is shown by the letter from the seventeen Latvian Communists.

The lack of freedom is often criticized. One exile Estonian experienced this when he went swimming in the Tallinn Bay. He was surprised to see a fisherman sitting there for hours on end without catching a single fish. The visitor approached the fisherman and asked him why the fish did not bite. When he himself was a boy he had often been fishing there and always caught fish. The fisherman answered: "Well, you know, nowadays no one dares open his mouth in this country . . ."

Another day, our visitor from the West was sitting on a bench in the park on Toompea Hill, overlooking the old castle at Tallinn. A Soviet soldier sat down beside him. The visitor enjoyed the beautiful view and happily exclaimed: "Thank God for all this beauty!" The soldier sat silent, thought for a while, and then sullenly muttered: "I thank Comrade Brezhnev instead!" The two men started to talk and the soldier kept on thanking Lenin, Stalin, and Brezhnev for every achievement in the Soviet Union. The visitor from abroad finally lost his temper and asked: "And whom are you going to thank when Brezhnev dies?" – The soldier answered: "Well, then I will thank God . . ."

Such stories and rumors are common in the Baltic Republics and other East European countries and have a certain information value. This is a consequence of the official unwillingness to accept free information and discussion. Based on the experience in Soviet Union and other closed societies of various ideological colours, the following proposition could perhaps be formulated: in societies where free information and discussion of sensitive questions is minimal, unofficial information, mainly in the form of rumors, becomes infinite. Unfortunately, there seems also to be an inverse relation between the quantity of the unofficial information and the quality of it. Almost uncontrollable rumor-mongering thus becomes the rule in societies with censorship and controlled information. But, on the other hand, many people do not seem to believe even the rumors they themselves help to spread.

CHAPTER 11

Human rights in the Baltics

When discussing human rights in the Baltic States it is necessary to distinguish between the time of Stalin's terror and the present situation. In one single night, between the 13th and 14th of June 1941, tens of thousands of Balts were deported in cattle trucks to prison camps or forced exile in Russia and Siberia.

The mass deportations did not stop with the Second World War. The largest wave came with the collectivization of agriculture towards the end of the 1940's. Tens of thousands of Balts, mainly farmers, were deported during a few days in March, 1949.

Altogether, 140,000 Estonians have been removed by force during the years that have elapsed since the Soviet occupation took place. About 155,000 Latvians and 300,000 Lithuanians have been deported during the same period.

The Case of Mart Niklus

The terror did not cease altogether with Stalin's death. This is illustrated by the fate of Mart Niklus.

Mart Niklus was a young, promising scientist from Tartu. His main interests were languages and birds. He acted as interpreter at the International Ornithological Congress in Leningrad in the spring of 1956. He attended a study circle in Swedish in his spare time.

During the autumn of 1956, the circle received a visit from some Finnish students. It often happened during the Finns' visit that complete strangers gave them letters for friends and relations abroad – letters that they did not send the usual way because of censorship. The Finns, therefore, did not think it particularly unusual when Niklus gave them an envelope containing some ten photographs and asked them to see that a certain person abroad received them. These pictures were later published in Estonian newspapers abroad.

The Soviet reaction came quickly. The authorities declared that the subject matter of the pictures was anti-Soviet and thus criminal. One of the pictures showed a jamming transmitter in Tartu which broadcast constant interference signals, twenty-four hours a day, in order to prevent people from listening to the Voice of America's programs in Estonian. Another picture showed a block of apartments where some of the windows were missing and the back wall was so cracked that wooden props had to be used to prevent the walls from collapsing. A third picture showed an elderly woman looking for offal and the like at the municipal garbage dump.

The pictures were genuine, but they showed a different side of reality than that officially preferred. Mart Niklus was sentenced to 15 years of hard labor for having smuggled the pictures out of the country. The Russian dissident Anatoly Marchenko tells us in his book, *My Testimony*, that he came across Niklus in various camps. Niklus did not give in during his imprisonment, and he even led a hunger strike. Niklus was released in 1964 and his name has since then figured several times in dissident circles. He was, for instance, a close friend of the Russian poetess Natalya Gorbanevskaya, until she was arrested, sent to a mental hospital, and later exiled to

France. She had been a contributor to *Chronicle of Current Events*, the underground publication of the Soviet civil rights movement. Niklus would have been the principal witness for the defense at Gorbanevskaya's trial, but his evidence was not accepted by the court.

Branded by the authorities as "an Estonian nationalist", Mart Niklus could not work in his own profession. He had to be satisfied with temporary part-time jobs as a substitute teacher. On September 30, 1976, Niklus was teaching at the 7th Secondary School in his home town, Tartu. In the middle of his lesson he was called out of the classroom by a militiaman showing a search warrant. Niklus pointed out that the warrant was not properly authorized, and left the school. But the militiamen followed and pulled him into a car. Mart Niklus did not resist. He was taken to a police station and held until evening.

Meanwhile, militiamen searched his home and confiscated (1) a paper signed by Alexander Solzhenitsyn, (2) Niklus' autobiography, (3) a children's book in French, and (4) an Estonian translation of the musical "Jesus Christ Superstar". The search was made to see if Niklus had used his typewriter to duplicate illegal literature.

After release, Niklus resumed his temporary work. But on October 8, 1976, he was arrested again. The formal reason for his arrest was his "resistance to the militia" on September 30. According to paragraph 182 of the Soviet Estonian Constitution, this is punishable by up to five years corrective labor, that is, detention in a labor camp. Niklus reportedly tore up his Soviet passport upon arrest and declared that he wished to renounce his Soviet citizenship.

Niklus immediately started a hunger strike in the KGB prison in Tallinn where he had been taken. He was soon set free this time. In August, 1977, he was once again arrested after meeting other Baltic dissidents. World opinion might help keep Mart Niklus from further arrests and intimidation.

The Case of Fricis Menders

Fricis Menders was born in Riga in 1885. At the age of 19, he joined the Revolutionary Social Democratic Party when it was founded. Menders played an active part in the 1905 Revolution. The following year he was arrested by the Tsarist police and deported to Siberia.

He managed to escape and go abroad, where he remained for ten years until the 1917 Revolution. Menders became Doctor of Law at the University of Bern in Switzerland and participated in a number of Social Democratic International Congresses as a representative for Latvia. He was a member of the Latvian National Council, which declared Latvia's independence on 18 November 1918. He was also a member of the Latvian delegation which in 1920 declared an armistice with Soviet Russia and made peace with Germany. Between the wars, Menders was one of the leading publicists, a member of Parliament, and also the leader of the Social Democratic Party in Latvia, and an internationally known politician. He was a member of the Executive Committee of the Socialist International.

During his long life, Menders was persecuted not only by the Tsar's Okhrana, but also by today's KGB. When Ulmanis abandoned parliamentary democracy in Latvia in 1934, and instituted an authoritarian regime, Menders was arrested together with many others of the left. He was forced to spend six months in one of the penal camps of the Ulmanis period.

During the Soviet regime Menders was arrested for the first time in 1948. He was interrogated for several months in Riga and then sentenced *in absen-*

tia, and against his denial, to ten years hard labor in Siberia. He was sent to Dubrovlag in the Mordovian Autonomous Republic, where many dissidents are still kept today.

Menders was sentenced for "anti-Soviet activities" during the previous "bourgeois period", and also for possessing "anti-Soviet literature". The last accusation was dropped with the amnesty for camp prisoners of 1955. Menders was released.

A new accusation was brought against Menders at the beginning of 1960. It was later withdrawn, as Menders persistently denied all accusations and international opinion had been mobilized. The KGB, however, confiscated three thousand typewritten pages during an illegal search of his house. These papers constituted the manuscript of Menders' memoirs for the period up to the Soviet occupation in 1940. Menders was questioned every day for several weeks after the search of his house. The interrogators brought up a lot of details from his memoirs and accused Menders of having written these with anti-Soviet intent. The memoirs were not returned when the accusation was withdrawn.

More than six decades after having been first arrested by the Tsarist regime, Menders was again arrested in 1969, this time by Soviet security police. He was then 84 years of age, and suffered from heart trouble, but was nevertheless sentenced to five years exile in Soviet Russia for alleged anti-Soviet activities.

Menders was accused of having met a young Latvian–American historian, Paulis Lazda, and of having handed over to him certain papers which were described as having anti-Soviet content by the KGB. Menders was taken to court in spite of his denial and in spite of the fact that the papers were in Lazda's handwriting.

233

The accusation of anti-Soviet propaganda was legally doubtful. Menders' papers – if they were his – were not published or circulated in any way, and should thus not have been labeled as propaganda. Menders was sentenced after only three days of hearings at the Supreme Court of the Latvian Soviet Republic. The trial did not satisfy the Criminal Code procedure rules.

Menders was prematurely released in early 1971, but he was now an old and broken man. Perhaps those in power in Moscow did not want Menders to die in exile because of the reaction, both abroad and at home. He died soon after his release.

In 1914, Lenin wrote that Menders was "the most important of the Latvian Mensheviks" and "also our most dangerous opponent".[1] Thus the treatment of Menders can be explained, but not excused. Menders was never willing to compromise with the communists. He was a living symbol for the Democratic Left in Latvia.

The Case of Janis Jahimovics

Janis Jahimovics (in Russian: Ivan Yakhimovich) graduated from the faculty of history and philology at the Latvian State University. He then worked as a teacher, until in 1960 he became chairman of a collective farm near Kraslava, Latvia. On January 22, 1968, Jahimovics, then 37, addressed a letter to Mikhail Suslov and the Central Committee of the Communist Party of the Soviet Union. Jahimovics, who was himself a Party member, protested the persecution of the Russian writers Yury Galanskov, Aleksander Ginzburg and other "energetic, brave, and high-principled members of our younger generation . . . Too bad for us if we are not capable of

---

[1] Lenin's *Collected Works*, Vol. 20, p. 335–335 (Russian edition).

reaching an understanding with these young people. Ideas cannot be murdered with bullets, prison and exile."[2]

In March 1968, Jahimovics was expelled from the Communist Party. In May he lost his job. This did not keep him from signing another protest letter, together with four dissident Russian Communists: A. Kosterin, General Pyotr Grigorenko, V. Pavlinchuk, and S. Pisarev. They expressed support for the policies of the Communist Party of Czechoslovakia. The signatories were well aware that they were voicing opinions contrary to those of the Soviet government, which was secretly planning the invasion of Czechoslovakia.

On March 24, 1969, Jahimovics was arrested. His house was searched. He was illegally deprived of his residence permit – the police simply crossed out the permit stamp in his internal Soviet passport. So he was unable to find work.

Some hours before his arrest Janis Jahimovics had written a moving letter of farewell. He speaks about himself, his family, and his friends – Russian dissidents Pavel Litvinov, Larissa Bogoraz, Pyotr Grigorenko, Alexander Solzhenitsyn, and others. He also explains his own political principles. Still considering himself a communist, Jahimovics stated that for communists there is only "one lord, one sovereign – the people. But the people are made up of living persons, of real lives. When human rights are violated, especially in the name of socialism and Marxism, there cannot be two positions".[3]

Janis Jahimovics acted according to his beliefs and objected to the violation of human rights. He was found to be mentally unsound by the Soviet authorities. After a follow-up examination at the Serbsky

[2] *AS* 11.   [3] *AS* 102.

235

Institute in Moscow in January, 1970, he was placed in a psychiatric hospital in Riga for compulsory treatment. Jahimovics was released in 1971.

Another Latvian, the journalist Ivars Zukovskis, also openly criticized the Soviet intervention in Czechoslovakia. In 1969, he was sentenced to five years in a labor camp. After serving this sentence, he was rearrested when the KGB found on him a petition addressed to the UN Commission for Human Rights. Zukovskis was imprisoned for six months. Then in August, 1974, Zukovskis was sentenced to another two years hard labor on the trumped-up charge of shoplifting.

The Case of Gunars Rode

Gunars Rode, Viktor Kalnins, and five other Latvians were arrested and sentenced in 1962. They were charged with treason, anti-Soviet propaganda, and membership in anti-Soviet organizations. Rode and his friends had founded the "Baltic Federation" and the "Latvian National Organization" to fight for the independence of Estonia, Latvia, and Lithuania. At the time of his arrest Gunars Rode, born in 1934, was a biology student at the University of Riga and a driver with the Transporation Department of the City of Riga.

Gunars Rode was given the severest penalty at the trial, 15 years. But his spirit remained unbroken in camp and prison. He initiated hunger strikes and other activities to protest against the illegal treatment of prisoners. One year he also organized a silent memorial ceremony around a self-made Latvian flag on his country's national independence day, November 18, thus demonstrating his hope for the restoration of Latvian sovereignty.

A Russian dissident, Lev Kvachevsky, who in 1971 was with Rode in the Vladimir prison and now lives in the West, reported after his release that Rode was in ill health: "He had a problem with his stomach; he could not eat. For four months we kept asking for a doctor's examination of him. Finally he was taken from our cell. We believed that he was being taken to a hospital. Later we learned that he had merely been transferred to another cell. We found out that he had been near death. From the cell, he was taken directly to the operating table. The surgeon said afterwards that he missed death by two hours."

Another Russian dissident and fellow prisoner, Vladimir Bukovsky, confirmed this story in 1976. As a consequence of hard labor, undernourishment, and the absence of medical assistance, Rode had become a total invalid, Bukovsky said. He suffered from a serious enteric ailment, twisting of the bowels, but received no medical help whatsoever. In the spring of 1976, Rode went on a hunger strike in order to force his transfer to a hospital. When this proved of no avail, Bukovsky and four fellow prisoners tried to break open Rode's isolation cell. As punishment for his action, Bukovsky was transferred to solitary confinement, where he was kept until he was exchanged for the Chilean Communist leader, Luis Corvalán.

The *Chronicle of Current Events* carried two items on Rode in issue no. 40, dated 20 May 1976. Rode and two fellow inmates of the Vladimir prison had been punished with seven days in solitary confinement for protesting against uneatable food. The same issue reported that Gunars Rode had been allowed to return to Riga for a visit to his father's grave. It was then suggested to Rode that he should appeal for clemency. Rode refused. The next issue of *Chronicle* (no. 41, dated August 3, 1976), carried the text of a telegram of congratulations sent by Soviet political prisoners on the occasion of the 200th

Anniversary of the Declaration of Independence of the United States of America. The telegram was signed by 15 prisoners, among them Gunars Rode and Sergei Soldatov, one of the Tallinn Four (see Chapter 1). Gunars Rode was finally set free on May 13, 1977, and a year later received permission to leave for Sweden.

The Right to Emigrate
Article 13:2 of the UN Declaration of Human Rights is receiving more and more attention. It reads:

> Everyone has the right to leave any country, including his own, and to return to his country.

This right is also protected by the 1965 Convention against Racial Discrimination and the 1960 Convention of Civil and Political Rights. Both have been signed by the Soviet Government. But at the same time any attempt to leave the Soviet Union without permission may be punishable by death, according to Article 64 of the Russian Criminal Law and corresponding articles in the penal codes of other union republics. Able-bodied Balts have found it very difficult to obtain emigration permits. Therefore they have on several occasions tried to flee the country. A few Lithuanians succeeded in escaping on board a Soviet trawler in the autumn of 1972. Their dramatic escape, together with some Ukrainians, from the Black Sea to Greece ended happily, although Soviet ships endeavoured to find the lost boat.

The Soviet Coast Guard was more successful when a sailor from the Baltic States, at roughly the same time, jumped off a trawler into the Baltic Sea, and, protected by the darkness of night, managed to make his way to a Danish fishing vessel near Gotland. Soviet Coast Guard ships caught up with the

Danish vessel, the Soviets boarded it in spite of protests from the Danish crew, and with guns in hand forced the fugitive to return. His name remained unknown.

Most Balts who would like to escape never get as far as the fugitive on board the Danish fishing vessel. The borders of the Baltic States to the West are sealed. The Baltic coast is guarded by mines, radar, and coast guards. Even the sand along the coast is raked in order to find footprints.

People have been relocated from the Baltic coastal areas and they have to have special permits to visit their old homes, which have often been turned into military bases.

Some Balts have in their desperation hijacked airplanes in order to escape to the West, others have jumped off Soviet ships in harbor or at sea. I would like to relate the fates of four Balts, all of which are concerned with the right to free emigration from the Soviet Union.

The Case of Jonas Kazlaukas

Jonas Kazlaukas, an internationally known linguist, was born in 1930.[4] He became a member of the Communist Party and the Head of the Linguistic Department of the University of Vilnius.

In 1968, he was invited to lecture at Pennsylvania State University in the USA. The Soviet Ministry for higher Education declined the invitation in March, 1970, without informing Kazlaukas. During the summer of 1970 Kazlaukas learned from an American colleague that he had declined the invitation and was dismayed. On October 8, 1970, Kazlaukas disappeared and six weeks later his body was discovered

---

[4] See William R. Schmalstieg, "Jonas Kazlaukas's Contributions to Lithuanian Linguistics", *Lituanus* No. 1, 1972.

in the river Neris, which flows through the capital of Lithuania.

After an unusually long delay, a medical report was published, stating that there was no evidence of physical violence and that Kazlaukas had committed suicide. According to information from Lithuania, Kazlaukas committed suicide after protesting against not being allowed to travel and then being placed in a mental hospital by force.

The Case of the Brazinskas's
In the middle of October 1970, a 46 year-old Lithuanian by the name of Pranas Brazinskas, and his 15 year-old son Algirdas forced at gunpoint a Soviet passenger plane to change course, and land at the Turkish town of Trabzon on the Black Sea. An air hostess was hit by a ricochet bullet and died. The elder Brazinskas had previously been sentenced to ten years hard labor and deportation to Uzbekistan for having supplied Lithuanian guerillas with arms.

The Soviet government demanded that the father and son be extradited from Turkey. Their hijacking was the first one in the whole of the Soviet Union to succeed, so the Soviet authorities wanted to show, at all costs, that this sort of crime did not pay. The Brazinskas's were branded as ordinary criminals by the authorities. The father was accused of having "stolen from his mother, beaten his wife, pilfered from his employer and served a prison sentence." The Turkish authorities stated, however, that no money was found on them.

Four Turkish lower courts agreed to the Brazinskas's demand to be considered as political refugees. As such they could both claim the right to political asylum. The Turkish Supreme Court decided to everyone's surprise not to declare them political refugees, which meant that the two might be extra-

240

dited and condemned to death according to current Soviet law.

After six years in Turkish prisons, Pranas and Algirdas Brazinskas were set free in 1976. They are now in the United States, where the immigration authorities are deciding their fate.

The Case of the Simokaitis
The other known case of Lithuanians hijacking a Soviet passenger plane is that of a married couple called Simokaitis. At the beginning of November, 1970, Vytautas Simokaitis, aged 34, and his 21 year-old wife Grazina tried to get an Aeroflot plane, en route from Vilnius to the seaside resort of Palanga on the Baltic Sea, to change its course and aim for Sweden. The couple were overpowered and the attempt did not succeed. In January, 1971, Simokaitis was sentenced to death by the Lithuanian Supreme Court and his pregnant wife was given three years hard labor.

These sentences gave rise to violent protests in several Western countries. Because of the wave of international protest the death sentence was changed to fifteen years hard labor. Just as in the case of the two Latvian Jews, sentenced to death for a planned hijacking at the trials of December 1970 in Leningrad. Simokaitis was sentenced according to the paragraph in the Soviet Criminal Law which says that any attempt to leave the country illegally may be punished by death.

The Case of Simas Kudirka
A fourth case that is known in the West concerns Simas Kudirka, a 40 year-old sailor. On November 23, 1970, he defected from the Soviet ship *Sovetskaya Litva* to a United States Coast Guard vessel. The two ships were at the time moored side by side off the

coast of New England, because of negotiations about fishing rights.

Kudirka asked for political asylum. In spite of this, the captain of the American ship, after receiving strict orders through the chain of command, allowed Soviet sailors to board his ship, render Kudirka unconscious, and then take him back to the Soviet vessel.

The trial of Kudirka took place in Vilnius in May 1971, before the Lithuanian Supreme Court. The investigation before the trial had been carried out by the KGB and the indictment was treason.

When the chairman of the Court pronounced the name of the counsel for the defense, Kudirka declared his decision to dispense with the counsel: "If my counsel is an honest man and intends to defend me conscientiously, it will only be detrimental to him. If he is not an honest man and intends to play the part of a second prosecutor, as often happens at political trials in Lithuania, then I think that my case is not complicated enough to need two prosecutors."

Kudirka declared himself not guilty. He stated that he had not committed treason against his country, which was Lithuania. He did not consider that Russia, which is today called the Soviet Union, was his country.

Kudirka gave a four hour speech in his own defense, explaining the background for his attempt at defection. He said that he came from a poor family. When Lithuania was incorporated into the Soviet Union in 1940, national oppression was added to the social injustices. Kudirka also described how he and his fellow countrymen experienced the mass deportation of Lithuanians in 1941 and 1944 to Russian and Siberian camps. Many of his acquaintances joined the guerilla forces against the Soviet authorities, but most of them came to a sad end. Kudirka left school after eight years and decided to become a sailor. He wanted to see the world and hoped that at sea and abroad he would be able to forget the tragedy of his people.

In his speech for his defense Kudirka quoted Marx and Lenin to show the differences between socialist theory and practice in Lithuania. Kudirka also related how the KGB men had suggested that he publicly denounce the Lithuanian "bourgeois nationalism" in exchange for a milder sentence. Kudirka declared that he refused to sell his country, Lithuania, at the price of his personal freedom.

Kudirka also pointed out that he was not a criminal according to international law, nor according to the United Nations' Declaration of Human Rights, nor according to the Soviet Constitution. He had one request to the Lithuanian Supreme Court and the Government of the Soviet Union – to allow Lithuania to become a free and independent country again. Kudirka was sentenced to ten years hard labor in a strict régime camp and lost all his possessions.

Simas Kudirka had to spend only some three and a half years in the labor camp. It was discovered that his mother once had held United States citizenship. Because of this, and concerted efforts of Lithuanian–Americans, the United States Government pressed the Soviet government to release Kudirka. He was allowed to emigrate to the United States in 1974.[5]

---

[5] Jurgis Gliauda has written a documentary novel on the Kudirka case, *Simas*, Manyland Books, 1971. See also Kudirka's own account together with an American writer, Simas Kudirka/Larry Eichel, *For those still at sea*. Dial Press, New York 1978.

CHAPTER 12

May Estonia, Latvia, and Lithuania be free and independent states!

Among the persons arrested and deported when the Baltic States were occupied and annexed by the Soviet Union was the President of the Estonian Republic, Konstantin Päts. His fate in captivity remained unknown, although various rumors circulated in Estonia and abroad. The International Committee of the Red Cross reported in 1974, that according to information supplied to them by the Soviet government, Päts died on January 16, 1956. The Soviet authorities, however, would not reveal his place of death nor the place of his burial.

In June 1977 three messages written by President Päts in Soviet captivity reached the free world. Although these messages do not show precisely when or where they were written, they are unmistakably in his handwriting and bear his signature and fingerprints. One of the messages must have been written in 1953 or 1954 since it mentions the approach of his 80th birthday, which was on February 23, 1954.

These three letters of Konstantin Päts are of considerable interest even today. They confirm the fact that he never voluntarily resigned his Presidency and that even in Soviet captivity he remained an ardent supporter of the right of self-determination of the Estonian, Latvian, and Lithuanian nations.

The original messages are on file at the Consulate General of Estonia in New York. The following translations into English have been certified by the Consul General of Estonia, Mr. Ernst Jaakson.

In his first message, Päts describes his personal fate:

Since the year 1940, I am being held without a court order, without any charges, as a prisoner in Russia in a hospital for the Jewish poor, where I, as President of the Republic of Estonia, am being subjected to degradation in every way and my life threatened. As a result of my advanced age and undescribably difficult conditions of life, my health has deteriorated here very much. It is difficult to describe all that, how ruthless force has been used here against me. All my personal belongings which I had along with me have been taken away. I have even been refused to use my own name. Here I am only No. 12. I don't even have permission to correspond with my family and to receive any help from them. The food here is bad, I have become weak, my hearing and eyesight have weakened. My protests that I am being held here without any lawful basis are being disregarded. For my selfprotection I do not even have that support which in other places is offered by societies for the prevention of cruelties to animals. I will soon be 80 years old, there are few days of life left for me. Having been born free, I would also want to die in freedom.

No sentence has been passed upon me. I have lived as a free human being and I wish to end my days of life in freedom. I am still the President of the Republic of Estonia and I have the right (word illegible) to expect corresponding treatment, as my home country is a free and independent state. I hope that a just public opinion will extend its protection also to my human rights and will help to bring about my release from this terrible place of imprisonment where brute force and unlimited injustice reign. I am here as President of the Republic of Estonia.

K. Päts (Signature)
(Fingerprint)

In the second message, President Päts addresses his own Estonian countrymen as well as Latvian and Lithuanian freedom fighters:

Compatriots!

I greet you in our fighting homeland, in Russian prisons, abroad, and in your place of banishment, and wish you all the best and a steadfast spirit, and strength in your justified resistance. Soon we will be free.

I also send greetings to the heroes of resistance of the Lithuanian and Latvian peoples, and to all refugees.

I am proud, our steadfast people, be courageous and confident, and try to achieve our great goal, namely that our homes should remain free in our free homeland.

K. Päts (signature)
(Fingerprint)

And in his third message, President Päts appeals to the Secretary General of the United Nations and to world opinion not to forget the fate of the three small Baltic nations. The Estonians, Latvians, and Lithuanians still dream of the day, when they will be able to participate as free and independent nations in the world community.

To the Secretary General of the United Nations:

I turn to the United Nations and the entire civilized world with the request to help the people of Estonia, Latvia, and Lithuania against whom the Russian occupants are using ruthless force and who, therefore, could perish.

I declare the annexation of the Baltic states, which was carried out in the year 1940, a brutal violation of international law and a falsification of the free will of the annexed peoples.

Save these peoples from complete annihiliation and allow these peoples to decide freely their own fate. Establish an agency of the authority of the United Nations in the Baltic States so that the citizens of the Baltic States could under their supervision and control freely express their true will through a vote of the people.

May Estonia, Latvia, and Lithuania be free and independent states!

K. Päts (signature)
(Fingerprint)

Annotated Bibliography

I have selected only books and pamphlets in English, French and German, also on Baltic history. Especially valuable works are marked with an asterisk.

Journals and yearbooks:

*Acta Baltica, Institutum Balticum, Königstein-im-Taunus, West Germany. Yearly since the early 1960's.

Baltic Review, New York. Published quarterly up to 1971 by the Estonian Committee within the Assembly of Captive Nations of Europe, ACEN.

Baltische Briefe, West Germany. Monthly for Baltic Germans in the Federal Republic.

*BATUN Newsletter. Irregular newsletter on human rights in the Baltic Republics and the activities of the Baltic Appeal to the United Nations, BATUN, 2789 Schurz Ave, Bronx, New York 10465.

Bulletin from the Institute for the Study of the USSR, Munich. Monthly until 1972.

Chronicle of Current Events, Moscow. Underground organ of the democratic movement in the Soviet Union, published in English by Amnesty International, 10 Southampton Street, London WC 2E 7HF.

Chronicle of Human Rights in the USSR, Khronika Press, 505 Eight Avenue, New York, NY 10018. Edited by one of the leading Soviet dissidents, Valery Chalidze, now in American exile.

Current Abstracts of the Soviet Press, New York. Monthly.

Current Digest of the Soviet Press, New York. Weekly.

Jahrbuch des baltischen Deutschtums, Carl-Schirren-Gesellsachft, Lüneburg, West Germany. Baltic German yearbook.

*Journal of Baltic Studies. Scientific quarterly published

by the Association for the Advancement of Baltic Studies, AABS, 366-86th Street, Brooklyn, NY 11209, USA. AABS has also published the proceedings of its Conferences on Baltic Studies.

*Lituanus. Quarterly devoting itself not only to Lithuanian subjects but also the cultural and political development in the neighbouring Baltic republics, Estonia and Latvia. Subscriptions from P.O. Box 9318, Chicago, Illinois 60690, USA.

Mitteilungen aus baltischem Leben. Quarterly published by Baltische Gesellschaft in Deutschland. Much biographical material.

Newsletter from Behind the Iron Curtain. Monthly published by the Estonian Information Center and the Latvian National Foundation in Stockholm. Subscriptions from Box 45 030, S-104 30 Stockholm, Sweden.

*Radio Liberty Research Bulletin, Munich. Excellent coverage of dissent in the Baltic republics and general development in the Baltic republics and other parts of the Soviet Union.

World Literature. An International Literary Quarterly published by Oklahoma University Press, Norman, Oklahoma with reviews also of Baltic literature in the homelands and in exile.

Also general journals like Index on Censorship, Osteuropa, Problems of Communism, Slavic Review, Soviet Analyst, Soviet Studies, Survey and others occasionally have interesting articles with reference to the Baltic republics.

Baltic States generally:

Ames, Ernst O. F. (ed.), The Revolution in the Baltic Provinces, London 1907.

Apse, Jan, The Baltic States, London 1940.

Babris, Peter, Baltic Youth under Communism, Research Publishers, Arlington Heights, Illinois 1967.

*The Baltic States, Royal Institute for International Affairs, Oxford University Press, London 1938.

The Baltic States and the Soviet Union: Reprinted from a Report of the Council of Europe, Stockholm 1962.

*The Baltic States 1940–1972. Documentary Background and Survey of Developments presented to the European Security and Cooperation Conference, Baltic Committee, PO Box 16042, 10321, Stockholm 1972.

Bilmanis, Alfreds, The Baltic States, Latvian Legation, Washington D.C. 1943.

Bilmanis, Alfreds, Baltic Essays, Latvian Legation, Washington D.C. 1945. Latvian envoyé to Moscow in the early 1930's and then in Washington 1935–1948. For a sixteen-page bibliography of his writings on Baltic affairs see Res Baltica (below).

Buchen, J. (ed.), The Baltic and Caucasian States, London 1920.

Bukss, Michael, Die Russifizierung in den baltischen Ländern, Latgalischer Verlag, München 1965.

Chambon, Henri de, La tragédie des nations baltiques, Ed. de la Revue Parlamentaire, Paris 1946.

Coates, William, Russia, Finland and the Baltic, London 1940.

Davies, Ellen Chivers, A wayfarer in Estonia, Latvia and Lithuania, Methuen, London & New York 1937. Travelogue.

Ehret, Joseph, Baltisches Schicksal, Basel 1970.

Ehret, Joseph, Adam der Europäer, Basel 1978.

Gehrmann, K., Die baltischen Staaten. Eine Brücke zwischen Ost und West, Berlin 1939.

Gimbutas, Marija, The Balts, Praeger, New York & London 1963. Prehistory and early history of Baltic tribes.

Graham, Malbone W J:r, New Governments of Eastern Europe, Henry Holt and Co, New York 1927.

Graham, Malbone, "Stability in the Baltic States" in R. L. Buell (ed), New Governments in Europe: The Trend toward Dictatorship, Thomas Nelson and Sons, New York 1934.

Jackson, Hampden J., The Baltic, Clarendon Press, Oxford 1940.

Kaelas, Aleksander, The Worker in the Soviet Paradise, Boreas, London 1947.

Kaelas, Aleksander, Human Rights and Genocide in the Baltic States, Stockholm 1950.

Kalme, Albert, Total Terror: An Exposé of Genocide in the Baltics, Appleton/Century Crofts, New York 1951.

Kazlauskas, B., L'entente baltique, Librairie de Recueil Sirey, Paris 1939.

Kirchner, Walter, The Rise of the Baltic Question, University of Delaware, Newark 1954. Mostly on the 16th century.

Klesment, Johannes, Legal sources and Bibliography of the Baltic States, Praeger, New York 1963.

*Landsmanis, Arturs, Persist or Perish, Soviet Russia destroying Baltic Peoples, Latvian National Foundation, Stockholm 1976.

Macartney, C. A. & Palmer, A. W., Independent Eastern Europe, Macmillan, London 1962.

Manning, Clarence A., The Forgotten Republics, Columbia University Press, New York 1959.

Meiksins, Gregory, The Baltic Riddle, New York 1943.

Meissner, Boris, Die Sowjetunion, die baltischen Staaten und das Völkerrecht, Verlag für Wissenschaft und Politik, Köln 1956.

Meuvret, Jacques, Histoire des pays baltiques, Paris 1934.

Montford, Henri de, Les nouveaux etats de la Baltique, Paris 1933.

Newman, Bernhard, Baltic Roundabout, London 1939.

Newman, Bernhard, Baltic Background, R. Hale Publishers, London 1948.

Newman, Edward W. P., Britain and the Baltic, Methuen, London 1930.

Oras, Ants, Baltic Eclipse, W. Gollanz, London 1948.

*Page, Stanley W., The Formation of the Baltic States, Harvard University Press, Cambridge, Mass. 1959.

Pennar, Jaan, Nationalism in the Soviet Baltics, in Erich Goldhagen (ed.), Ethnic Minorities in the Soviet Union, Praeger, New York 1968.

Pennar, Jaan, Bakalo, Ivan I., Bereday Georg Z. F., Modernization and Diversity in Soviet Education with Special Reference to Nationality Groups, Praeger, New York 1971.

251

*Pick, Frederick William, The Baltic Nations, Boreas, London 1945.

Problems of Mini-Nations: Baltic Perspectives, New York 1973. Selected papers of the Third Conference on Baltic Studies organized by the Association for the Advancement of Baltic Studies, AABS.

Pusta, Kaarel R., The Soviet Union and the Baltic States, John Felsberg, New York 1942. Estonian envoyé to Western European governments during independence.

*Rauch, Georg von, Geschichte der baltischen Staaten, Kohlhammer Verlag, Stuttgart 1970. Also in English.

Raud, Villibald, The Baltic States as a British Market: the Smaller Nations in the World's Economic Life, P. S. King and Staples, London 1943.

Raymond, Ellsworth & Martin, John Stuart, A Picture History of Eastern Europe, Crown Publishers, New York 1971. Chapters on the Baltic States.

Reddaway, Peter, Uncensored Russia. The Human Rights Movement. Jonathan Cape, London 1972. Annotated text of the "Chronicle of Current Events".

Reddaway, Peter & Bloch, Sidney, Russia's Political Hospitals. The Abuse of Psychiatry in the Soviet Union, Gollancz 1977.

Reddaway, William Fiddian, Problems of the Baltic, Cambridge University Press, Cambridge, 1940.

*Rei, August, The Drama of the Baltic Peoples, Vaba Eesti Kirjastus, Stockholm 1970. Head of state and Social Democratic leader in independent Estonia.

Rei, August, Nazi-Soviet Conspiracy and the Baltic States. Diplomatic Documents and Other Evidence, Boreas, London 1948.

Res Baltica. A Collection of Essays in Honor of the Memory of Dr Alfred Bilmanis 1887–1948, A. W. Sijthoff-Leyden, Netherlands 1968.

Rutter, Owen, The New Baltic States and Their Future, Methuen, London 1925.

Schaper, E., Die baltischen Länder im geistigen Spektrum Europas, Zürich 1964.

Spekke, Arnolds, Balts and Slavs, Their Early Relations, Alpha Printing Co, Washington D.C. 1965.

Suduvis, N. E., Allein ganz allein: Wiederstand am baltischen Meer, West Germany 1964.

Swettenham, John Alexander, The tragedy of the Baltic
States, Hollis and Carter, London 1952.

Tarulis, Albert N., Soviet Policy toward the Baltic States
1918–1940, University of Notre Dame Press, Notre
Dame, Indiana 1959.

Tillett, Lowell, The Great Friendship. Soviet Historians
on the Non-Russian Nationalities, University of North
Carolina Press, North Carolina 1969.

Third Interim Report, 83rd Congress. 2nd Session, Select
Committee to Investigate Communist Aggression and
the Forced Incorporation of the Baltic States into the
USSR, US House of Representatives, Washington
1954. New edition by William S. Hein & Co, Buffalo,
New York 14 209, USA 1972.

Valters, M., Das Verbrechen gegen die baltischen Staten,
Atlanta Verlag, USA 1962.

Warner, Oliver, The Sea and the Sword. The Baltic
1630–1945, Jonathan Cape, London 1965.

Weiss, Hellmuth, Die baltischen Staaten in Die Sowjetisierung Ost-Mitteleuropas. Untersuchungen zu ihrem
Ablauf in den einzelnen Ländern 1945–1957, Frankfurt-
am-Main-Berlin 1959.

Vitols, Kaasik, Kajeckas, Les annexions des états baltes,
Stockholm 1946.

Wittram, Reinhold, Baltische Geschichte. Die Ostsee-
lande Livland, Estland, Kurland 1180–1918, München
1954. Baltic German historian on the history of Germans in the Baltic provinces.

Woods, Ethel Gertrude, The Baltic Region, London 1932.

*Zarins, Aina, Dissent in the Baltic Republics: A Survey of
Grievances and Hopes, Radio Liberty Research Bulletin No 496/76, Munich 1976.

Estonia:

Aspects of Estonian Culture, Boreas, London 1961.

Cathala, Jean, Portrait de l'Estonie, Paris 1937.

Chambon, Henri de, La République de l'Estonie, Ed. de la Revue Parlementaire, Paris 1936.

*Documents from Estonia on the Violation of Human Rights, Estonian Information Centre, Stockholm 1977.

Eliaser, Elga, Estonia, Past and Present, Estonian Information Centre, Stockholm 1965. Estonian-born correspondent for *Daily Telegraph* in Scandinavia.

Estonian Events. Mimeographed news bulletin published in 1967–72 by political scientist, Rein Taagepera of University of California.

*Hehn, Jürgen von, Rimscha, Hans von & Weiss, Hellmuth, Von den baltischen Provinzen zu den baltischen Staaten. Beiträge zur Entstehungsgeschichte der Republiken Estland und Lettland, 1917–1918, J. G. Herder-Institut, Marburg/Lahn 1971.

Käbin, Johannes, Estonia, Yesterday and Today, Progress Publishers, Moscow 1971. First Secretary of the Communist Party of Estonia.

Kaelas, Aleksander, Das sowjetisch besetzte Estland, Estonian Information Centre, Stockholm 1958.

Kant, Edgar, Bevölkerung und Lebensraum Estlands, Tartu, Estonia 1935.

Kareda, Endel, Technique of Economic Sovietization, Boreas, London 1947.

Kareda, Endel, Estonia in the Soviet Grip, Boreas, London 1949.

Kareda, Endel, Estonia – the forgotten nation, Toronto 1961.

Kreep, Endel, & Uustalu, Evald, Outlines of Estonian Geography and History, Stockholm 1961.

Kruus, Hans, Grundrisse der Geschichte des estnisschen Volkes, Tartu 1932. Histoire de l'Estonie, Paris 1935. Kruus joined the new government after the Soviet take-over in 1940 but was later demoted when he refused to become a puppet.

*Küng, Andres, Estland zum Beispiel. Nationale Minderheit und Supermacht, Seewald Verlag, Stuttgart 1973.

Mägi, Artur, Das Staatsleben Estlands während seiner Selbstständigkeit, Stockholm 1967.

Martna, Mihkel, L'Estonie, Paris 1920.

Martna, Mihkel, Estland, die Esten und die estnische

Frage, Olten, Germany 1919. Leader of the Estonian "Menzheviks".

Müürisepp, Aleksei, The Estonian People on the Road to a New Life, State Publishing House, Tallinn 1961. Leading Estonian Communist until his death in 1970.

Nodel, Emanuel, Estonia. Nation on the Anvil, Bookman Associates, New York 1963. Polish-born historian who passed his student examination in Estonia and is now Assistant Professor of History at the Western Michigan University in the United States.

Nodel, Emanuel, Strategy and Tactics of the Estonian Communist Party: 1917–1940, A Case Study of Soviet Penetration of the Baltic. Pending publication.

Parming, Tönu & Järvesoo, Elmar (eds), A Case Study of a Soviet Republic. The Estonian SSR, Boulder, Colorado 1978. Scholarly.

Pekomäe, Vello (ed), Estonia in Pictures and Words, EMP publishers, Stockholm 1955.

Pullerits, Albert, Estonia: Population, Culture and Economic life, Eesti Raamat, Tallinn 1935.

Raud, Villi ald, Estonia: a Reference Book, Nordic Press, New York 1953. A follow-up to Pullerits' book.

Raun, Linda, The Estonians, HRAF Press, New Haven, Connecticut 1955.

Raun, Toivo, The Revolution of 1905 and the Movement for Estonian National Autonomy, Princeton, New Jersey 1969. Doctoral dissertation.

Seth, Ronald, Baltic Corner. Travel in Estonia, Methuen, London 1939. Published also under the title Estonian Journey: Travel in a Baltic Corner, McBride, New York, 1939.

Survel, Jaak, Estonia Today, Boreas, Lodnon 1947.

Ten Aspects of Estonian Life, Eesti Raamat, Tallinn 1967. Probably also later editions.

Tomingas, William, The·Soviet Colonization of Estonia, Kirjastus Kultuur, New York 1972.

Tumulus, George, I am an Estonian. The Baltic and the Metamorphoses of the Russian Empire, Exposition Press, New York 1959.

Uluots, Jüri, Grundzüge der Agrargeschichte Estlands,

Tartu 1935. So far the last prime minister of independent Estonia.

Uuemaa, E. & Valdvere, F., Economic Development of Estonia, Ministry of Economic Affairs, Tallinn 1937.
*Uustalu, Evald, the History of the Estonian People, Boreas, London 1952.
Villecourt, L., L'Esthonie, Paris 1932.
*Walter, Gert, Estland – Geschichte und Gegenwart einer jungen Sowjetrepublik, Verlag der Nation, Berlin. No printing year, probably 1969. East German of Baltic German origin describes a journey to his native land in the middle 1960's.

Latvia:

Balodis, Francis, Die Letten, Riga 1930.
Bilmanis, Alfreds, Latvia in the making, Riga 1928.
Bilmanis, Alfreds, Latvia as an Independent State, Washington D.C., 1947.
Bilmanis, Alfreds, A History of Latvia, Princeton 1951.
Bobe, M., and others (eds), The Jews in Latvia, Association of Latvian and Estonian Jews in Israel, Tel Aviv 1971.
Cakste, Janis, Die Letten und ihre Latvija, Stockholm 1917.
Carson, George B. (ed.), Latvia: An Area Study, Chicago 1956. Two volumes.
Ceichners, Alfreds, Was Europa drohte. Die Bolschewisierung Lettlands 1940–1941, Riga 1943.
Eldelber, Max (ed.), Latvia, Copenhaguen 1938.
Grant-Watson, Herbert A., Latvian Republic, London 1965.
Hehn, Jürgen von, Lettland zwischen Demokratie und Diktatur, Jahrbücher für Geschichte Osteuropas, Beiheft 3, Isar-Verlag, München 1957.
Hehn, Jürgen von, Rimscha, Hans von & Weiss, Hellmuth, Von den baltischen Provinzen zu den baltischen Staaten. Beiträge zur Enstehungsgeschichte der Republiken Estland und Lettland 1917–1918, J. G. Herder Institut, Marburg/Lahn 1971.

Jegers, Benjamin, Bibliography of Latvian Publications Published Outside Latvia 1940–60, Part I: Books and Pamphlets, Part II: Serials, Music, Maps, Programmes and Catalogues, Daugava publishers, Stockhom 1968 and 1972.

King, Gundar, Economic Policies in Occupied Latvia, Pacific Lutheran University Press, Tacoma, Washington 1965.

Latvia – Past and Present, Latviju Gramata, Waverly, Iowa 50 677, USA.

Ozolin, Jan A., Amber Land or Latvia Past and Present, Kobe 1922.

Pauaux, R., Portrait de la Lettonie, Paris 1937.

*Rutkis, Janis (ed), Latvia Country and People, Latvian National Foundation, Stockholm 1967.

Salts, Alberts, Lettlands Wirtschaft und Wirtschaftspolitik, Riga 1930.

Segreste, M., La Lettonie, Paris 1930.

*Silde, Adolfs, Die Sowjetisierung Lettlands, Bundesinstitut für Ostwissenschaftliche und Internationale Studien, Münster, West Germany 1967.

*Silde, Adolfs, Resistance Movement in Latvia, Latvian National Foundation, Stockholm 1972.

Spekke, Arnolds, History of Latvia, Latvian National Foundation, Stockholm 1951.

Spekke, Arnolds, Latvia and the Baltic States, London 1949.

Speeke, Arnolds, Latvia and the Baltic Problem, London 1954.

Svabe, Arveds, Agrarian History of Latvia, Riga 1929.

Svabe, Arveds, The Story of Latvia, Latvian National Foundation, Stockholm 1949.

Svabe, Arveds, Histoire du Peuple Letton, Stockholm 1953. Same as above.

Urch, Reginald Oliver Gilling, Latvia – Country and People, London 1938.

Voss, Alberts, Lenin's Behests and the Making of Soviet Latvia, Progress Publishers, Moscow 1970. First Secretary of the Communist Party of Latvia.

Watson, H. A. G., The Latvian Republic, London 1965.

257

Zalts, Alberts, Latvia's National Economy in 20 Years, Riga 1938.
Zolmanis, Emils, Latvia among the Baltic States, Riga 1931.

Lithuania:

Audenas, Juozas (ed), Twenty Years Struggle for Freedom of Lithuania, Supreme Committee for the Liberation of Lithuania, New York 1963. Ex-minister of agriculture in independent Lithuania.
Baltramaitis, Casimir V., (ed.), Lithuanian Affairs, Lithuanian Press Club, New York 1945.
*Bourdeaux, Michael, Land of Crosses, London 1979. On religion, dissent and persecution in contemporary Lithuania.
Chambon, Henri de, La Lithuanie moderne, Ed. de la Revue Parlementaire, Paris 1933.
Chase, Thomas G., The Story of Lithuania, Stratford House, New York 1946.
*Gerutis, Albert (ed), Lithuania 700 years, Manyland Books, New York 1967. Bibliography.
Harrison, Ernest J., Lithuania 1928, Hazell, Watson and Viney, London 1928, British vice Consul in Lithuania.
Hellmann, Manfred, Grundzüge der Geschichte Litauens und des liatuischen Volkes, Darmstadt 1966.
Jurgela, Constantine R., History of the Lithuanian Nation, Lithuanian Cultural Institute, New York 1948.
Klimas, P., Der Werdegang des litausichen Staates, 1919.
Living in Freedom. A Sketch of independent Lithuania's Achievements, Lithuanian Information Service, Augsburg 1948. On cultural life.
Maciuika, Benedict V. (ed.), Lithuania in the last 30 years, HRAF Press, New Haven 1955.
Norem, Owen J. D., Timeless Lithuania, Amerlith Press, Chicago 1943. Latest US ambassador to independent Lithuania.
Pakstas Kazys, Lithuania and World War II, Lithuanian Cultural Institute, Chicago 1947.
Paleckis, Justas, Das sowjetische Litauen, SWA Verlag,

258

(East) Berlin 1948. First head of government in Lithuania after Soviet take-over in 1940.

Pelekis, K., Genocide: Lithuania's Threefold Tragedy, Venta, West Germany 1949.

Petruitis, J., Lithuania under the Sickle and Hammer, Cleveland 1945.

Sabaliunas, Leonas, Lithuania in Crisis, Nationalism to Communism 1939–1940, Indiana University Press, Bloomington and London 1972. Extensive bibliography.

Salkauskis, St., Sur les confins de deux mondes, Genéve 1919.

Senn, Alfred Erich, The Emergence of Modern Lithuania, Columbia University Press, New York 1959.

Simutis, Anicetas, The Economic Reconstruction of Lithuania after 1918, Columbia University Press, New York 1942.

Stukas, J. J., Awakening Lithuania, a study on the Rise of modern Lithuanian Nationalism, Madison, New Jersey 1966.

Tauras, K. V., Guerilla Warfare on the Amber Coast, Voyages Press, New York 1962.

Vaitiekunas, Vytautas, Lithuania, Assembly of Captive European Nations, New York 1965. Revised edition in 1968.

*Vardys, Stanley V. (ed.), Lithuania under the Soviets. Portrait of a Nation 1940–1965, Praeger, New York 1965. Bibliography.

*Violations of Human Rights in Soviet Occupied Lithuania, Published annually by Lithuanian American Community, Inc., 708, Custis Road, Glenside, Pennsylvania 19038, USA.

TWO MEMORANDA TO UNO FROM ESTONIA

To the General Assembly
of the United Nations Organization

The Estonian Democratic Movement and the Estonian National Front present to the General Assembly of the United Nations the following MEMORANDUM, concerning the fate of the Estonian nation.

In view of the fact:

that existence of different nations constitutes the riches of the humanity;

that as a result of forcible levelling and assimilation of national cultures the humanity grows poorer;

that national independence is main condition for the survival of a nation and her culture;

that one of the basic features in the development of the world during the last decades has been the emergence and growth of independent national states — members of the UNO;

that the International Covenant of Economic, Social and Cultural Rights (art. 1), the Declaration of the Granting of Independence to Colonial Countries and Peoples (par. 2) as well as other analogous UNO documents declare the right of all nations to self-determination, under which they shall freely determine their political status, and exercise their economic, social and cultural development;

that in accordance of the Universal Declaration on Human Rights (art. 21, par. 3) the power of government lies in the peoples' will, which must be expressed through periodic and unfalsified elections ... and forms, that guarantee the freedom of voting;

that Estonia, a former internationally recognized independent state and member of the League of Nations (beginning from 1921) was in 1940 forcibly deprived of her national independence and reduced in fact to the status of a colonial territory;

that as a result of such status and the policy of the Soviet government, aimed at the gradual assimilation of all nationalities living on the Soviet territory into a Russian-dominated nation, there has arisen a serious threat as to the further national, political and spiritual existence of the Estonian nation;

that the states—signatories of the Atlantic Charter (including the Soviet Union) committed themselves (art. 3) to promote restoration of sovereign rights and self-government to those peoples, who have been forcibly deprived of them;

that the aforementioned commitment has not been fulfilled solely in the case of the three Baltic nations, including Estonia;

that under the colonial rule the Estonian nation has not been guaranteed the fulfilment of the articles 3, 8, 9, 10, 11, 12, 13, 14(1), 18, 19, 20, 21, 26(2), 27(2) of the Universal Declaration on Human Rights, articles 1, 8(1d), 13(3), 15(3) of International Covenant on Economic, Social and Cultural Rights and articles 6, 7, 9, 10, 12, 14, 17, 18, 19, 21, 22 of the International Covenant on Civil and Political Rights

the Estonian Democratic Movement and the Estonian National Front
DEMAND:

1. Restoration of the independent Estonian state in the frontiers fixed by the 1920 Tartu peace-treaty between the Estonian Republic and Soviet Russia;
2. admission of Estonia as a former member of the League of Nations to United Nations membership;

To these ends the Estonian Democratic Movement and the Estonian National Front consider necessary:

a) to liquidate the existing colonial administration, which does not correspond to the art. 21. par. 3 of the Universal Declaration of Human Rights, depends entirely on the Soviet central government and is an instrument of the latter's imperialist and chauvinistic aims;

b) to liquidate the Soviet military bases on Estonian soil and withdraw from Estonia all Soviet military personnel (who, under the agreement between Estonia and the Soviet Union were stationed for 10 years only, the agreement expired in 1949);

c) up to the formation of national organs of government through free democratic elections to place Estonia temporarily under the UNO administration and to introduce to Estonia the UNO's peace-keeping forces;

d) pending the UNO administration, opportunity for return to Estonia must be given to all persons of Estonian nationality, who have been forcibly deported from Estonia (including these detained on political reasons), or who have left Estonia at their own will, also to all other persons, who have been citizens of the Estonian Republic, and to their descendants;

e) to restore normal political life and to create conditions for really free democratic elections (under the supervision of the UNO observers) in order to form a representative body of the Estonian people — the Constituent Assembly.

All political parties and groups, who respect the democratic principles and the right of peoples to national independence, may participate in the elections to the Constituent Assembly.

In the elections to the Constituent Assembly suffrage belongs to all those persons at least 18 years old, who have been (or among whose parents at least one has been) citizens of the Estonian Republic, or who were born on the Estonian territory.

The Estonian Democratic Movement and the Estonian National Front are convinced that only the implementation of the aforementioned considerations and demands permits the United Nations Organization to exercise consistently her obligations which lie on her in accordance with the articles 1, 2, 4, 5 of the Declaration on the Granting Independence to Colonial Countries and Peoples, article 1 par. 3 of the International Covenant on Civil and Political Rights and articles 103, 104, 105 of the UNO Charter.

The Estonian Democratic Movement and the Estonian National Front demand the UNO to take effective steps in order to abolish the immoral, inhuman and illegal Soviet colonial rule in Estonia and to compel the Soviet Union not to hinder the restoration of the legal rights and national sovereignty to the Estonian nation.

Estonians will never accept the colonial status of their fatherland.

At present, when even the smallest nations of the world have been recognized the right to national independence, the Estonian nation looks forward to urgent and real help from the United Nations Organization.

Tallinn, October 24, 1972

the Estonian
Democratic Movement

the Estonian
National Front

To the Secretary General
of the United Nations Organization
Mr. Kurt Waldheim

Your Excellency,

The Estonian National Front and the Estonian Democratic Movement address to you a Memorandum, which applies for the restoration of the independent Estonian state with the aid of the UNO as well as for admission of Estonia to the UNO membership. In doing so we are guided by the fact that the three Baltic States (incl. Estonia) are the only states — former members of the League of Nations — who after the World War II have experienced no implementation of the 3rd article of the Atlantic Charter, relating to the restoration of sovereign rights and self-government to those nations who have been forcibly deprived of

hem. We would like to bring to your attention the well-known fact that the fate
of the Baltic states was determined in 1939-1940 not by the peoples of these
states, but through a secret deal between two imperialist powers, who fixed their
respective spheres of influence at the expence of their smaller neighbours. All
subsequent developments in the three Baltic states (incl. an electoral farce of
1940, on the basis of which Estonia was »admitted» to the Soviet Union) must
be seen as efforts to give a more decent and legal form to an action that really
was an annexation of small states by a great power, carried out under the military occupation and with the use of a brutal force.

This annexation was never recognized by the democratic states of the world.
As the result of this the Estonian nation has been denied an opportunity to
shape freely her destiny in her own national interests and possibility to be represented in the community of world nations.

In addition to the loss of political independence a serious threat to the very
existence of the Estonian nation as such has gradually arisen: a perspective of her
assimilation among the Russians, settling unhindered and in growing numbers on
the Estonian territory; an assimilation which is planned and favoured by the
soviet government.

The following tables indicate proportional changes among various nationalities living in Estonia:

TABLE I

Year	Total population in thous.	Estonians in thous.	Estonians %	Russians* in thous.	Russians* %	Other nationalities in thous.	All non-Estonians in thous.	All non-Estonians %
1934**	1 064	980	92,1	60	5,6	24	84	7,8
1959	1 197	893	74,6	267	22,3	37	304	25,4
1970	1 356	925	68,2	381	28,1	49***	430	31,8
Increase 1934—70	+292	—55	—5 6	+321	+436,0	+25	+346	+312,0

Notes:
  * Including Ukrainians and Byelorussians
 ** Excepting the areas near Petseri and Narva, inhabited mostly by
    Russians; after the World War II those areas were separated from
    Estonia and merged with the Russian Federation
*** Now mostly Russianized

As the Table II indicates, migration from other Soviet Republics (mainly
from the Russian Federation) has considerably increased during the last decade.

From the overall increase during the years 1961-70 (152 000) the mechanical increase totalled 92 500, i.e. 61 %. At the same time considerable percentage of the natural increase is due to the local Russian population.

TABLE II Increase of population 1951—1970*

Years	Total increase	Natural increase	Migrants from other Soviet Republics	Average annual increase
1951—70	270,1	124,1	146,0	13,5
1951—55	58,5	30,5	28,0	11,7
1956—60	59,7	34,2	25,5	11,9
1961—65	75,1	32,0	43,1	15,0
1966—70	76,8	27,4	49,4	15,4
1970	19,0	6,4	12,6	19,0

* In thousands

Notes:
Data concerning the post-war period are obtained from the statistical year-book "Narodnoye Hozyaistvo Estonskoi SSR v 1970 godu", Tallinn 1971.

The influx of Russian migrants has been officially justified by the need of manpower for rapidly expanding industry. In fact, economically groundless boosting of industry serves as a cover for Russification. During the period of 1940-1970 total Soviet industrial output has increased by 1188 %, that of Estonia by 2779 %; industrial output in Estonia has increased annually by 11,7 %, the productivity by 7,6 % only. The gap is being filled up with the help of Russian emigrants who receive various facilities at the expense of local population, e.g. cheap communal flats out of order. At the same time the majority of Estonians have to build the so-called co-operative flats at their own expense. The Russians are concentrating mainly in big towns and big factories, which are subordinated directly to Moscow and have no connection with the economy and needs of Estonia.

Your Exellency, we are aware that your native country was — almost at the same time as Estonia — forcibly annexed by her big neighbour. Your country has benefitted by the victory of democratic powers in the World War II. Due to that fact her independence has been restored and you — as a representative of your country — are the Secretary General of the world's largest representative body. Our country has so far been denied restoration of her lost national independence and when our representatives (in the lull between German and Soviet occupation in September 1944) set up an Estonian National Government, which appealed for the implementation of the article 3 of the Atlantic Charter, they were arested by the Soviet authorities and sent to Russian labour-camps. Since the political field was left open to semi-russianized colonial bureaucracy. These self-tyled »Lost sons of people» have no right to speak on behalf of the Estonian people. Actually they are not elected by the people, but appointed to their posts by Soviet colonial administration. Such collaborators exist among every subdued nation as they existed also in Austria during the German occupation. At the same time the majority of Estonian people is so intimidated and remembers so well the bloody bachanalias of Stalin era, that they consider the display of any discontent equal to suicide.

You may ask: why bother the UNO with such old problems at the moment, when the world body is overburdened with more urgent issues? Some people in the West may also say: you are not directly assimilated at the moment, you do not starve, you are doing comparatively well economically, some of you are allowed to visit the western countries, you have got your national culture etc. As result your situation is really not so bad.

We reply: the problem of existence and independence of an once recognized nation cannot grow old — it is simply long overdue and therefore the more urgent. If it didn't emerge at once after the World War II (at the Potsdam Conference) it is because in our case the aggressor found herself — as a result of the attack by her former partner — in the camp of democratic states. These states didn't cope with the delicate problem of her former annexations, hoping probably to come to terms with her on more urgent and important issues. So they practically ignored the fate of the Baltic states. The result of that policy of neo-ppeasement, that naive faith in the goodwill and reliability of the totalitarian tate was more annexation in the eastern part of Europe, more aggression in Korea etc.

Why, then, cannot we accept the concept, according to which our present situation is comparatively tolerable?

We cannot accept it

- because existence without any real guarantee as for the future, with constantly increasing influx of Russian colonial element is worse than no existence at all;
- because liberties and rights that are hypocritically proclaimed, on paper, but never allowed to be implemented, are worse than no liberties at all;
- because overt colonialism tends to produce slaves or freedom-fighters, but the system of disguised colonialism, pseudo-liberties and double-talking produces only spiritual bastards and double-talkers, a kind of people, who fear even their minds thinking about certain truths and drawing conclusions (security men hear!) or who are accustomed to think one way and speak the other way.

Such system of double-talking, constant intimidation and oppression, lack of any guarantees as concerns security of an individual and future of a nation, the system of direct or indirect lies, one-sided and distorted information, lack of spiritual and political freedom, any real alternative and responsibility tends to distort the consciousness of the nation to such extent that she becomes

265

accustomed to see in the unnatural natural, in the lie a truth, in dictatorship and terror the highest form of democracy, and as a result is ready to merge without resistance in the »great Russian nation» under the cover of the so-called Soviet nation theory.

In the present state of affairs there are only two alternatives left for the Estonian people:

a) if she doesn't resist, she is allowed to Russianize slowly and gradually;

b) if — on the contrary — she offers active resistance, the whole nation will be dealt with quickly and brutally, the intellectual and other active elements of the nation will be jailed and deported, the rest of the population subjected to intense Russification and repressions. One must not miss the fact that the Soviet colonial rulers will never feel themselves safe and secure in their illegally and unjustly seized posessions until all non-Russian population of those posessions is not Russified.

We would like to remind you that denial of truth and democratic forms of government, regime of military occupation and oppression of spiritual freedom, subjugation of national culture to communist censorship and propaganda, lack of independent thinking and action, lack of freedom of conscience can never be compensated by show of certain progress in economy and living-standard, still meagre and onesided and exagerated by the propaganda machinery, especially in comparison with that of the neighbouring Finland.

We would also like to remind you that the price of any important administrative, scientific or cultural post, the price of any foreign journey (which depends on the recommendation of the local Communist Party bransch) is in fact intellectual and moral self-abnegation.

The UNO is helping to national independence many nations, who have never had such independence in the modern sense of the word. Even the smallest nations and territories (e.g. Maldives, Nauru etc.) have been recognized the right to be independent states. On the 29th of August, 1972, the UNO recognized Puerto Rico as a territory, which has inalienable right to self-determination and independence, despite of the fact that the Puerto Ricans have had several occasions to express freely, their will, occasions that the Estonians have never had under the Soviet colonial rule.

We find that the responsibility of the UNO towards the three Baltic States, who have precedent of internationally recognized national independence and who have lost it not by their own fault, is much greater.

Immediately after the end of the World War II and before the beginning of the Potsdam Conference, a western author wrote as follows:

». . . the history of Estonia, Latvia and Lithuania puts a question to the peacemakers of tomorrow: will they accept the lesson of the past and restore those Small States to their rightful place of independence so that the Baltic nations can once more live their lives in liberty, contributing, as before, to European peace and progress? That is the BALTIC QUESTION. Unless it is answered aright, the Peacemakers of tomorrow must fail us.»

266

We ask now: Will the Peacemakers of today fail the Baltic nations once more? That is the question to which we expect answer from the community of world nations.

Tallinn, October 24, 1972

the Estonian
Democratic Movement

the Estonian
National Front

Index

269

271